# NATURAL REMEDIES

## AN ESSENTIAL A–Z GUIDE

This is a Starfire Book
First published in 2001

02 04 05 03

1 3 5 7 9 10 8 6 4 2

**Starfire** is part of
The Foundry Creative Media Company Limited
Crabtree Hall, Crabtree Lane, Fulham, London, SW6 6TY

Visit the Foundry website: www.foundry.co.uk

ISBN 1 903817 22 6

A copy of the CIP data for this book is available from the British Library

Printed in China

SPECIAL THANKS TO EVERYONE INVOLVED WITH THIS PROJECT:
Anna Amari, Frances Banfield, Lucy Bradbury, Roger Buckley, Helen Courtney, Claire Dashwood,
Giskin Day, Karen Fitzpatrick, Vicky Garrard, Phil Hempell, George Keyes, Lesley Malkin,
Geoffrey Meadon, Sonya Newland, Colin Rudderham, Mel Shaw, Andrea Simmonds,
Graham Stride, Helen Tovey, Helen Wall, Sharon Weiss, Nick Wells.

# NATURAL REMEDIES

## AN ESSENTIAL A–Z GUIDE

AUTHOR - KAREN SULLIVAN

GENERAL EDITOR - TRICIA ALLEN

STAR
FIRE

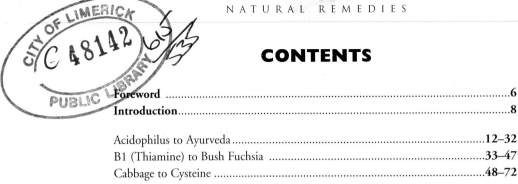
# CONTENTS

# THEMES

Each A–Z entry is tagged by themes which can be followed as threads throughout the book.
*Sometimes you will find two entries with identical names in this book, however, thematically they *are* different. For example, the same topic may fall under Aromatherapy *and* Herbalism (the icons for each entry will be different).

 Aromatherapy      Herbalism      Home Remedies      Nutrition

 Flower essences      Homeopathy      Natural Health

# FOREWORD

As we move into the twenty-first century, complementary and alternative medicine has become the first preference of health care for many and its popularity is rapidly increasing. Each year, more and more people are choosing to consult a natural therapy practitioner and the sales of natural remedies are higher than ever before. The number of colleges training complementary practitioners are growing, an increasing number of universities are offering degree courses in complementary and alternative medicine, and the number of students wishing to train and practise these therapies is on the rise.

The government acknowledged the growth of this trend by commissioning the House of Lords Select Committee on Science and Technology to research the field of complementary and alternative medicine. Twenty-nine different natural therapies were investigated, and the report published in November 2000 issued recommendations on the areas of regulation, education and training, and research and development. Complementary and alternative medicine is now being taken seriously; it is an important, fast-growing industry that is here to stay.

It is not so long ago that natural remedies were the mainstay of medicinal treatment, and this is still the case in many parts of the world. Modern medicine has worked many miracles over the last few decades and few would deny the life-saving properties of modern surgical methods and drugs. Is it possible, however, that in applauding these developments, we have thrown the baby out with the bathwater. Conventional medical approaches have embraced new technologies and the vast array of chemical drugs produced by the pharmaceutical industry, yet have ignored the lessons of the past which demonstrate that natural therapies and remedies are highly effective in curing many common ailments. Furthermore, the side effects from many of the drugs prescribed today give serious cause for concern, especially if we consider the number of patients in hospital due to ill effects from these drugs.

Nowadays many people choose to consult complementary therapists because they are concerned about taking chemical

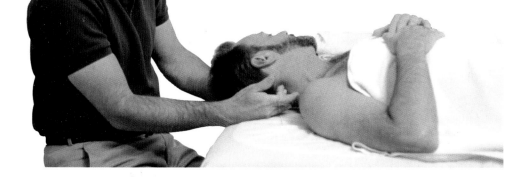

medications and also because they are looking for long-term solutions to their health problems, rather than just short-term relief from the symptoms. Patients tend to want a health practitioner that will offer them a full consultation that takes into account the whole of their disease process and treats the underlying cause, rather than just having the symptoms of their disease palliated or suppressed.

I have been a homeopathic practitioner for over 10 years. In that time, I have seen the number of homeopaths in my area increase tenfold, and yet we all achieve busy practices, with approximately 15 to 20 patients every week. Also, there are ever-increasing numbers of other complementary therapists in the area, as well as new health care shops opening. The patients who consult me are varied, including pregnant women, parents with young children, businessmen and women, teenagers and the elderly. Although the patients and their symptoms are all very different, they all have the same desire to be treated holistically with natural remedies.

It has been my pleasure and privilege to write the foreword, and read and edit this excellent and timely book on natural remedies. This book encompasses a wide range of natural remedies: from herbalism to aromatherapy, homeopathy to flower essences, nutrition to home remedies. Simple to use, with clear guidelines about the complementary and alternative therapies available today, this book is highly informative and I would have no hesitation in recommending it to anyone with an interest in natural remedies.

TRICIA ALLEN BSc (Hons) LCH MARH, Homeopath

# INTRODUCTION

Since the beginning of civilization, we have looked to nature to provide us with remedies for healing the body, mind and soul. Throughout time various tribes, communities and societies have had their own healers, methods and medicines, and by using the natural remedies available to them, discovered many effective ways of healing. Many ancient societies produced highly evolved systems of medicine, as can be seen from the Ayurvedic practices in India and traditional Chinese medicine in China, both of which were based on natural remedies and holistic methods of diagnosis and treatment. In many parts of the world, these practises continue today, and it is estimated that 80 per cent of the world's population still rely on plants as their first form of medicine. Moreover, herbs are the basis for many of the drugs used by modern medicine and continue to be used in scientific research to find cures for today's diseases.

Until the early part of the twentieth century, every family had a supply of their favourite home remedies, including plants, herbs and foodstuffs that could be used to treat minor medical emergencies, or prevent a common ailment from becoming more serious. The knowledge of how to use these natural remedies was passed down from generation to generation, becoming part of the folklore of each family and community. When illness struck, the cause was investigated and, more often than not, the treatment could be found in the garden, in a field, or in the cupboard.

During the middle of the twentieth century, society began to change its outlook towards natural remedies. The advent of modern medicine, with its many miracles, also led to a growing dependency on doctors and an increasingly stretched health care system. The growth of the pharmaceutical industry has meant that there are indeed palliatives and cures for most disease symptoms, however, we have become accustomed to putting our health completely in the hands of doctors, or instead purchasing medicinal drugs to instantly make us feel better. We are no longer in touch with our bodies, so when we become ill, we rely on others to treat us.

Increasingly, however, we are learning that the conventional medical system is not infallible. Modern medicine may make us feel better in the short term, but it does so by palliating or suppressing the symptoms, not by curing their cause. For example, cough mixtures will suppress a cough, but the natural reflex of the body to expel mucous from the lungs will also be suppressed. This means that, in the long run, our bodies will be less able to fight off illness and infection.

The growth in complementary and alternative medicine has been unprecedented. Nearly 20 per cent of the British population regularly use alternative or complementary therapies, including acupuncture, aromatherapy, herbalism, homeopathy and reflexology; spending more than £500 million annually in the process. An estimated eight out of ten British people have tried a complementary therapy or remedy, and as

consumers we spend £150 each year on herbal medicines alone: largely because they are perceived to be safer and more effective than medicinal drugs.

Why the sudden surge of interest in natural remedies? The fact is, that despite conventional medical disdain, there is now a growing body of evidence proving that natural remedies work. In clinical trials comparing drug and herb treatments, some herbs have been coming out on top. For example, it has been proved that St John's wort is as effective as the pharmaceutical antidepressants available to treat mild depression, and there is evidence that large doses of the mineral selenium can protect against cancer. Research conducted in a Rudolf Steiner vegetarian community has shown that the children living there suffered from 40 per cent fewer allergies than children raised more conventionally, yet they had never been treated with medicinal drugs.

What is more, our approach to our bodies and to health care in general has changed. People have become tired of the all-to-familiar five-minute consultation with the doctor and also with the prescription that inevitably follows: there are clearly other aspects of patients' lives that need to be taken into consideration. Far from asking questions about emotional health, sleep patterns, diet and exercise, many conventional doctors tend to trot out the old adage 'eat less fat', and bang the symptoms on the head with a drug. Nowadays we expect more. We want to sit down with someone who will listen to us and consider the whole picture, making links between our lifestyle, our past and familial history, the totality of our symptoms and our overall health on every level. This is how the practitioners of complementary and alternative medicine work.

The evidence in favour of this approach is overwhelming. Just 20 years ago, the British Medical Journal (BMJ) suggested that complementary medicine 'ought to be as extinct as divination by examination of bird's entrails'. Recently, the BMJ has produced a twelve-part series on complementary and alternative medicines. In Europe, complementary medicine plays an important role in preventative and overall health care. In France, one-third of the population use homeopathic medicines and 39 per cent of French family physicians prescribe them. Twenty per cent of all German physicians prescribe homeopathic medicines and 45 per cent of Dutch physicians consider homeopathy an effective form of medicine.

Studies show that many natural therapies and remedies are effective. We are now aware of the positive health benefits of taking supplements, such as antioxidants, and massaging with aromatherapy oils. One study showed that people using acupuncture take 79 per cent fewer prescription drugs, while another showed that asthmatic children were found to improve dramatically within the first few days of taking *Ginkgo biloba* extract. This is not just a new trend in New Age thinking: natural therapies and remedies offer a safer alternative to conventional medicine, and their efficacy is on the brink of receiving wide scientific support.

Natural therapies are holistic, taking into consideration the mind, body and spirit as equally important elements to good health. Natural remedies work by bringing these three elements into balance, producing a sense of well-being, which in turn allows healing to take place. Even better, natural remedies work to prevent illness, yet treat the cause of disease when it does set in, reducing the duration and possibility of recurrence. As our bodies are literally encouraged to heal themselves, we become stronger, healthier, and more resistant to the rigours of modern-day life. Natural remedies work on insidious health problems – that are often the result of stress – and have the potential to wipe out a host of niggling health conditions (otherwise an array of medicinal drugs would be needed to help). Why is this the case? Simply because, once the cause is eliminated, symptoms disappear. For example, you can continue to use inhalers for your asthma for years and years, but once you cease the medication, the symptoms return unabated. If you address the cause of your asthma, then you will actually have a good chance of eliminating it once and for all.

This book is part of a range of encyclopedias which offer authoritative and easy-to-use information on a wide range of subjects. Organized in alphabetical order, this book enables the reader to cross-reference easily between the entries. There are seven thematic strands in the book: Aromatherapy, Flower Essences, Herbalism, Homeopathy, Home Remedies, Natural Health and Nutrition. Each theme is represented by a distinctive icon (see page 4), enabling the reader to find information either by name or by theme.

KAREN SULLLIVAN
London, June 2001

## ACIDOPHILUS

Acidophilus (also known as *Lactobacillus acidophilus*) is a source of friendly intestinal bacteria (flora). Healthy bacteria play an important role in our bodies, and unless they are continually supplied with some form of lactic acid or lactose (such as Acidophilus) can die, causing a host of health problems. Many doctors and health practitioners recommend taking Acidophilus alongside oral antibiotics, which can cause diarrhoea, destroy the healthy flora of the intestines and lead to fungal infections. Acidophilus may also help to ensure vaginal health.

The best sources are natural, unflavoured and live yoghurt.

### Properties and Uses
- Keeps the intestines clean
- Prevents vaginal thrush
- Aids the absorption of nutrients in food
- Relieves and prevents constipation and flatulence
- Maintains intestinal health

## ACONITE

*Aconitum napellus*

The homeopathic remedy Aconite is made from monk's hood, also known as wolf's bane, and the whole plant is used to prepare the remedy. It is appropriate for conditions that come on suddenly and which are often very acute, sometimes as a result of exposure to cold. Illnesses may follow a fright, particularly in young children.

Conditions that respond to aconite are those characterised by intense pains, such as neuralgia. The sufferer cannot bear to be touched and will seem hot

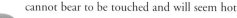

headaches; inflammation; sudden colds or fevers; a red, raw, sore throat; violent sudden nausea and vomiting, and croupy coughs, particularly those that come on after exposure to cold or dry air, will all respond to Aconite. It can also be used to treat shock and any trauma, either emotional or physical, to which it will respond.

In the case of sudden illness, take Aconite first, and then go on to other remedies if required.

### Properties and Uses
- For sudden and intense symptoms
- For ailments from exposure to the cold or after a fright
- For very high fevers and restlessness
- For onset of cramp
- For burning pains
- To quench thirst for cold water
- To reduce red inflammations
- ))))➤ *Homeopathy*

## ACUPRESSURE

Acupressure is one of the most ancient healing traditions, perhaps predating acupuncture itself. The Chinese discovered that pressure on specific points of the body could relieve common health problems. Acupressure is based on the same concept of meridians and acupoints in acupuncture but fingertip pressure is applied rather than needles. The aim is to balance the flow of energy within the meridians to ensure that all organs and body systems are functioning well. In this way disease is prevented or cured.

Acupressure is similar to *Shiatsu* in that it involves the use of finger pressure on acupuncture points to stimulate the smooth flow of *chi* (energy) through the channels of

*ABOVE LEFT: All types of yoghurt (including the organic variety, pictured here) are a rich source of Acidophilus, a form of lactic acid needed in constant supply by the intestine-friendly bacteria in our digestive tract.*
*LEFT: The Aconite homeopathic remedy is prepared from monk's hood and can be used to treat intense pains, such as neuralgia, or help lessen the effects experienced after a trauma or violent shock.*
*RIGHT: Acupuncture is an ancient Chinese medical technique practised as part of Traditional Chinese Medicine (TCM). As seen here, hair-thin needles are inserted through the skin at specific points to help redirect and redistribute chi, or vital energy, along the body's channels.*

the body. Unlike *Shiatsu*, acupressure involves mostly thumb and fingertip pressure, although it can also incorporate massage along the meridians. Pressure is used evenly and applied in the direction of the flow of the meridians. Pressure may also be applied using small wooden sticks with rounded ends for single points or rollers for covering several points simultaneously.

Acupressure is used to relieve a number of common ailments including headaches, back pain, fatigue, constipation, and is particularly useful for stress-related disorders such as digestive problems, mood swings, insomnia and even asthma. It can be self-administered, although knowledge of acupoints and meridians is essential to ensure that the proper points are being treated.

))))➤ *Acupuncture, Shiatsu, Traditional Chinese Medicine*

## ACUPUNCTURE

Acupuncture works by balancing the body's energy to encourage it to heal itself. It can be used to treat a wide range of conditions, including disorders for which conventional medicine has not been able to find a cure or even a cause.

Acupuncture is a medical technique practised in Traditional Chinese Medicine (TCM) and consists of inserting hair-thin needles into the skin at specific points, called acupuncture points or acupoints. It has been used for more than 4,000 years and is used not only for relieving pain but also for curing disease and improving overall health.

Chinese medical practitioners believe that a vital force, called *chi*, flows through our body in channels, or meridians. When this vital force, or energy, becomes blocked or stagnant, disease and disharmony result. Acupuncture works by stimulating or relaxing points along the meridians to unblock energy and encourage its flow. Twelve major meridians are identified in acupuncture, although practising acupuncturists make use of 59 major and minor meridians and up to 1,000 acupuncture points along the channels.

The first consultation will last for up to 90 minutes, and your therapist will take great trouble to make an accurate diagnosis, since the success of the treatment depends upon it. He will ask you questions about your health, lifestyle, medical history, symptoms, sleep patterns, sensations of hot and cold, any dizziness, eating habits, bowel movements, emotional problems, relationships and many other factors. He will also note various elements of your appearance, and take pulse readings from each wrist. There are six basic Chinese pulses, three on each wrist. He will then decide on a course of treatment to restore your energy and ensure that you experience optimum health.

The needles will be inserted into the skin and manipulated to calm or stimulate a specific point. He will use up to eight needles, which will either be left in for about 30 minutes, or removed very quickly. Your acupuncturist may also suggest some Chinese herbal treatment, or dietary or lifestyle changes, to go alongside the treatment.

The needles are typically inserted 0.3 to 1 cm ($^1/_{10}$ to $^4/_{10}$ in) deep, but some procedures require the needles to be inserted as deep as 25 cm (10 in). The acupuncture points are then stimulated either by gentle twirling, by heat, or by stimulation with a weak electrical current. Acupuncture points can also be stimulated by pressure, ultrasound and certain wavelengths of light. Occasionally herbs are burnt at acupuncture points and this technique is called moxibustion.

Acupuncture does not hurt but you will feel a tingling sensation when the needle enters, and a little discomfort if the correct acupuncture points are addressed. After treatment you may feel quite profoundly different – either elated or perhaps exhausted.

The World Health Organisation (WHO) recognizes the use of acupuncture in the treatment of a wide range of medical problems, including abdominal pain, allergies, constipation, diarrhoea, indigestion, anxiety, depression, insomnia, nervousness, neurosis, cataracts, gingivitis, poor vision, tinnitus, toothache, poor athletic performance, chronic fatigue, immune system tonification, stress, arthritis (including juvenile), back pain, muscle cramping, muscle pain or weakness, neck pain, headaches, migraines, bladder dysfunction, asthma, bronchitis, the common cold, sinusitis, tonsillitis, childhood illnesses and flu. Conditions like cancer, Myalgic Encephalomyelitis (ME), irritable bowel syndrome (IBS) and allergies, which have not been satisfactorily explained or treated by conventional medicine have been, in some cases, cured by acupuncture.

➠ *Traditional Chinese Medicine*

## AGNUS CASTUS

*Vitex agnus-castus*

 The fruit of a pretty Mediterranean shrub, half-hardy in the UK.

### Properties and Uses
- Balances hormones
- Relieves premenstrual sydrome (PMS) with irritability, breast pain and water retention
- Helps menopausal symptoms, especially mood swings and depression; take with sage for hot flushes

- Helps restore a regular menstrual cycle when coming off the contraceptive pill or when the cycle has been disrupted

### Dosages
- The best time to take these berries is first thing in the morning, before breakfast. One cup of the decoction, or 20–30 drops of the tincture in a little water, daily, will usually suffice.

➠ *Herbalism*

## AGRIMONY

*Agrimonia eupatoria*

A wild plant with small yellow flowers on tapering spikes like church spires. A Bach flower remedy, Agrimony is for those who hide their problems and inner selves behind a cheerful face, masking real feelings of unhappiness and unworthiness. They are the life of a party and will make jokes, perhaps even inappropriately. The person who needs Agrimony finds it hard to deal with the darker, less pleasant parts of life and extreme emotions. They are reluctant to burden others and dread arguments, pursuing peace at all costs. This course can lead to an inner anguish and distress, often masked by alcohol or drugs.

Agrimony helps us love ourselves as we are and to cast aside the mask we wear; it helps us cope with the difficult sides of our nature and use humour appropriately.

## Key Notes

- The person who needs Agrimony will put on a brave face of cheerfulness
- Other distractions may include drink, drugs and dangerous, thrill-seeking hobbies or occupations
- They may be restless sleepers or unable to sleep without help

))))➤ *Bach Flower Remedy, Herbalism*

## ALEXANDER TECHNIQUE

The Alexander Technique was developed by Frederick Matthias Alexander, who believed that 'Every man, woman and child holds the possibility of physical perfection; it rests with each of us to attain it by personal understanding and effort'.

The Alexander Technique is not a therapy as such, but a process of re-education, which aims to teach us to rediscover our natural poise, grace and freedom and use our bodies more efficiently. It is taught in lessons where the practitioner is referred to as a teacher, not a therapist, and the individual participating in the lessons is known as a pupil, not a patient or client.

The Alexander Technique works on the principle that mind and body form a complex and integrated whole. As a holistic system, the technique is not taught in order to alleviate specific ailments, such as a stiff neck or aching back, but is concerned with addressing the source of such problems. However, it has been found that in the process of restoring harmony to the whole person, specific problems often disappear.

When taught by a qualified teacher, the Alexander Technique is safe for everyone to use. Young children do not usually need it as they have natural poise and balance, but they can be taught it as a preventative technique. Children with physical handicaps, such as polio and scoliosis of the spine, can also benefit from it. The technique is perfectly safe to learn at any stage of pregnancy. Pregnant women may find that it helps them

cope with their changing shape and the pressure it puts on their spine. Many women who learnt it during pregnancy believe it enabled them to have an easier labour.

The Alexander Technique is not a cure for any condition or illness, although many symptoms appear to improve during practice. To date, there is not much scientific evidence for the benefits of this technique, but students and teachers report an improvement in numerous problems. Stress-related conditions, general fatigue and lethargy, anxiety, breathing disorders, back, neck and joint pain are believed to be improved. It has also been shown to help in the recovery from illness or injury and is believed to increase self-awareness and improve both personal and professional relationships. Actors, singers and dancers claim it enhances their performance and sports men and women believe it improves their co-ordination and helps them to use their energy more efficiently.

*LEFT: Vitex agnus-castus.*

*RIGHT: The Alexander Technique re-educates people about their posture, grace and poise. It is often accompanied by dance movements and massages, which help render the body more flexible.*

## ALLERGY TESTING

There has been some recent controversy about the efficacy of conventional allergy tests. *Which?* magazine in the UK found them to be unreliable and, they decided, a waste of money. Other experts do not agree. All severe allergies will be picked up by one of two tests (see below). What can be difficult to assess is food intolerance, the symptoms of which do not often show up until much later.

There are two main types of tests:

- The skin-prick test is normally carried out in a doctor's or consultant's office: it involves placing a drop of the substance being tested on the patient's forearm or back and pricking the skin with a needle, allowing a tiny amount to enter the skin. If the patient is allergic to the substance, a weal (a mosquito bite-like bump) will form at the site within about 15 minutes.
- A radioallergosorbent test (RAST) requires a blood sample which is sent to a medical laboratory where tests are done with specific foods to determine whether the patient has produced antibodies to that food. This test is often used on young children who might become distressed by frequent pricks and, in the case of people who have eczema or other skin conditions, might make the results difficult to assess.

There are alternatives to conventional allergy tests. Hair mineral analysis is useful, as is a technique called auricular cardiac reflex (ACR) in which practitioners check for changes in pulse when food or chemicals suspected of being harmful are placed within the body's electrical field. Best of all, perhaps, is applied kinesiology which works on the theory that foods or chemicals to which an individual is sensitive cause muscle weakening as a result of changes in the body's electrical field. Practitioners place suspect substances in the hand or under the tongue and check for muscle weakening in the arms or legs for example.

))) *Diagnosis*

## ALLIUM CEPA
Red Onion

The onion, grown worldwide, has been used across many continents and by many religions for its healing properties. The whole red-onion bulb is used and its potent oil stimulates the tear glands and nasal mucous membranes, causing the eyes and nose to water. In homeopathy, it is used to treat any condition that includes these symptoms, such as colds and hayfever.

*Allium cepa* is particularly good for colds and hayfever symptoms: profuse mucous discharge, smarting and swollen eyes, sneezing, sore nose and upper lip from the irritation caused by streaming. It is also useful for burning or neuralgic pain that moves from side to side or, in children, neuralgic pain which accompanies earache, molar toothache which moves around and headaches occurring behind the forehead. The early stages of laryngitis can also be helped.

*LEFT: Sneezing is often the result of a very mild case of allergy to some inhaled or ingested airborne substance. Allergy testing is an effective way of profiling an individual's tolerance to allergic substances through skin-prick and radioallergosorbent (RAS) tests.*
*RIGHT: The Aloe Vera plant.*
*ABOVE RIGHT: An image of the almond plant, flowers and seeds from Stephenson's and Churchill's nineteenth-century botanical papers.*

## Properties and Uses

- For hayfever and colds
- For burning and irritating nasal discharge
- For profuse watery discharge from eyes
- For headache, toothache, earache in children, stuffiness, cough, neuralgia, colic in babies
- Symptoms improve in cool, fresh air and worsen in warm, stuffy rooms or cold, damp conditions

))))▶ *Homeopathy*

## ALMOND OIL

Sweet almond oil is often used as a carrier oil in aroma-therapy treatments, acting as a base for blending essential oils for the purpose of massage or other forms of treatment. Almond oil is one of the best carrier oils because it is not sticky, and is light enough for regular use on most skin types. Rich in vitamins, this oil is particularly good for dry skin and blends well with other oils. It can be used for face or body massage in people of all ages.

))))▶ *Carrier Oils*

## ALOE VERA

Known as *Kumari* in Ayurvedic medicine, Aloe Vera is used in many therapeutic disciplines, including Western herbalism, folk medicine and Ayurveda. The gel and the leaves of the Aloe Vera plant are used therapeutically. The gel is normally used for healing (see opposite), while the latex of the leaves is a powerful cleansing agent and a laxative.

Aloe gel can cause skin irritation in some people. If irritation persists discontinue use. Aloe Vera contains a powerful laxative, anthraquinone, which can cause diarrhoea and intestinal cramps. If you use Aloe juice or supplements as a laxative, do it under the guidance of a physician and never exceed the recommended dosage.

## Properties and Uses

- In Ayurveda, Aloe Vera is used for all three doshas to bring balance
- Aloe Vera relieves inflammation, soothes muscle spasms, purifies the blood and cleanses the liver
- Fresh Aloe gel, scooped or extracted from the spongy leaves of the plant, can be spread on the skin to heal burns, scalds, scrapes, sunburn and wounds
- Apply the gel directly to the outer eyelid to treat conjunctivitis
- Commercially packaged products use stabilized Aloe which has none of the fresh herb's healing properties

## Key Notes

- Drink the Aloe juice for internal conditions, apply the gel externally. To soothe wounds, clean first with soap and water. Cut several inches off an older leaf, slice it lengthways and apply the gel to the wound. Allow it to dry. You can then leave the gel on the wound for several hours, or wash it off and reapply if it is painful.

))))▶ *Ayurveda, Herbalism*

## AMINO ACIDS

Amino acids are organic compounds that comprise the building-blocks of proteins in the body. A number of amino acids play an essential role in building our bodies. There are many different amino acids, about 20 of which are the main constituents of proteins; only about half of these are classified as essential nutrients – that is, necessary in the human diet.

Proteins are essential substances in our diets because of their constituent amino acids. Nutritionally, complete proteins are those that contain the right concentrations of amino acids which humans cannot synthesize from other amino acids or other sources. An adequate diet, however, may be achieved by consuming the correct mixture of proteins, some of which might be deficient in one amino acid but rich in another. Some of these amino acids are used directly as building-blocks in the synthesis of new proteins, while others may be used to supply energy and still others, particularly when large amounts of proteins are consumed, may be excreted in urine. Amino acids are necessary to make almost all elements in the body, including hair, skin, bone, tissue, antibodies, hormones, enzymes and blood.

Experts suggest that amino acids should not be supplemented without the supervision of a trained practitioner.

## ANACARDIUM

*Anacardium orientale/semecarpus*

Grown in the East Indies, the Hindus use the acrid black juice of this nut to burn away moles, warts and other skin complaints. The Arabians used the juice for a number of conditions, such as mental illness, memory loss and paralysis. Homeopathically, cardol, the juice extracted from the pith between the shell and kernel, is used to make the remedy which is prescribed for 'tight' feelings of pain.

This remedy is useful when there is a feeling of tightness or constricted pain. Other conditions that may be relieved are itchy skin, piles, constipation, indigestion, duodenal ulcers (which feel better immediately after eating, but cause discomfort two hours later) and rheumatism. It is particularly beneficial for those who suffer from an inferiority complex and who want to prove themselves, or for those who feel that they have been humiliated and want to vent their anger.

The Anacardium constitutional type normally has a pale face, blue rings around the eyes, a strong moral sense, feels guilty, is easily offended, lacks self-confidence and likes dairy produce.

### Properties and Uses
- Relieves constricted pain, plugged ear, nose or back passage
- Helps with loss of memory, leading to harsh behaviour, obsessive/compulsive behaviour and fixations
- The patient will normally be irritable and/or suffering from nervous exhaustion

*ABOVE: Different types of amino acids are contained in all varieties of meat.*

*ABOVE RIGHT:* Anacardium orientale.

*RIGHT:* Angelica archangelica.

- Suitable for conditions with a tight feeling of constriction, duodenal ulcers, blocked gut or anus
- Symptoms usually improve immediately after eating, when lying on the affected part, after rubbing and tend to worsen around midnight, after washing in hot water and using a compress

## ANGELICA
*Angelica archangelica*

The healing properties of Angelica were so revered in antiquity that it was called 'the root of the Holy Spirit'. There are over 30 varieties of Angelica grown around the world; at least 10 are highly valued in Traditional Chinese Medicine (TCM). Many more are used in Ayurvedic medicine, Western herbalism, aroma-therapy and folk medicine. The root and the seeds are used to produce the essential oil which has a musky sweet, woody scent.

Take care not to use this remedy during pregnancy or if you are a diabetic. Do not use on skin exposed to sunlight as Angelica oil tends to attract insects.

### Properties and Uses
- Angelica is a tonic and stimulant that seems to strengthen the im-mune system.
- Detoxifying and diuretic properties stimulate the circulation and lymphatic system to eliminate toxins from the body, making it useful for cellulite, arthritis and fluid-retention problems.
- Relieves indigestion, flatulence and benefits digestive problems caused by stress
- Angelica's expectorant properties are beneficial in treating colds, bronchitis and respiratory infections.
- Good for dull, congested or irritated skin and is believed to have an affinity with the female reproductive system.

⟫⟫ *Ayurveda, Chinese Herbalism, Herbalism*

## ANGELICA
*Angelica archangelica* and *Angelica sinensis*

In the West, Angelica has been associated with magic and sorcery for centuries. Necklaces of Angelica leaf were thought to provide protection against spells and illness, and its presence in a garden or cupboard was a defence against charges of witchcraft. Chinese Angelica, or *Dong Quai*, has been used in Asia for thousands of years and is enjoying renewed popularity as a gynaecological aid. Ayurvedic practitioners prescribe the herb for menstrual problems, as well as arthritis, abdominal pains and flu. Western herbalists use Angelica for convalescence, persistent fevers, indigestion and weak digestion in general, colic and cramping pains, coughs, poor circulation and general weakness with feelings of cold.

Fresh Angelica roots are poisonous so they must be dried to eliminate all hazard. Do not use with hyper-tension or heart disease. Pregnant women should avoid the overuse of Angelica.

### Properties and Uses
- In Ayurveda, Angelica balances all three doshas. It is a wonderful expectorant and digestive aid.
- Prepare the leaves and seeds as an infusion for a mild treatment, or use the root in a decoction for a stronger effect
- Angelica is pungent and sweet, heating and moisturizing. It is a stimulant, expectorant, tonic, emenagogue, carminative and diaphoretic
- Angelica has antibacterial properties, and has been used to induce menstruation and abortion
- In Chinese herbalism, Angelica is used for blood-deficient symptoms such as a pale complexion, tinnitus, blurred vision, palpitations and is commonly used for all menstrual disorders, such as irregular menstruation, amenorrhoea or dysmenorrhoea (painful periods)

- It is essential for pain in general as it moves the blood, including abdominal pain, traumatic injury and even arthritic pain; it is useful for dry stools and helps heal sores

### Dosage

- For an infusion, use one teaspoon of the powdered leaves or seeds in a cup or teapot. Add one cup of boiling water. Steep for 10–15 minutes. Strain. For a decoction, take three teaspoons of the powdered root. Add three cups of water and bring to the boil. Cover and simmer for five minutes. Remove from the heat and let stand for 15 minutes.

))))➤ *Aromatherapy, Ayurveda, Chinese Herbalism, Herbalism*

## ANISEED

*Pimpinella anisum*

Aniseed works mainly on the stomach, intestines and lungs, and its powerful oil is extracted for a wide variety of therapeutic uses.

### Properties and Uses

- Expectorant, antispasmodic, carminative, anti-microbial, aromatic
- The volatile oil in aniseed provides the basis for its internal use to ease griping, intestinal colic and flatulence; it also has an expectorant and antispasmodic action and may be used for bronchitis, for tracheitis where there is persistent irritable coughing, and for whooping cough

- Externally, the oil may be used in an ointment base for the treatment of scabies; the oil by itself will help in the control of lice
- It has mild oestrogenic effects which explains the use of this plant in folk medicine to increase milk secretion, facilitate birth and increase libido

### Dosage

- Infusion: the seeds should be gently crushed just before use to release the volatile oils. Pour one cup of boiling water over one to two teaspoonfuls of the seeds and let it stand covered for 5–10 minutes. Take one cup three times daily. To treat flatulence, the tea should be drunk slowly before meals.
- Oil: one drop of the oil may be taken internally by mixing it into half a teaspoonful of honey.

## ANT CRUD

*Antimonium crudum*

This homeopathic remedy is prepared from black sulphide of antimony, which occurs naturally as an ore. It is known as the 'pig's remedy', because it is most appropriate for those with a large appetite, and when the stomach and digestive system are affected.

Ant Crud is useful for treating an upset stomach and vomiting caused by overeating. Vomit is normally acidic. Children who will benefit from Ant Crud may be irritable and fretful, but will not want attention. In low dosages, Ant Crud can be taken for long periods of time to treat calluses and corns on the feet.

*ABOVE LEFT: Angelica archangelica.*
*ABOVE: Antimonium crudum.*
*RIGHT: Pimpinella anisum (aniseed).*

**Properties and Uses**
- For irritability and fretfulness
- For treating a thick white coating on the tongue
- For lumpy discharge
- For rough, hardened, cracked skin
- For nostrils, corners of the mouth and sore, cracked feet
- For sensitive feet
- For sensitivity to cold

**Key Notes**
- Symptoms worsen in damp weather
- Symptoms worsen in Sun and heat
- The Ant Crud type tends to be peevish, gloomy and sulky, often sentimental
- Adults can feel depressed, even suicidal, and generally want to be left alone
- This type tends to be voraciously hungry, never feeling satisfied

## ANTIMONIUM TART

Antimony potassium tartrate is a poisonous crystalline salt which has no colour or odour and is used as a fix for leather, textiles and in insecticides. In the past, it was used in conventional medicine as an emetic for internal worms, to induce vomiting and as an expectorant. Homeopathically, it is used to treat gastric disorders and chest complaints.

The Ant Tart type tends to be pale and sickly-looking with dark rings around the eyes and a cold sweat on the face. The individual may look run down, and will hate being disturbed or fussed over when ill.

### Properties and Uses

- For people who are irritable, anxious and despairing
- For chest complaints and coughs with rattling breathing and great difficulty in bringing up phlegm
- For stomach upsets with nausea, weakness and cold sweats
- For people who are uninterested in food and drink
- To treat drowsiness
- Symptoms improve when sitting up, after vomiting

and in cold air; they worsen in stuffy rooms and, if wearing too much, with movement or when lying down

### Key Notes

- This remedy is particularly good in the very young or the very old who are too feeble or weak to help themselves, for instance by helping them cough up phlegm. Wet, cold conditions bring on thick, excess mucus in the air passages, leading to rattling breathing. Sour food or drink can lead to gastric problems, intense nausea and lack of thirst.
- Other symptoms which can be treated include headaches with the sensation of having a tight band around the head, a face cold to the touch, a thickly coated tongue, fluid retention (leading to bloated legs) and nausea.

## ANTIOXIDANTS

Much of the cell damage that occurs in disease is caused by highly destructive chemical groups known as free radicals. These are the products of oxidation, a process that naturally occurs in our body as we breathe. Today, because of increasing levels of pollution in the air, there are more free radicals than ever before. In small quantities free radicals can fight off bacteria and viruses, but in larger quantities they encourage the ageing process and cause premature damage to our cells.

Free-radical damage is believed to be the basis for the ageing process and for the visible signs of ageing, such as greying hair, wrinkles, skin changes and muscle wastage. Free radicals can be formed by exposure to radiation and toxic chemicals, such as those found in cigarette smoke, over-exposure to the Sun's rays or various metabolic processes, such as the process of breaking down stored fat molecules for use as an energy source.

*LEFT: Antimonium tart can treat headaches, especially those that manifest themselves through a constricted feeling around the head.*
*ABOVE RIGHT: A number of nutrients contained in fruit act as antioxidants to provide protection against free radicals operating in the environment.*
*CENTRE RIGHT: Gingko biloba (The plant pictured) when taken in supplement form can help minimize the damage exerted by free radicals.*

Free radicals are normally kept in check by the action of free-radical scavengers which occur naturally in the body and which act to neutralize the free radicals. The body makes these as a matter of course. There are also a number of nutrients that act as antioxidants, including vitamin A, betacarotene, vitamins C and E and the minerals selenium and zinc.

Although many antioxidants can be obtained from food sources, such as fresh fruit and vegetables, it is difficult to get enough of them from these sources to prevent the generation of free radicals caused by our polluted environment, the number of chemicals in our foods and many other factors. Free-radical damage can be minimized by taking supplements of key nutrients, such as the ones listed above, and the following:

- Alpha-lipoic acid
- Bilberry
- Coenzyme Q10
- Cysteine
- Grapeseed extract
- *Ginkgo biloba*
- Glutathione
- Green tea

There are a variety of different combination supplements now available on the market, and these are probably the easiest and most effective forms in which to take these nutrients.

Many trials have shown that additional antioxidant vitamins, such as 2000 mg of C and 400 mg of E daily, can significantly reduce the number of heart attacks, strokes, cataracts and other diseases, and slow down the process of ageing. The following also represents promising research.

Vitamin E has been found to enhance a variety of immune-system responses by reducing blood stickiness, the harmful effects of toxins such as cigarette smoke, the damage caused by the Sun (when applied topically) and halving the risk of heart attack in those with heart disease. Vitamin E also prevents cataracts and, when taken with vitamin A, improves some cases of hearing loss. It is essential for skin health, and age spots are one of the key deficiency signs.

Selenium is the other most important antioxidant and it has now been proven that it decreases the rate of cancer and increases life span. Selenium deficiency is

also signalled by age spots, cataracts, cancerous changes, infections, muscle inflammation and heart disease, so it has an undoubted effect on many parts of the body. In research studies, selenium supplements have been found to improve kidney function, help prevent liver cancer, enhance immune function, improve thyroid function, treat skin conditions and reduce the symptoms of arthritis.

Over 150 studies show that antioxidants significantly reduce the risk of cancer at virtually all major sites of the disease.

))))➤ *Minerals, Vitamins*

## APIS

*Apis mellifica*

The bee is known for its unique ability to produce honey and for its painful sting. In homeopathy, Apis is used to treat stinging pain and inflamed, burning skin which has swollen up and is painful to touch. Found commonly in Europe, Canada and America, the whole live bee is used homeopathically, including its sting, and is dissolved in alcohol.

Apis is used for complaints, such as bites, stings and urticaria, when the skin becomes swollen, red and itchy, or burns and stings, and is sensitive to the touch. It is also used for urinary tract infections, such as cystitis and for urine and fluid retention. Allergic reactions which affect the nose, eyes and throat, including anaphylactic shock, when watery swelling occurs, and complaints in which joints become swollen, such as arthritis, can also be treated. It is also good for fever accompanied by dry skin, a sore throat, severe headache and lack of thirst. During pregnancy, take care to avoid Apis below a 30c potency.

Apis types tend to be protective of their own territory, irritable and difficult to please. They spend hours trying to do things without making headway and love to organize other people's lives. They have a 'stinging' retort or respond harshly to those who cross them.

### Properties and Uses

- Relieves hot stinging pain, smarting, watery swellings
- Reduces sensitivity to touch
- Lowers fever accompanied by dry skin
- Relieves violent headache
- Helps lack of thirst
- Helps scant urination
- Reduces restlessness
- Diminishes jealousy and irritability
- Helps unpredictability
- Symptoms improve under cool conditions, but worsen when touched, in heat or during sleep

## APPLE

*Malus species*

Apple has many uses in traditional medicine and the old adage 'to eat an apple going to bed, will make the doctor beg his bread' has been justified by its many health-giving properties. Modern research shows that apples are excellent detoxifiers and apple juice – even from the supermarket shelf – can destroy viruses in the body. Pay attention, however, to how many apple seeds you actually ingest as they can be toxic when taken in large amounts.

### Properties and Uses

- Cleans teeth and strengthens gums
- Lowers cholesterol levels
- Antiviral action
- Detoxifies
- Protects from pollution by binding to toxins in the body and carrying them out
- Neutralizes indigestion
- Prevents constipation
- Soothing with antiseptic properties
- Eat raw apples regularly as a detoxificant for gout and rheumatism
- To prevent viruses from settling in and to reduce their duration, eat an apple (or a glass of apple juice) three times a day
- Raw, peeled and grated apples can be used as a poultice for sprains
- For indigestion, heartburn and other digestive disorders, eat an apple with meals

- Use as a poultice for rheumatic and weak eyes
- Two apples a day can reduce cholesterol levels by up to 10 per cent
- As a treatment for intestinal infections, hoarseness, rheumatism and fatigue, increase your daily intake to up to l kg (2.2 lb)
- For curative purposes, as an alternative to eating the whole fruit, drink 600 ml (1 pt) of naturally sweet apple juice a day
- Grated apple, mixed with live yoghurt, may be helpful in cases of diarrhoea

## ARG NIT

*Argentum nitricum*

Silver nitrate, the source of this remedy, was given the names 'Hell Stone' or 'Devil's Stone' because of its corrosive effect. Silver nitrate is extracted from the mineral acanthite, the main ore of silver. Safe in small doses, large amounts are poisonous, causing breathing problems and damaging the kidneys, liver, spleen and aorta, and overdosing affects the skin, turning it permanently blue. In homeopathy, the remedy is most frequently used for nervous and digestive complaints.

Arg Nit is mainly used for fear and anxiety, usually brought on by stress, and can help problems, such as claustrophobia, dangerous impulses and stage fright. It can also control the overwhelming feeling that something awful is about to happen. It is very useful for digestive problems, such as diarrhoea and vomiting, particularly if the symptoms are brought on by nerves and headaches which begin slowly and are caused by overeating sweet foods. It also helps other conditions such as asthma, colic in babies, epilepsy, warts and sore throats. During labour, it can help bring relief when bearing down.

The Arg Nit type looks stressed, is often prematurely old, with hollowed features and wrinkles. They tend to be in jobs where rapid responses and a good memory are necessary. Outwardly exuberant and happy, they also suffer from internal turmoil and emotional in-stability, meaning that they cry easily, or lose their tempers. They will fret about what might happen in the future. Arg Nit types often prefer salty foods, dislike cold food and crave sweetness.

### Properties and Uses

- Relieves fears, anxiety, phobias, palpitations, sweating
- Relieves mental exhaustion
- Helpful for people under stress who find it hard to control their emotions, leading to irrational thoughts and impulses
- Helpful for people under pressure who push themselves because of a fear of failure
- Helps digestive complaints brought on by nerves and tension
- Helps with effects of excessive intake of sweet foods
- For bloating and flatulence
- Relieves tension in the neck
- Relieves headaches caused by overwork
- Symptoms improve in fresh air, cool conditions and if pressure is applied, but worsen in heat, at night, under stress and if lying on the left side

))))➤ *Amino Acids*

*LEFT: In homeopathy,* Apis mellifica *is effective in treating red, inflamed skin.*
*ABOVE LEFT: Cox's apples.*
*ABOVE: The homeopathic remedy* Argentum nitricum *is suitable for people under pressure or who are anxious.*

## ARGININE

L-arginine is one of the most important and useful amino acids with a significant role in muscle growth and repair, helping to regulate and support key components of the immune system. It is also extremely important for male fertility. A non-essential amino acid, it is capable of being synthesized in the body and it is therefore not crucial that we get additional amounts in our daily diet. It is, however, essential for children.

Take on an empty stomach and avoid consuming in excess as it could cause mental and metabolic disturbances, nausea and diarrhoea. Prolonged high doses may be dangerous to children and to anyone with liver or kidney problems.

The best sources are raw cereals, chocolate and nuts.

### Properties and Uses

- Boosts immunity
- Fights cancer by inhibiting the growth of tumours
- Builds muscle and burns fat by stimulating the pituitary glands to increase the secretion of growth hormone
- Helps to promote the healing of burns and other wounds
- Helps to protect the liver and detoxify harmful substances
- Increases low sperm count in men

### Dosage

- The optimal intake is unknown, but doses of up to 1.5 g appear to be safe.
- Take Arginine with lysine, which inhibits herpes attacks in carriers

))))➤ *Amino Acids*

## ARNICA

*Arnica montana*

Arnica has been used for its healing properties for centuries. It grows in the mountain regions of Europe and Siberia. In folk remedies it was used for aches and bruises and in conventional medicine for rheumatism, gout and dysentery. When in flower the whole fresh plant is used externally as a cream for sprains and bruises, and internally to treat shock, often following an injury.

Arnica is an effective first-aid treatment for bruising, sprains and strains. Internally, it can help control bleeding and stimulates the healing of damaged tissue. It is also useful for shock, either after an injury or emotional trauma. It can be used for long-term joint and muscle complaints such as osteoarthritis. Internal treatment can aid external conditions such as boils. Remember not to use arnica cream on broken skin.

The arnica type is morose and, when ill, denies there is a problem, preferring to be left alone. They are often morbidly imaginative.

### Properties and Uses

- Relieves bruises, sprains, pain and shock from injury
- First remedy to consider in any physical trauma
- For fear of being touched or being approached when in pain
- For nightmares
- For use if feeling sore and bruised in whole body or affected part
- For use after dental work, surgery, or childbirth.
- Will promote rapid healing and prevent haemorrhage
- For hot head and cold body
- Symptoms improve during movement and when lying down with the head lower than the feet; they worsen after prolonged movement or rest, under light pressure and in heat

## AROMATHERAPY

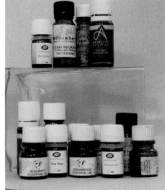

Aromatherapy involves the use of essential oils, which are the life force of aromatic flowers, herbs, plants, trees or spices, for therapeutic purposes. The word aromatherapy literally means 'treatment using scents' and the therapy has evolved as a branch of herbal medicine. Unlike the herbs used in herbal medicine, essential oils are not taken internally but are inhaled or applied to the skin. Each oil has its own natural fragrance and therapeutic action. Treatment involves applying these oils to the body to improve physical, mental and emotional health.

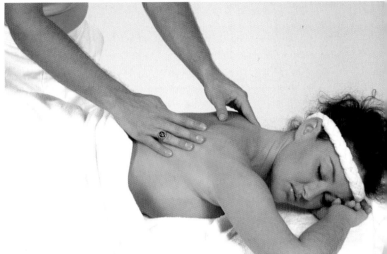

Essential oils enter the body by inhalation and absorption through the pores of the skin. Once in the body, they work in three ways: pharmacologically, physiologically and psychologically. The chemical constituents of the oils are carried in the bloodstream to all areas of the body, where they react with the body's chemistry in a way that is similar to drugs. Certain oils also have an affinity with particular areas of the body and their properties have balancing, sedating or stimulating effects on body systems. Once inhaled, aromatic signals are sent to the limbic system of the brain, where they exert a direct effect on the mind and emotions.

There are many ways to use essential oils at home. Massage and bathing tend to be the most popular, and techniques which involve applying oils to the body are usually more effective than inhalation. However, there are several other techniques which are particularly beneficial for certain conditions. These include steam inhalations, creams, lotions and shampoos, gargles and mouthwashes, neat applications (only appropriate for some oils), douches and compresses.

Aromatherapy is gentle enough to be used by people of all ages and states of health. It is nurturing for babies and children and offers comfort and care to the elderly. Pregnant women, and even seriously ill patients with cancer or AIDS, can benefit from professional treatment. The therapy has been shown to be particularly effective in preventing and treating stress and anxiety-related disorders, muscular and

rheumatic pains, digestive problems, menstrual irregularities, menopausal complaints, insomnia and depression.

Aromatherapy is compatible with conventional medicine and most other forms of holistic treatment. However, if you are taking other medication, consult your doctor first. Some oils are not compatible with homeopathic treatment. Aromatherapy is safe to use at home for minor or short-term problems providing you follow certain guidelines:

• Do not take essential oils internally unless advised by a registered and experienced aromatherapist
• Do not put essential oils in the eyes
• Keep all oils away from children
• Do not apply oils undiluted to the skin, unless it is stated that it is safe to do so

Consult a qualified practitioner for advice and treatment if you:
• Are pregnant
• Have an allergy
• Have a chronic medical condition, such as high blood pressure or epilepsy
• Are receiving medical or psychiatric treatment
• Are taking homeopathic remedies
• Have a chronic or serious health problem, or if a problem becomes severe or persistent
• Are treating an infant
⫸ *Essential Oils*

*ABOVE LEFT: Arnica cream can be used to soothe cuts, bruises and grazes on the skin.*
*LEFT: Essential oils used in aromatherapy.*
*ABOVE RIGHT: Woman receiving an aromatherapy massage.*

## ARSENIC

*Arsenicum album*

Arsenic has a rather questionable reputation as a murder weapon. Indeed, poisoning by arsenic is the mainstay of many murder mysteries. Thankfully, arsenic poisoning is no longer a common cause of death. In the past, small doses were given to treat syphilis, anthrax and to improve stamina. Arsenic is made of metallic crystals which cannot be destroyed. In homeopathy, a minute compound of arsenic is used, which works beneficially on the sensitive lining of the digestive tract and respiratory system.

*Arsenicum album* is given to those suffering from anxiety, being alone, fear of the dark, fear of failure, etc., which are caused by underlying feelings of insecurity. It is also useful for problems of the digestive system, such as indigestion, diarrhoea and vomitting, food poisoning and excessive eating, such as over-consumption of fruit or ice cream and drinking too much alcohol. Arsenic can be used to treat a range of conditions which particularly sting or burn, such as mouth ulcers, sore lips, eye inflammation, vomiting and burning pains in the rectum. Asthma, fatigue, fluid retention, especially around the ankles, can also be helped.

The *Arsenicum* type is elegant, organized and plans well in advance for every eventuality. They tend to be insecure and unconfident underneath, but they have strong ideas which make them intolerant of others. They want everything done perfectly and, of course, their way. They are restless and worry about their own health and that of their loved ones. *Arsenicum* people are chilly people who crave heat.

### Properties and Uses

- Relieves digestive disorders; fear and anxiety; regular, painful headaches; problems that are accompanied by a burning pain
- For fear of being alone, being robbed, or dying
- For anxiety, which causes restlessness and irritability
- For meticulous people who hoard and are possessive
- For headaches, dizziness, vomiting, diarrhoea, asthma caused by anxiety, fluid retention, cracked lips and ulcers

- Symptoms improve with movement, in warmth, when lying down with the head propped up, and are wor-sened on the right side in the cold, after cold food and drinks

## ASPARTIC ACID

L-Aspartic acid is a non-essential amino acid which has been used for many years in the treatment of chronic fatigue. Studies confirm the efficiency of this amino acid in raising energy levels and in helping to overcome the side effects of drug withdrawal. Do not take with protein, such as milk, and do not take more than 1g without the supervision of your doctor.

### Properties and Uses

- Disposes of ammonia, helping to protect the central nervous system
- Helps treat fatigue
- Improves stamina and endurance

### Dosage

- Supplements are available in 250–500 mg tablets; take three times daily with juice or water

⟫⟫ *Amino Acids*

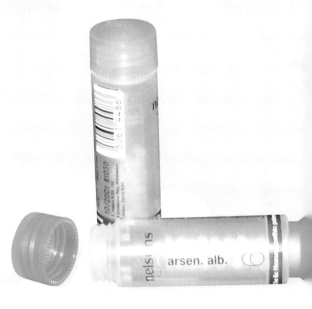

## ASPEN

 A slender silver-barked, deciduous tree with almost circular leaves which tremble with the slightest breeze, it grows to 9 m (30 ft) in height.

A Bach flower remedy, aspen is good for anxiety, apprehension and fear of things unknown. Dr Bach described it as being for 'vague unknown fear, for which there can be given no explanation, no reason'. The fear can be so deep-seated that the person may be too frightened to express it, or they may not acknowledge the sensation as fear, feeling as if burdened by doom and frozen somewhere inside by an unexplained and inexplicable dread or terror.

### Key Notes

- The person who needs aspen may feel frightened, a sense of dread and that something awful may happen. This may be extreme enough to affect appetite, produce palpitations and interrupt sleep patterns bringing nightmares.
- Aspen is suitable for the fears and nightmares of children.
- Aspen brings on a reassurance that there is nothing to fear. It helps us to face the unknown openly with courage and trust.

))⟩ *Bach Flower Remedies*

*LEFT: The tiny concentration of* Arsenicum *found in homeopathic tablets (pictured) is beneficial to the lining of the digestive and respiratory systems. BELOW: Bach flower remedies.*

LEFT: A type of astragalus.
NEAR RIGHT: Auricular therapy is a type of acupuncture which focuses on targeting the ear to treat dysfunctions, pains and imbalances occurring in other parts of the body.
FAR RIGHT: Edward Bach (pictured), the creator of the Bach flower remedy theory.

## ASTRAGALUS

*Astragalus membranaceus*

Used in both Chinese and Western herbalism, astragulus is an important herb for immune function, and for adrenal gland function and digestion. In Chinese medicine it is known as *Huange Qi* and, in that discipline, is widely used for spleen disorders.

According to Chinese medicine, astragulus tonifies the spleen and benefits the *chi*. It also helps water balance problems, such as retention, by regulating the opening and closing of pores and reducing swelling. It is a great tonifier and particularly useful if severe blood loss occurs. It is useful for spleen-deficient symptoms, such as lack of appetite, fatigue and diarrhoea. Its action is upwards and outwards, so it can help with a prolapsed uterus or with uterine bleeding. It is used in prescriptions to help the immune system fight viruses, fight frequent colds and help excessive sweating.

### Properties and Uses

- Good for oedema and sores full of pus that have not yet discharged, and is also used in post-partum fever from a severe loss of blood
- Decoction or tincture for chronic fatigue, persistent infections, night sweats, multiple allergies and glandular fever
- Modern research shows that the herb helps to counteract tiredness and lack of appetite in patients undergoing chemotherapy and radiotherapy for cancer
- Soothing and healing for stomach ulcers

### Key Notes

- The root can be bought in Chinese herb shops. It is often used as a soup stock with other nourishing herbs for people with severe immune deficiencies.
- A safe herb for home use, but severely debilitated patients should always be seen by a professional herbalist who will prescribe according to the individual's condition and circumstances. Always tell the hospital if you are taking herbal medicine in conjunction with their treatment.

)))▶ *Chinese Herbalism*

## AURICULAR THERAPY

Auricular therapy is ear acupuncture. According to auricular therapists there are many benefits:

- It provides quick access to diagnostic information.
- You do not have to be treated with needles. Therapists can use very fine, small needles that go in to a depth of only one millimetre, but they can also use light therapy, electrotherapy or very small magnetically-charged ball bearings, which press on the relevant points.
- You can have semi-permanent treatment. Small needles can be embedded in the ear or small ball bearings can be taped over the necessary points for up to a week at

a time. This way you can press on the point when you feel the need.

- It is less invasive than body acupuncture and so is better for those patients who are anxious about their problem or the treatment, or who are reluctant to undress for treatment.
- It is an effective form of pain control with an immediate calming effect.

The ear is believed to mirror the shape of the foetus in the womb: the lobe represents the head, and points relating to the tongue, eyes, tonsils, teeth and ears are all found on the lobe. The rest of the points are positioned 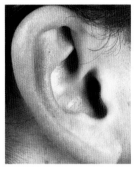 on the ear where they would exactly match the organs to which they correspond if a miniature foetus were super-imposed over the ear. Opinions vary as to how many points there are on the ear, some say there are 200, others say it is over 300, but each one relates to a specific organ or area of the body. Needling, or otherwise stimulating a point on the ear, affects the corresponding organ or meridian in the same way that stimulating a point on the body would.

Auricular therapy is an example of holographic therapy – the belief that small bits of the body can reflect the whole person. Therapists use the analogy of a mirror to explain the concept. If you look in a mirror it reflects your image, but if you smash the mirror into hundreds of pieces each small piece will still reflect your whole image. The Chinese consider the ear to be perfect for holographic therapy because it is a reflection of the kidneys, and to advocates of traditional Chinese medicine, the kidneys are the root of all.

))))▶ *Acupuncture*

## AUSTRALIAN BUSH FLOWER ESSENCES

The Australian Aboriginals have always used flowers to heal the emotions as did the ancient Egyptians. They were also very popular in the Middle Ages. In the fifteenth century Paracelsus wrote about how he collected dew from flowering plants, diluted it and used the liquid to treat imbalances. This healing method was rediscovered by Dr Edward Bach through the use of English flowering plants. Today our society and its needs are totally different from those of 60 years ago. There has been a great need for remedies that will help people deal with the issues of the modern world – self-awareness, sexuality, communication skills and spirituality to name but a few. The answer to this need has come from the Australian plants, developed and researched by naturopath, Ian White.

The bush remedies not only help give clarity to one's life but also the courage, strength and commitment to follow and pursue one's goals and dreams. They help to develop a higher level of intuition, self-esteem, spirituality, creativity and fun. The more the essences are used, the more one is likely to experience greater awareness and happiness in one's life.

))))▶ *Bach Flower Remedies*

## AVOCADO

*Persica americana gratissima*

Avocados are the fruit of a small, sub-tropical tree. They are rich in vitamins A, some B-complex, C and E, and potassium. Because they contain some protein and starch, as well as being a good source of monounsaturated fats, avocados are considered to be a perfect, or complete food. Traditionally avocados have been used for skin problems. The pulp has both anti-bacterial and anti-fungal properties. Do not eat avocados or take any product containing avocado if you have been prescribed the antidepressants monoamine oxidase inhibitors (MAOI).

### Properties and Uses

- Excellent restorative food, particularly during convalescence
- Traditionally used for sexual problems
- For skin disorders
- Antioxidant
- Used to treat circulatory problems
- Aids digestive system
- Antibacterial and anti-fungal
- Avocado paste can be applied to rashes and rough skin to soothe and smooth
- Avocado oil can be used as a base oil for massage
- Eat an avocado each day when convalescing
- The pulp, applied to grazes and shallow cuts, and covered with sterile gauze, can prevent infection and encourage healing
- Eat regularly for digestive and circulatory problems
- The flesh of a ripe avocado soothes sunburnt skin; cut in half and rub gently over the affected area

## AYURVEDA

Ayurveda is the traditional system of healing practised in India and Sri Lanka. Like Traditional Chinese Medicine (TCM), Ayurveda is a complete system, with a variety of different components aimed at improving emotional, physical and mental health. The discipline is thousands of years old; Ayurveda was well established before the birth of Buddha, and some biblical stories reflect the wisdom of Ayurvedic teachings.

Ayurveda is comprised of many different branches, in order to consider all aspects of health and healing. For example, Ayurvedic medicine is only one spoke on the Ayurvedic wheel and to benefit fully from Ayurveda it is helpful to consider the other elements, including astronomy, meditation, yoga, colour therapy, massage, sound and music therapy, a form of aromatherapy, breathing exercises, and much more. While the approach is vastly different from conventional Western medicine in some ways, it can be considered a programme for living which addresses every part of human life, and puts it into the context of our environment, and even the Universe. That is not to say that every element of Ayurveda is essential for health and well-being, but by following a simple Ayurvedic approach, we can develop ways of keeping ourselves balanced in times of increasing stress, pressure and worry. Most importantly, however, we can adopt a lifestyle that works to create harmony, preventing illness and encouraging our bodies to heal much more quickly when we do become ill.

In Ayurveda, it is believed that everything within the Universe, including people, is composed of energy, or *prana*. It is because we are made up of constantly changing energy that our bodies, our emotions and our physical environment change in ways that can be both positive and negative. Ayurveda teaches how to encourage the balance of these energies, which means that we are at ease within our bodies and the world around us. Energy controls the functions of every cell, thought, emotion and action, and so all aspects of our lives – including our health, our sleeping patterns, our happiness and well-being, and even our success – can be affected by getting the balance right.

Ayurveda is a Sanskrit word derived from two roots, *ayu* and *vid*, meaning 'life' and 'knowledge'. *Ayus*, or daily life cycles, represents a combination of the body, the senses organs, the mind and the soul. This science of life embraces both preventative measures and therapeutic procedures, enabling us to improve general health and to become aware of our natural needs and how to satisfy them.

## B1 (THIAMINE)

Thiamine is involved in all key metabolic processes in the nervous system, the heart, the blood cells and the muscle. It is useful in the treatment of nervous disorders, and can protect against imbalances caused by alcoholism.

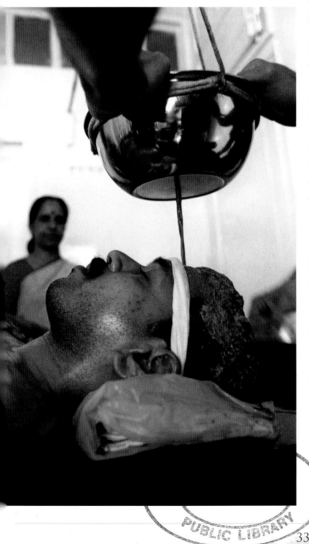

There are more cases of vitamin B1 deficiency than any other nutritional element – probably because of the high rate of alcoholism in our society.

Sources of B1 include all plant and animal foods, but good sources are wholegrains, brown rice, seafoods and pulses. It is also found in pork, milk, eggs, organic meats and barley.

### Properties and Uses

- Protects against imbalances caused by alcohol consumption
- May help to treat heart disease
- May be useful in the treatment of neurological disease (particularly those caused by B1 deficiency)
- May help to treat anaemia
- May improve mental agility
- May help to control diabetes linked to deficiency
- Useful in the treatment of herpes and infections
- Helps to convert sugar to energy in the muscles and bones

### Dosage

- Heavy drinkers, smokers and women who are pregnant or taking the pill should increase normal dosage to up to 100–300 mg per day
- Should be taken if you experience an increase in stressful conditions; most effective as part of a good B-complex supplement
- Thiamine is non-toxic, but it is not recommended that you take more than 400 mg daily

))))▶ *Vitamins*

*LEFT: A patient receives treatment comprising an Ayurvedic massage with medicated oils aimed at improving blood circulation.*
*TOP RIGHT: A glass of milk is rich in Vitamin B1 (thiamine).*

## B2 (RIBOFLAVIN)

Riboflavin is a water-soluble member of the B-complex family of vitamins. It is crucial for the production of body energy and has antioxidant qualities. Riboflavin is not stored in any significant amount in the body and deficiency is common. Riboflavin is non-toxic in most doses, but it is not recommended that you take in excess of 400 mg per day, unless supervised by a registered practitioner.

The best sources are milk, eggs, fortified breads and cereals, green leafy vegetables and fish.

### Properties and Uses
- Works with enzymes to metabolize fats, protein and carbohydrates
- Aids vision
- Promotes healthy skin, hair and nails
- Promotes healthy growth and reproductive function
- Boosts athletic performance
- Protects against anaemia

### Key Notes
- Pregnancy, breastfeeding, taking the pill and heavy drinking all call for an increased intake.
))))▶ *Vitamins*

## B3 (NIACIN)

Niacin takes the form of nicotinic acid and nicotinamide, and is a fairly recent addition to the family of B-complex vitamins, named as a vitamin in only 1937. Niacin has been shown to lower blood cholesterol, and other body fats, and is useful in the prevention of heart disease. It may also help to prevent diabetes.

The best sources for B3 are meat, fish, wholegrain cereals, eggs, milk and cheese.

### Properties and Uses
- Prevents and treats schizophrenia
- Aids in cell respiration
- Produces energy from sugar, fat and protein
- Maintains healthy skin, nerves, tongue and digestion

*LEFT: Brown bread is a good source of vitamin B2 (riboflavin), which is not stored in the body in vast amounts and must be restocked constantly through balanced nutrition.*
*RIGHT: Eggs are a rich source of vitamin B12 (cobalamin).*

- May lower cholesterol and protect against heart disease
- Reduces blood pressure

### Key Notes
- Large doses may be used therapeutically, but should be taken under the supervision of a doctor or practitioner.
- In high doses, niacin may cause depression, liver malfunction, flushing and headaches.
))))▶ *Vitamins*

## B5 (PANTOTHENIC ACID)

Pantothenic acid is a vital component of living cells. Chemical processes within the body convert it to an intermediary catalyst called coenzyme A which is critical for the production of energy which drives cell function. The best sources for B5 include most grains, vegetables and meats but this vitamin is especially plentiful in liver, yeast, salmon, eggs and dairy products.

### Properties and Uses
- Helps lower high cholesterol levels
- Alleviates arthritic pain

### Key Notes
- It works in conjunction with all other B vitamins.
))))▶ *Vitamins*

## B6 (PYRIDOXINE)

Pyridoxine is necessary for vitamin B12 to be absorbed. B6 is required for the functioning of more than 60 enzymes in the body and is required for protein synthesis. Of all the B vitamins, B6 is the most important for a healthy immune system, and it is thought to protect the body against some types of cancer.

The best sources for B6 are meat, fish, milk, eggs, wholegrain cereals and vegetables.

### Properties and Uses
- Boosts immunity

- Helps to control diabetes
- Assimilates proteins and fats
- Helps prevent skin and nervous disorders
- Treats symptoms of PMS and menopause
- Acts as a natural diuretic
- Protects against cancer

### Key Notes

- Should always be taken as part of a B-complex supplement, and in equal amounts with B1 and B2.
- Vitamin B6 is toxic in high doses, causing serious nerve damage if more than 2 g per day is taken. Some people report side-effects with doses as low as 100 mg.

))))➤ *Vitamins*

## VITAMIN B9 (FOLIC ACID)

Folic acid is a water-soluble vitamin which forms part of the B-complex family. It is also known as vitamin Bc or vitamin B9. Low levels of folic acid may lead to anaemia. Folic acid is essential for the division of body cells, and needed for the utilization of sugar and amino acids.

Recent findings indicate that folic acid can prevent some types of cancer and birth defects, and it is helpful in the treatment of heart disease. Most folic-acid deficiency is the result of a poor diet because it is abundant in leafy green vegetables, yeasts and liver. Taken from just before conception, and particularly in the first trimester of pregnancy, folic acid can prevent spina bifida.

The best source are green leafy vegetables, wheatgerm, nuts, eggs, bananas, oranges and organ meats e.g. liver.

### Properties and Uses

- Improves lactation
- May protect against cancer
- Improves skin
- A natural analgesic
- Increases appetite in debilitated patients
- Needed for metabolism of RNA and DNA
- Helps form blood
- Builds up resistance to infection in newborns and infants

- Essential for genetic code transmission
- Prevents spina bifida

### Key Notes and Dosage

- There are many people at risk of deficiency, including heavy drinkers, pregnant women; elderly and those on low-fat diets. Supplementation at 400–800 mcg is recommended for those at risk.
- Take with a multivitamin and mineral supplement.
- Folic acid is toxic in large doses and can cause severe neurological problems. High doses may cause insomnia and interfere with the absorption of zinc in the body.

))))➤ *Vitamins*

## B12 (COBALAMIN)

Cobalamin is a water-soluble member of the B-complex vitamin family, and it is the only vitamin that contains essential minerals. B12 is essential for the healthy metabolism of nerve tissue and deficiencies can cause brain damage and neurological disorders.

B12 was once considered to be a wonder drug and was given by injection to rejuvenate. B12 may also reduce the risk of cancer and the severity of allergies, as well as boosting energy levels. Low levels of B12 result in anaemia.

Good sources of B12 include liver, beef, pork, eggs, cheese, fish and milk.

### Properties and Uses

- Necessary for maintenance of the nervous system
- Improves memory and concentration
- Required to utilize fats, carbohydrates and proteins
- Increases energy
- Promotes healthy growth in children
- May protect against cancer
- Protects against allergens and toxic elements

### Dosage

- Doses of between 5–50 mcg should be adequate for most people; higher dosages should be supervised. Best taken as part of a B-complex supplement.
- Although Vitamin B12 is not considered to be toxic, it is not recommended that you take more than 200 mg daily, unless recommended by a registered practitioner.

))))➤ *Vitamins*

## BACH FLOWER REMEDIES

This delightful therapy is misleadingly simple, but the results can be dramatic. Flower essences, or flower remedies, as they are more commonly known, are used therapeutically to harmonize the body, mind and spirit. The bottled flower remedies are said to contain vibrations of the Sun's energy, absorbed by the flowers' petals when immersed in Sun-warmed water. The remedies use the vibrational essence of the flowers to balance the negative emotions which lead to, and can be symptoms of, disease. They are a simple, natural method of establishing personal equilibrium and harmony.

Flower remedies do not work in any biochemical way and, because there is no physical part of the plant remaining in the essence, its properties and actions cannot be detected or analysed as if it were a drug or herbal preparation. Therapists believe the remedies contain the energy or 'memory' of the plant from which it was made and work in a way that is similar to homeopathic remedies – on a vibrational basis.

Some of the remedies are known as 'type remedies'. Your type of essence is effectively the remedy that is most compatible with your personality or basic character, and it can be taken when the negative side of your character threatens the positive. The difficulty with a type remedy lies in analysing your character and deciding which remedy best matches it. For example, if you are a perfectionist and work hard to achieve results, this would be a positive side of your character. However, if you become obsessive about this work, aggressive and difficult to please, and demand too much of other people, then the negative side of this characteristic has taken over: the appropriate essence would redress the balance.

Flower remedies are ideal for home use as they are simple to make and use. They are made in water, preserved with alcohol and employ the ability of flowers to change and enhance mood, and to balance negative emotions which may contribute to disease.

Negative emotions depress the mind and immune system, and contribute to ill health. Some of the most common negative emotions include fear, uncertainty, loneliness, oversensitivity to influences and ideas, despondency, excessive concern for the welfare of others and despair. Just before physical symptoms set in, you may notice tearfulness, irrational fears (of being alone, for example), depression or anxiety. These are all negative emotional states that can be addressed using flower remedies.

Bach flower remedies work to rebalance negative emotions, improving well-being which will then lead to good physical health. They can be used to prevent and treat illness by working on the emotions.

Flower remedies can complement other types of therapies such as herbalism, homeopathy or aromatherapy, or be used alone. They are simple and effective and can be used to:

- Provide support in times of crisis
- Treat the emotional symptoms produced by illness
- Address a particular recurring emotional or behavioural pattern
- Help prevent illness by identifying negative emotional states that are the precursors to ill-health

Remedies act quickly and there should be an improvement within days, although it may take months to fully address a long-standing pattern.

### Dosage

- Up to five different essences may be chosen and mixed together at any time
- Put 2 drops of each essence in a 30 ml dropper bottle filled with water, and take 4 drops on the tongue or in a little water, four times daily

## BARLEY

*Hordeum sativum vulgare*

Barley is rich in minerals (calcium and potassium) and B-complex vitamins, which make it useful for convalescents, or people suffering from stress. Barley has been used for its restorative qualities, in medicine and in cooking, for thousands of years. Malt is produced from barley.

## Properties and Uses

- Anti-inflammatory – particularly for the urinary and digestive systems
- Taken daily, it may lower cholesterol levels
- Barley water can be used in the treatment of respiratory disorders, and eases dry, tickling coughs
- Barley water can be used for urinary tract infections and cystitis, and can ease flatulence and colic
- Cooked barley is easily digested and nutritious, and is a traditional remedy for constipation and diarrhoea
- Barley water reduces acidity in the spleen if drunk twice a day for a month
- Make a poultice of barley flour to reduce inflammation of the skin
- Barley may help to prevent heart disease, as it promotes the normal functioning of the heart and stabilizes blood pressure
- Eat in soups and stews when convalescing; barley is very nutritious

## BARLEY/WHEATGRASS

Barley grass is high in calcium, iron, the entire range of essential amino acids, chlorophyll, flavonoids, vitamin B12, vitamin C and many minerals and enzymes. As a food it helps to heal the stomach and aids both colon disorders and pancreatitis. It is also an effective anti-inflammatory.

Wheatgrass is a rich, nutritional food that became popular under the auspices of Dr Ann Wigmore, the founder of the Hippocrates Health Institute in Boston, USA. Wheatgrass contains a huge number of vitamins, minerals and trace elements. According to Dr Wigmore, 2.25 kg (1 lb) of wheatgrass is equal in nutritional value to nearly 70 kg (31 lb) of vegetables.

Because wheatgrass is a living food, there are various and rather spectacular claims made. For example:

- It helps to eliminate cancerous growths
- It helps mental health problems
- The molecular structure of chlorophyll (in which wheatgrass and barley grass are rich) resembles that of haemoglobin (the oxygen-carrying protein of the red blood cells); this means that wheatgrass is effective for a wide array of health complaints related to blood deficiency

- In experiments on anaemic animals, blood counts returned to normal after four or five days of treatment

))))► *Chlorophyll*

## BATHS

Water therapy, in the form of baths or showers, can be used to improve circulation and increase vitality so that the vital force can work more efficiently. It can also be used to ease pain. Hot, cold and alternate hot and cold water are used to achieve specific effects. Hot water is initially stimulating but has a secondary relaxing effect. Cold water is also stimulating with an invigorating and tonic effect. Alternate hot and cold baths or showers stimulate blood and lymph circulation, help to remove congestion and have a tonic effect on body tissues.

))))► *Aromatherapy, Naturopathy*

*LEFT: Ripe barley.*
*ABOVE: Turkish steam baths.*

*LEFT: Bee pollen is found in bee hives, and has been used as a medicine for thousands of years.*
*BELOW: A Bach flower remedy, beech helps people who are lonely and isolated.*
*RIGHT: Atropa belladonna (deadly nightshade).*

### Properties and Uses

- Rich in amino acids and protein
- Helps to suppress appetite and cravings
- May help to improve skin problems, and retard the ageing process
- May help to treat prostate problems
- Energizes the body
- Regulates the bowels
- May help to boost immunity and diminish allergies

### Dosage

- 400 mg doses, taken daily, appear to be safe levels
- Always take pollen with food

## BEECH

*Fagus sylvatica*

The common beech tree is the source of this flower remedy. A Bach flower remedy, beech is effective for arrogant, critical and intolerant people. Beech types are overly dependent on the environment, have their own way and are very proud that they can cope. They think problems should be solved in their way and are intolerant of those who cannot see the wisdom of that approach. They do not understand that everyone has different strengths and experiences. They think 'cannot' means 'will not' and therefore become irritable and short-tempered with others. They may feel unsupported and unappreciated.

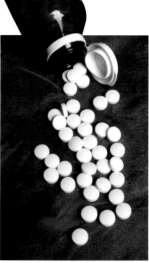

## BEE AND FLOWER POLLEN

In flowering plants the pollen-producing spores are located in the stamens of flowers. Flower pollen is said to be purer than bee pollen. Bee pollen is found in the hives themselves. It is rich in protein and amino acids and, along with honey, forms the basic diet of all the bees in the hive, except for the queen (see Royal Jelly). Pollen has been used as medicine around the world for thousands of years. If you suffer from hayfever or are allergic to bee stings you may suffer a reaction to bee pollen. Consult with your doctor before taking this supplement.

The best source is unpasteurized honey which contains small amounts of bee pollen.

## Key Notes

- People who need beech are often lonely and isolated. Lack of understanding and empathy leads to a narrow view and restricted expression.
- Beech fills hearts with empathy and opens eyes to see beauty without judgement. It teaches that we are all individuals with different methods for dealing with the world.

))))▶ *Bach Flower Remedies*

## BEHAVIOURAL THERAPY

Behavioural therapy, which was introduced at the turn of the twentieth century, is based on learning theories. It aims to predict and control behaviour using scientific means. It concentrates on observing and analysing behaviour and cognitive functioning, diagnosing unproductive habits and ways of dealing with life, and instituting changes in order to change and improve the outcome. Therapists discuss methods and expectations with patients, and the client agrees to participate at a negotiated level. Measures to monitor effectiveness are then established. The techniques used include:

- Counter-conditioning, which involves replacing an undesirable response to a stimulus with a new one
- Role playing, in which the therapist demonstrates more effective behaviours in a session, which the patients can then apply in real life
- Aversion conditioning, which involves pairing a stimulus that is attractive to the patient but would lead to undesirable results, with an unpleasant event or thought in order to break the pattern
- Desensitization, which involves relaxing the patient and then exposing them gradually and gently to anxiety-provoking situations

## BELLADONNA

*Atropa*

The deadly nightshade plant was used in witchcraft during the Middle Ages. *Bella donna* means 'beautiful woman' in Italian, and women used it in eyedrops to enlarge their pupils, making them more attractive. It is grown throughout Europe and the fresh leaves and flowers are used in homeopathy.

Commonly used for complaints with sudden onset, inflammatory states, fevers, tonsillitis, flu, earache – particularly on the right side. Helps severe, pounding headaches, jarred by eye movement, boils, sore breasts from breastfeeding, fits, cystitis, teething, sunstroke and scratching.

Belladonna types are normally strong, fit and healthy, lively and highly energetic when well. When ill, they can be restless, violent, agitated and stubborn.

### Properties and Uses

- Relieves sudden, intense inflammatory complaints, with flushing and throbbing pains
- For high fevers with staring eyes and dilated pupils
- Calms restless, excitable behaviour
- For wild hallucinations and nightmares
- For instances when the body is very hot with cold feet
- For sensitivity to light and the sun, and touch and movement
- For throbbing headaches
- For earaches, particularly on the right side
- For a bright red tongue and hot dry face
- Symptoms improve in warmth, standing up, with warm compresses and worsen when cool, on the right side, at 3 p.m., with movement, noise, light, pressure

## BELLIS PERENNIS

*Daisy*

This homeopathic remedy is similar to arnica, hypericum and calendula, and is mainly used following accidents, sprains and bruises. *Bellis perennis* is known as 'woundwort' or English arnica. It is most appropriate for wounds that are deeper within the body, such as in the abdomen or pelvis. The whole daisy plant is used to make this remedy.

*Bellis perennis* is best for injuries to the back or slipped discs, after major surgical operations, injuries or blows to the breasts, and where tumours develop from injuries. Helpful after Caesarean section and childbirth, and during pregnancy when there is lower back ache and the uterus feels sore and squeezed.

The *Bellis perennis* type is rather like the arnica type, and they tend to say they are well even when they are ill. When chronically ill, they may develop a sense of being downtrodden, becoming tired and wanting to lie down.

### Practises and Uses
- For tiredness when the sufferer wants to lie down
- For sciatica during pregnancy
- For sore joints and muscles
- For pains down the thighs and when the wrists feel contracted
- For bruised, sore feelings

- Waking at 3 a.m. and unable to get back to sleep
- Symptoms feel worse from touch, cold bathing, cold drinks, becoming chilled after hot baths, a warm bed and surgery, but improve from continued motion and cold applications

*LEFT: Bellis perennis (daisy).*
*ABOVE: Bergamot, the refreshing, essential oil from the Bergamot tree (illustrated here) is known to stimulate skin sensitivity towards the Sun.*
*RIGHT: Carrots are extremely rich in the carotenoid betacarotene.*

## BERGAMOT

The bergamot tree was originally cultivated in Italy, where the fruit has a history of use in folk medicine. The refreshing essential oil is expressed from the peel of the fruit, which resembles a small yellow orange. Outside Italy bergamot is perhaps best known as an ingredient in both Earl Grey tea and eau de cologne. Bergamot increases the skin's sensitivity to sunlight. Never use it undiluted on the skin and simply avoid if you have sensitive skin. Mix it with a carrier oil before adding to bathwater to ensure it disperses well in the water.

## Properties and Uses

- Joyous and uplifting bergamot is a powerful anti-depressant which has a wonderful balancing effect on moods
- As an antiseptic it is good for acne and boils, and other skin complaints such as oily skin, eczema and psoriasis; cuts and insect bites can also respond well to bergamot
- The oil inhibits viral activity; when diluted in alcohol it can be dabbed on cold sores, chicken pox and shingles
- The fragrance repels insects and the oil can be used to expel worms
- Bergamot has an affinity with the genitourinary system; it is a diuretic and a powerful urinary disinfectant, particularly good for cystitis; it can also be used for thrush and other types of vaginal itching and discharge
- As a digestive, bergamot is sometimes used to encourage appetite; it is also used to cool fevers

))))➤ *Essential Oils*

## BETACAROTENE

Betacarotene is known as a carotenoid, and is a precursor to vitamin A. It has antioxidant properties, and when food or supplements containing betacarotene are consumed, the betacarotene is converted to vitamin A by the liver. According to recent reports, betacarotene appears to help prevent cancer by neutralizing free radicals. Taking large amounts of vitamin A over a long period of time can be toxic, but no such overdose can occur with betacarotene.

The best sources of betacarotene are any brightly coloured fruits and vegetables, such as carrots, tomatoes, watercress, broccoli, spinach, cantaloupe and apricots.

## Properties and Uses

- Anti-carcinogenic
- Antioxidant
- Prevents and treats skin disorders and ageing of the skin
- Improves vision and prevents night blindness
- Improves the body's ability to heal
- Promotes growth of strong bones, hair, teeth, skin and gums

## Dosage

- The Recommended Daily Allowance (RDA) is now believed to be inadequate, and people with special needs (following illness, suffering from infections, with diabetes, for example), should have a higher level: 15,000 iu is considered to be the optimum dose.

))))➤ *Antioxidants, Vitamin A*

## BICARBONATE OF SODA

Bicarbonate of soda is a white powder used traditionally as a raising agent for baking. It is used in many natural remedies, and on its own for its soothing and neutralizing properties. Bicarbonate of soda should only be used externally on children and babies.

## Properties and Uses

- Anti-inflammatory, particularly for skin conditions
- Alkaline, which neutralizes acids
- A paste of bicarbonate of soda and water can be applied to nappy rash to reduce inflammation and irritation
- Drink a solution of bicarbonate of soda and hot water (one teaspoon for every 225 ml) to reduce flatulence and ease indigestion
- For bee stings, extract the sting and apply a paste of bicarbonate of soda and water to neutralize
- The juice of half a lemon mixed with one teaspoon of bicarbonate of soda and warm water will help ease a headache; drink every 15 minutes until pain is reduced

## BILBERRY

Also known as blueberry, the herb bilberry is a strong antioxidant that keeps capillary walls strong and flexible. It also helps to maintain the flexibility of the walls of the red blood cells and allows them to pass through the capillaries better. The entire plant is used in treatment. Bilberry contains fatty acids, flavonoids, iron, tannins and ursolic action. It can also interfere with iron absorption when taken regularly.

### Properties and Uses

- Helps to control insulin levels and strengthen connective tissues
- Inhibits the growth of bacteria and acts as an anti-inflammatory
- Anti-ageing and anti-carcinogenic
- It acts as a diuretic and urinary tract antiseptic
- Useful for hypoglycaemia, inflammation, stress, anxiety, night blindness and cataracts
- May help to halt or prevent macular degeneration

## BIOCHEMIC TISSUE SALTS

Biochemic tissue salts are homeopathically prepared and were introduced at the end of the nineteenth century by a German doctor, Wilhelm Schüssler. He believed that many diseases were caused by a deficiency of one or more of 12 vital minerals, and described exactly what each of them did in the body. He also listed the ailments he claimed could be cured by taking tissue salts as medicines in tablet form. A deficiency in each salt would manifest as particular symptoms. An imbalance in these salts would also cause a range of illnesses. Replacing them in small, easily absorbed doses restores balance and allows the body to heal itself.

Lack of *Calcerea phosphorica* (Calc Phos), for example, would show up as teething problems or an inability to absorb nutrients properly, while lack of magnesium phosphate (Mag Phos) would affect nerve endings and muscles. Replacing the missing mineral with a minute dose of the tissue salt can correct the problem.

The 12 tissue salts are listed in the homeopathic range of medicines, and hence are diluted, but the two therapies are quite different. While biochemics replenish the mineral deficiency believed to be causing the disease, homeopathic remedies are prescribed on a 'like cures like' basis, and are concerned with mental and emotional health as well.

Tissue salts can help many everyday aches and pains, and are used to treat simple symptoms that are usually self-healing, such as indigestion, colds, hayfever, stress, muscular pain, skin disorders, cuts and burns. Tissue salts can be used alongside homeopathic remedies.

The 12 tissue salts are: calcium fluoride (Calc Fluor), calcium phosphate (Calc Phos), calcium sulphate (Calc Sulph), iron phosphate (Ferr Phos), potassium chloride (Kali Mur), potassium phosphate (Kali Phos), potassium sulphate (Kali Sulph), magnesium phosphate (Mag Phos), sodium chloride (Nat Mur), sodium phosphate (Nat Phos), sodium sulphate (Nat Sulph), silicon dioxide (Silica).

They can be obtained from most health food stores, either as a single tissue salt or in a number of combinations that will address a number of complaints.

## BIOFEEDBACK

Biofeedback is a form of technologically supported relaxation therapy which was developed in the US. Patients are taught a series of relaxation exercises similar to Autogenic Training, but in biofeedback it is taken one step further and a patient's progress is monitored by machines which assess changes in heart rate, body temperature, muscle tension, skin conductivity and brain waves. Once training is complete, patients learn how to recognize their body's signals and reach a state of relaxation themselves, which is the basis of the therapy. Biofeedback trains patients to recognize the symptoms of stress, migraines, or whatever illness they suffer from, and then to take the appropriate steps to deal with them. The most common conditions which benefit from biofeedback are stress and anxiety related disorders such as insomnia, digestive troubles, headaches and high blood pressure.

)))➤ *Diagnosis*

## BIOFLAVONOIDS

Bioflavonoids were originally called vitamin P, and are also known as flavones. They accompany vitamin C in natural foods and are responsible for the colour in the leaves, flowers and stems of food plants. Their primary job is to protect the capillaries, keep them strong and prevent bleeding. Many of the medicinally active substances of herbs are bioflavonoids, which are non-toxic, and should be taken with vitamin C for best effect.

The best sources are citrus fruits, apricots, cherries, green peppers, broccoli and lemons. The central white core of citrus fruits is the richest source.

**Properties and Uses**
- Reduces bruising in susceptible individuals
- Protects capillaries
- Protects against cerebral and other haemorrhaging
- Reduces menstrual bleeding
- Has antioxidant properties, and encourages vitamin C's own antioxidant qualities
- Anti-viral activity
- Anti-inflammatory
- Anti-allergy
- May help to cure colds

)))➤ *Antioxidants, Vitamin C*

*LEFT: Vaccinium myrtillus (bilberry).*
*TOP RIGHT: Bioflavonoids are present in citrus fruits like lemons.*

## BLACK COHOSH

*Cimicifuga racemosa*

Also known as black snakeroot, black cohosh is a valuable herb that has a powerful action as a relaxant and a normalizer of the female reproductive system. It tones the womb and reproductive organs, and brings on menstruation or triggers labour. As it contains oestrogenic substances, this herb is useful for conditions where there is an oestrogen deficiency, such as menopause.

### Properties and Uses

- Emmenagogue, antispasmodic, alterative, nervine and hypotensive
- It may be used beneficially in cases of painful or delayed menstruation; ovarian cramps or cramping pain in the womb will be relieved

- Helps with the symptoms of PMS, including bloating, pain and emotional symptoms
- May help with skin complaints that occur cyclically
- Will give strength to weakened contractions during labour and will help the womb to shrink after childbirth
- It is very active in the treatment of rheumatic pains, but also in rheumatoid arthritis, osteoarthritis, in muscular and neurological pain
- Also useful in cases of sciatica and neuralgia
- As a relaxing nervine it may be used for nervous disorders and stress
- It has been found beneficial in cases of tinnitus
- It is also the basis of the homeopathic remedy *Cimicifuga racemosa*

### Dosage

- Use 10–30 drops of tincture diluted in water, or one teaspoon of root decocted to a cup of water

## BLACK-EYED SUSAN

*Tetratheca ericifolia*

A small scrubby plant of the Australian woodland. It is called 'black-eyed' as the drooping bell-like flowers have a core of black pollen-covered stamens surrounded by four mauve petals.

Black-eyed Susan is for people who are always rushing around and striving to get things done; the busy workaholics who do not have time for themselves or the people around them and expend all their energy outwards at a fast rate. The flower's petals protect the black centre, so the remedy helps one turn inward, slow down and pay attention to the inner rhythm.

### Key Notes

- People who need Black-eyed Susan are always 'on the go'. They hate waiting or delay as they rush to accomplish things quickly.
- Accompanying physical symptoms are irritability, poor digestion, restless sleep, general tension and stress. They may also have nervous rashes.
- Black-eyed Susan releases stress and helps slow down and find the inner peace to relax.

))))➤ *Australian Bush Flowers*

## BLUE BELL

*Wahlenbergia spp.*

A small perennial blue bell native to Australia. The small, blue, bell-like flowers appear in spring.

Blue bell is a remedy for the heart – it opens it wide to the flow of the Universe. People who need blue bell are emotionally closed and fearful. They fear that love will run out and they will be left with nothing. They may be possessive and greedy with objects standing as symbols for love.

### Properties and Uses

- For those who are emotionally closed and find it hard to share without keeping a mental tally of all emotional transactions
- For people who are possessive, greedy and possibly houseproud; for children who will not share
- For people suffering from congestive and containing symptoms such as indigestion, cramps, constipation or haemorrhoids

## BORON

Boron is a trace mineral found in most plants and it is essential for human health. Recent research has reported that boron added to the diets of post-menopausal women and prevented calcium loss and bone demineralization – a revolutionary discovery for sufferers of osteoporosis.

It is also claimed that boron will raise testosterone levels and build muscle in men, and is therefore often used by athletes and body builders. Boron is found in most fruit and vegetables, and does not appear in meat and meat products. Boron supplements are usually taken in the form of sodium borate.

Boron can be toxic, with symptoms including a red rash, vomiting, diarrhoea, reduced circulation, shock and coma. A fatal dose is 15–20 g, 3–6 g in children. Symptoms appear at about 100 mg.

The best sources of boron are root vegetables (such as potatoes, parsnips and carrots) grown in soil that is rich in the mineral.

### Properties and Uses

- External treatment of bacterial and fungal infections
- Lowers the incidence of arthritis
- Prevents osteoporosis
- Builds muscles

### Dosage

- No Recommended Daily Allowance (RDA), but it is suggested that you take 3 mg daily to prevent osteoporosis.

⟫⟫ *Minerals*

*LEFT: Cimicifuga racemosa (black cohosh).*

*ABOVE: Hyacinthus non-scriptus (bluebell).*

*RIGHT: Boron is found in most fruit and vegetables, but the best sources are root vegetables like carrots.*

## BREAD

Wholegrain bread is an excellent source of carbohydrates and B-complex vitamins, which maintain the health of the nervous system and ensure healthy functioning of body systems. Traditionally, bread was used as a poultice, and applied as a styptic to stop bleeding of wounds.

### Properties and Uses

- Nutritious
- Anti-inflammatory
- Apply cold bread to closed eyes to reduce the inflammation of conjunctivitis and soothe itching
- Apply a warm bread poultice to infected cuts to reduce itching and pain
- Apply fresh bread to shallow wounds to help stop the bleeding
- Apply a hot bread poultice to ease the pain of a boil and help bring it out

## BREWER'S YEAST

Brewer's yeast is the same type of yeast that is used in the brewing process, and is quite different from the yeast that causes *Candida albicans*. It is a rich source of B vitamins and amino acids, as well as some minerals, in particular chromium and selenium. It also contains naturally occurring nucleic acids (DNA and RNA) which are said to enhance the immune system, among other things.

Brewer's yeast comes in tablets, and as a powder that can be sprinkled on food or drinks. It is not toxic and can be taken daily without any side-effects. Some experts suggest that it may cause yeast infections and chronic fatigue syndrome, but this has largely been disproved.

### Properties and Uses

- May reduce wrinkling and aid in the treatment of skin problems
- Works as a wound-healing agent
- Encourages the healing of burns

- Rich source of B vitamins which can help to relieve stress and nervous disorders
- Encourages immune activity
- Increases energy
- Use externally to detoxify skin

⟫⟫ *Homeopathic Remedies*

## BRYONIA

*Bryonia alba*

Found in central and southern Europe, the deadly root of this plant is bitter-tasting and kills within hours of ingestion. The homeopathic remedy, in which the fresh root is pounded to a pulp, was one of the first to be proved in 1834 by Samuel Hahnemann and is mainly used for conditions which start slowly and worsen with movement.

It is often used for coughs, colds, headaches and flu which develop slowly and are accompanied by dryness (for instance, in the throat) and great thirst. Byronia is also useful for joint inflammation such as rheumatism and osteoarthritis, chest and abdominal inflammation, pleurisy, pneumonia, constipation and mastitis. People who need bryonia are like bears with sore heads.

Bryonia types are materialistic and fear poverty. They are anxious and irritable if their financial security is threatened. Rather plodding by nature, this type is straightforward and reliable, if somewhat meticulous and critical.

### Properties and Uses

- Relieves pressure for acute complaints with slow onset, painful with movement
- For ailments accompanied by dryness of the mouth, lips, eyes, chest, throat and there is great thirst
- For those who are reluctant to move or speak
- For people who are heavy-headed and irritable

*BELOW LEFT: In homeopathic remedies, the fresh root of bryonia is finely ground into a pulp from which tablets are then made.*
*BELOW: Arctium lappa (burdock).*

- For people who want things, but cannot pin-point what, and then refuse what is offered
- For excessive sweating
- For headaches and stabbing pains, worse for movement
- For people who worry about business when ill
- Symptoms improve after rest, when pressure is applied to the area and worsen with movement

## BURDOCK

*Arctium lappa* or *Arctium minus*

Burdock is a common wayside plant with large leaves and purple flowers. Both the root and the leaves are used, and both are antimicrobial. It is most commonly used for skin diseases, such as acne, or dry, scaly skin conditions. It acts by pushing toxins out on to the surface of the skin, but it can be given as a diuretic to help flush out toxins from the liver and kidneys.

### Properties and Uses
- Blood cleanser and alterative, diuretic and lymphatic cleanser
- Good for rheumatism and gout
- Lowers blood-sugar levels, making it very useful for diabetes
- For eruptive and stubborn skin conditions, especially when hot and inflamed: acne, spots, boils and rashes, psoriasis, rheumatism and gout
- For skin and liver problems, used with dandelion root
- For chronic cystitis and loss of appetite

### Dosage
- Two teaspoons of dried root, decocted, daily or one teaspoon of the tincture twice daily for some months
- For lack of appetite take the tincture three times daily, before meals, in a little water or fruit juice: 5–10 drops for children and 20 drops for adults

## BUSH FUCHSIA

*Epacris longiflora*

A low shrub, the bush fuchsia flowers throughout the year with bright red, elongated bell-like flowers hanging in a row from the stem. The leaves are small and heart-shaped.

Bush fuchsia is used to balance the hemispheres of the brain so that the rational left side and creative right side can be expressed with confidence. It is useful for all problems with learning difficulties, or translating marks from the page (words, symbols, music) into physical action. It also gives the confidence to express these more completely when performing or speaking in public.

### Key Notes
- The person who needs bush fuchsia may be nervous and stammer. Although intelligent, people who need this remedy may be slow or unable to learn. They may avoid situations which highlight this or become shy. There may also be difficulties with determining left and right, up and down.
- Bush fuchsia is specific for children with dyslexia or learning difficulties. It rebalances the mind, aiding concentration and confidence.
- This remedy also releases energy to rebalance the mind, and open it up to new possibilities.

))))▶ *Australian Bush Flowers*

- _Draws out infection
- Red cabbage leaves form the basis of a good cough syrup
- Make cabbage a regular part of your diet to reduce the risk of cancer
- A cabbage poultice can be applied to boils and infected cuts to draw out the infection and disperse pus
- Applied to bruises and swelling, macerated cabbage leaves will encourage healing
- Dab white cabbage juice on mouth ulcers and gargle for sore throats
- A warm cabbage compress on the affected area will reduce headaches and some neuralgias
- Drink fresh cabbage juice to reduce the discomfort of gastric ulcers and bronchial infections
- A cabbage leaf, lightly pounded, can be placed directly on the breast to relieve mastitis
- Raw cabbage juice is said to be useful for the treatment of ulcers, psoriasis, chronic headaches, asthma, cystitis and bronchitis; drink 25–50 ml daily for best effects

## CABBAGE

*Brassica oleracea*

Cabbage has traditionally been used for medicinal purposes as well as for cooking. It has anti-inflammatory properties, and contains chemicals that can prevent cancer. The ancient Greeks used fresh white cabbage juice to relieve sore or infected eyes, and cabbage juice from the stem is a good remedy for ulcers. Traditionally, the Romans and Egyptians would drink cabbage juice before big dinners to prevent intoxication; cabbage seeds are said to prevent hangovers.

Do not eat red cabbage raw. Avoid cabbage if you suffer from goitre, or take monoamine oxidase inhibitors (MAOI) antidepressants. Cooked red cabbage can cause constipation and irritation of the colon due to the large quantities of iron.

### Properties and Uses

- An excellent anti-inflammatory
- Contains lactic acid, which acts to disinfect the colon
- Used to reduce the pain of headaches and rheumatic disorders
- Soothes eczema and other itching or weeping skin conditions
- Anti-cancer

## CALC CARB

*Calcarea carbonica*

This homeopathic remedy is derived from the mother-of-pearl in oyster shells. This remedy is most often used to help problems relating to the teeth and bones. It is particularly good for broken bones which are slow to heal, backache and joint pain.

It is used to treat bones and joints which are slow to develop or slow to heal after injury and relieves complaints which may be due to this, such as backache. It also helps slow-growing teeth and pain during

teething. Right-sided headaches, premenstrual tension, heavy periods, menopause problems, thrush, eczema, arthritus, asthma and digestive problems can also be helped.

The Calc Carb type is shy, quiet and sensitive. They appear to be withdrawn, but are really more afraid of making fools of themselves. When well, they are happy and work hard. When ill, they become slightly depressed and require constant reassurance. They tend to be overweight but healthy.

### Properties and Uses

- Frequently indicated for very young children
- Treats many anxieties and fears
- For fear of the dark, ghosts and monsters
- For fear of small spaces, mice and thunderstorms
- For over-responsible people, slow but reliable
- For those who suffer from too much mental and physical exertion and who like to pace themselves
- Relieves joint aches and pains
- Speeds up slow development of teeth and bones
- Controls excessive sweating
- For sensitivity to cold and dampness
- For constipation
- Symptoms improve when lying on the affected side, late morning and in dry weather, and worsen with sweating, after exertion, in the damp and cold, on waking and before a period

))))➤ *Biochemic Tissue Salts*

## CALC FLUOR

*Calcarea fluorica*

One of the 12 tissue salts, Calc Fluor is used homeopathically and mainly in pregnancy. It is used to improve the elasticity in the skin, veins or glands. As a tissue salt it helps with piles, varicose veins, cold sores, cracked tongues and lips. Physical symptoms relieved include inflamed skin and stretch marks in pregnancy, swollen glands, and enamel deficiency of teeth.

*ABOVE LEFT: Cabbage has long been valued both for its nutritive as well as its curative properties.*
*LEFT: The homeopathic remedy* Calcarea carbonica.
*RIGHT: The homeopathic remedy* Calcarea flourica, *one of the 12 tissue salts.*

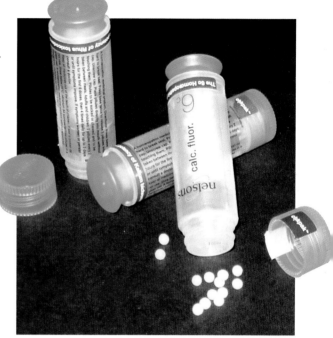

There is no real Calc Fluor type, but there may be an obsession with financial ruin and trivia.

### Properties and Uses

- Helps dilated veins, poor teeth, swelling around the joints
- For gastritis with green discharges
- For people with no strong mental or emotional indications
- Symptoms become worse at the beginning of motion, from cold and damp; they become better from continuous motion

))))➤ *Biochemic Tissue Salts*

## CALC PHOS

*Calcarea phosphorica*

Calcium phosphate is a mineral salt which is the main constituent, along with collagen, of bones and teeth. A natural version is the mineral apatite. For homeopathic use, it is prepared chemically from dilute phosphoric acid and calcium hydroxide, which form fine particles of calcium phosphate. These are then filtered and dried. The remedy is also used as a tissue salt and used to treat bone and teeth complaints.

Used to treat slow growth and growing pains in children, for instance, when the fontanelles are slow to close in an infant, painful teething and numbness, and tingling attributed to growing. It is also used to treat bones that are healing slowly. Slow recovery after illness due to weakness and fatigue, digestive problems such as diarrhoea and indigestion and recurrent throat infections can be helped.

The Calc Phos type tends to be thin with dark hair and long legs. They will seem discontented and unhappy, although they will be friendly. They dislike routine. Babies are irritable, requiring constant attention and are easily bored.

### Properties and Uses
- Relieves painful bones and teeth, digestive complaints and growing pains
- Helps slow-healing fractures
- For weak digestion
- For restlessness and dissatisfaction
- For those who hate getting up in the morning
- For those who need constant stimulation
- Symptoms improve in dry, warm weather and worsen in cold, damp weather, when worrying, after sexual or over-exertion

## CALCIUM

Calcium is an important mineral and recent research shows that we get only about one-third of what we need for good health. Calcium is essential for human life – it makes up bones and teeth, and is crucial for messages to

be conducted along the nerves. It ensures that our muscles contract and our hearts beat, and it is extremely important in the maintenance of the immune system, among other things.

There are many groups at risk of calcium deficiency – in particular the elderly – and because it is so important to body processes, our bodies take what they need from our bones, which causes them to become thin and brittle. Calcium is used therapeutically for allergies, depression, panic attacks, insomnia and hyper-activity, and extra should be taken during pregnancy and while breastfeeding.

Please note that doses exceeding 2000 mg per day may cause hypercalcaemia (calcium deposits in the kidneys), but since excess calcium is excreted, it is unlikely to occur unless you are also taking excess quantities of vitamin D.

The best sources of calcium are milk, cheese and dairy produce, leafy green vegetables, hard tap water, salmon and other tinned fish, eggs, beans, nuts and tofu.

### Properties and Uses
- Treats and prevents osteoporosis
- Prevents cancer
- Useful in the treatment of high blood pressure
- Helps to prevent heart disease
- Useful in treating arthritis
- Helps keep skin healthy
- Alleviates cramps in the legs
- Encourages regular beating of the heart
- Soothes insomnia
- Helps the body to metabolize iron
- Necessary for nerve impulse transmission and muscular function

### Dosage
- Experts recommend that calcium be taken in a good multivitamin and mineral supplement, although extra doses may be given up to 1000 mg per day
- More calcium is needed by women after the menopause, and while pregnant and breastfeeding

▶ *Minerals*

## CALENDULA

*Calendula officinalis*

Known as marigold, or calendula, the whole flower tops or petals of the common garden plant are used therapeutically. Calendula is one of the best herbs for treating local skin problems. It may be used safely wherever there is an inflammation on the skin, whether due to infection or physical damage. It may be used for any external bleeding or wounds, bruising or strains. It will also be of benefit in slow-healing wounds

BOTTOM LEFT: *Calcium is a major constituent of bones and teeth.*
ABOVE: Calendula officinalis *(calendula).*

and skin ulcers. It is ideal for first aid treatment of minor burns and scalds.

## Properties and Uses

- Anti-inflammatory, antispasmodic, lymphatic, astringent, emenagogue, antimicrobial
- Internally acts as a valuable herb for digestive inflammation and thus it may be used in the treatment of gastric and duodenal ulcers
- As a cholagogue it will aid in the relief of gall bladder problems and also through this process help indigestion
- Has marked anti-fungal activity and may be used both internally and externally
- Also used in the treatment of delayed menstruation and painful periods

## Dosage

- Infusion: pour a cup of boiling water on to 1–2 teaspoons of the florets and leave to infuse for 10–15 minutes. This should be drunk three times a day. External use as a lotion or ointment for cuts, bruises, diaper rash, sore nipples, burns and scalds.
- Tincture: 1–4 ml three times a day.

))))▶ *Homeopathy*

## CALENDULA
*Calendula*

The common, or pot, marigold has been used for centuries for its healing properties. It is a popular herbal medicine and is used for its anti-inflammatory and anti-microbial qualities in conditions ranging from skin complaints to cancer. As a cream, ointment or tincture it is a common first-aid treatment for cuts, grazes and scalds in both herbal and homeopathic medicine. Homeopathically, the fresh leaves and flowers of the plant are used to make the remedy and a cream for external use.

It is well-known for its cleansing antiseptic qualities and to promote healing by aiding clotting. After childbirth, it is often used by midwives in baths or lotions to aid perineal tears. After tooth extraction profuse bleeding can be controlled by gargling with calendula in cooled boiled water.

Ensure cuts are clean before use so that rapid healing does not close in dirt or germs. Do not use for puncture wounds or deep cuts, as rapid healing may seal the infection inside the wound.

As a homeopathic remedy, it can be given after a bad wound to prevent sepsis. Give after surgery, as well as Arnica, to help wounds heal.

## Properties and Uses

- Relieves cuts, grazes, minor wounds, perineal tears after childbirth and mouth ulcers
- Symptoms improve when lying still or walking and worsen in damp weather, in draughts and after eating
- Take after surgery
- Take to prevent sepsis in wounds
- For people who may be irritable or frightened, but have no obvious mental symptoms

))))▶ *Herbalism*

## CANTHARIS
*Lytta vesicatoria* or *Cantharis vesicatoria*

The homeopathic remedy cantharis is made from Spanish fly, a bright green beetle that is native to southern Europe and western Asia. It emits a rapid-acting irritant, cantharidin, causing blistering, hence its other common name. The remedy is made using the whole beetle, dried and powdered.

Ailments treated are those characterized by burning or stinging, particularly urinary tract infections such as cystitis with frequent but painful urination, insect bites, burns and scalds, infections, burning abdominal pains and stinging diarrhoea. It is also for infections that spread rapidly or conditions that quickly deteriorate. Mental problems such as rage, agitation leading to violence, excessive sexual desire and severe anxiety can be relieved.

Cantharis types tend to be bursting with ideas, but rather confused. They have maniacal tendencies, tend to explode with anger, and have a very strong sex drive.

### Properties and Uses

- Relieves conditions accompanied by stinging or burning sensations, rapidly spreading infection and stings
- Important remedy in cystitis with burning pains
- For use after burns, with sting pains
- For those with a thirst, but no wish to drink
- For a burning sensation in the stomach
- For sweating and palpitations
- For infections that rapidly worsen
- Symptoms improve in the warmth, with massage, after flatulence or burping and at night, and worsen with movement, after drinking coffee or cold water and in the afternoon

## CARNITINE

L-carnitine is a non-essential amino acid, which is necessary for many functions in the body, the most important of which is its role in regulating fat metabolism – in other words, transporting fat across membranes to the energy burning parts of cells. The more carnitine available, the faster the fat is transported, and the more fat is used for energy. Recent studies show that carnitine may be useful in the treatment of some forms of heart disease and in muscular dystrophy. Food sources of carnitine include meats and dairy foods.

### Properties and Uses

- Regulates the metabolism of fat
- Helps to break down branched-chain amino acids
- Controls ketone levels in the blood

### Dosage

- L-carnitine supplementation is believed to be safe between 1.5–2 g daily, although experts recommend that you only take it for one week a month; 500 mg daily is thought to be adequate dosage for improving athletic performance
)))➤ *Amino Acids*

## CARRIER OILS

When essential oils are used for massage, they must be mixed into a base or carrier, as they are too concentrated and powerful to be used on the skin in an undiluted form. Carrier oils also provide the lubrication needed for the massage itself.

A carrier oil can be any unperfumed vegetable oil, such as soya, safflower or sunflower oils, although the oils most often used in aromatherapy are sweet almond oil and grapeseed oil. Some carrier oils have therapeutic qualities of their own – for example, peach kernel, avocado and apricot kernel are rich and nourishing, and high in vitamin E. Olive oil has many healing properties, although its strong odour sometimes masks the scent of the oil itself.

A good ratio of oils is three drops of essential oil for every 5 ml of carrier oil.
)))➤ *Grapeseed Oil, Olive Oil, Peach Kernel*

## CARROT

*Daucus carota*

A member of the *Umbelliferae* family, which also includes celery and parsnip, the carrot is a widely grown vegetable. Carrots were first used as medicinal herbs rather than as vegetables, and today they have the dual

*ABOVE: Olive oil (pictured) can be used as a carrier oil, however, its strong smell sometimes overpowers the scent of the essential oil being used.*
*ABOVE RIGHT: Samuel Hahnemann, who invented the mixture, Causticum Hahnemanni.*
*RIGHT: Carrots were used medicinally before they were eaten as vegetables.*

purpose of acting as therapeutic agents, and providing the best source of betacarotene (a form of vitamin A) in the human diet. They are rich in vitamins A, B, C and E, and the minerals phosphorus, potassium and calcium. Chinese medical practitioners suggest eating carrots for liver energy.

Eating an excessive quantity of carrots may cause the skin to yellow temporarily. Also carrot seeds are a nerve tonic and will induce abortion, so avoid during pregnancy.

### Properties and Uses

- Energizing, anti-inflammatory, antiseptic
- Cleanses the system of impurities
- Contains calcium which will encourage healthy skin, hair and bones
- Carrot oil restores tone and elasticity to skin
- Drink fresh, raw carrot juice daily to energize and cleanse the body
- Fresh carrot juice will help to relieve the effects of stress, fatigue and illness on the body
- Carrot soup is a traditional home remedy for infant diarrhoea – it soothes the bowel and slows down bacterial growth
- Raw, grated carrots or cooked mashed carrots can be applied to wounds, cuts, inflammations and abscesses to discourage infection and encourage healing
- Dried carrot powder will restore energy, and can help to treat infections, glandular problems, headaches or joint problems

)))》 *Vitamin A*

## CAUSTICUM
*Causticum hahnemanni*

This remedy was invented and proved by Samuel Hahnemann and is unique to homeopathy. It is made chemically from quicklime (calcium oxide) and potassium bisulphate. Hahnemann found that it caused a burning taste in the back of the mouth and an acerbic sensation. It is used for a set of symptoms known as the causticum cough and for neuromuscular conditions.

Symptoms of the causticum cough include a raw, throat with a dry, tickly cough; a hard, racking cough; chest filled with mucus which is difficult to cough up; incontinence with the cough and coughing which is worse on breathing out. Also helps neuromuscular problems such as weakness, stiffness, neuralgia, tearing pains in the joints, muscles and bones, cramps, particularly affecting the vocal chords, bladder, larynx or right side of the face. Other conditions alleviated include dizziness when bending forward, heartburn in pregnancy, burning rheumatic pain, roaring in the ears, nasal soreness and tender scars.

The causticum type tends to have dark hair and eyes, sallow skin, be narrow-minded, and suffer from mental and physical exhaustion. They tend to be hypersensitive and weepy.

### Properties and Uses

- Relieves causticum cough
- For painless loss of voice
- For those who are very critical of others, particularly authority
- Imparts a strong sense of empathy
- Feels a strong sense of injustice
- For burning pains
- For warts
- For symptoms with a slow onset, gradual paralysis
- For tearing, bursting pain in joints, muscles, bones
- Symptoms improve in warm, damp weather, after cold drinks and washing, and worsen in dry, cold winds, with movement

## CAYENNE

*Capiscum annuum*

This fiery red pepper, used all over the world in cooking, is known to many Westerners by its Caribbean name, cayenne. It is widely used in Ayurvedic medicine, and has warming and mucus-relieving qualities.

Cayenne should not be given to children under the age of two. Use rubber gloves when chopping cayenne peppers, as they may burn the fingertips. If burning should occur, wash with vinegar several times, rinsing carefully. Discontinue use if the skin becomes irritated.

### Properties and Uses

- Can be used for arthritis and muscle soreness, and internally as a digestive aid and a treatment for colds, fever, toothache, diarrhoea and constipation
- Assists digestion by stimulating the flow of saliva and stomach secretions; it has analgesic and warming properties, increasing circulation; it also has strong digestive, carminative and emetic properties
- Cayenne acts as a decongestant and an expectorant
- Alleviates colds, gastrointestinal and bowel problems, and is used as a digestive aid
- Externally, cayenne treats arthritis and muscle soreness
- Creams containing cayenne are frequently used in the treatment of shingles

))))▶ *Ayurveda, Herbalism*

## CELERY

*Apium graveolens*

Hippocrates, the father of medicine, wrote that celery could be used to calm the nerves, and indeed, its very high calcium level is likely the reason for this phenomenon. The seeds, leaves and edible root of the plant are used. Celery is best eaten raw, and its juice is particularly useful. The seeds are rich in iron and many vitamins, including A, B and C, and can be used in the treatment of liver problems and high blood pressure. Celery seeds are used by Ayurvedic practitioners to reduce indigestion, a nervous stomach and ungrounded emotions. In aromatherapy, celery seed oil can be used to counteract jet lag, and exposure to smog and toxic environments.

Celery should not be eaten during pregnancy as it may cause the uterus to contract.

### Properties and Uses

- Reduces high blood pressure
- Digestive, reducing spasm in the muscle of the intestinal tract and acting as an anti-inflammatory
- Can ease insomnia
- May help in the treatment of arthritis and rheumatic disorders; in Japan, rheumatic patients are sometimes put on a celery-only diet
- Stimulates the thyroid and pituitary glands
- Possibly antioxidant
- Clears uric acid from painful joints
- Acts on the kidneys and is a mild diuretic
- Eat the seeds to treat arthritis (for which they act as an anti-inflammatory) and muscle spasms (antispasmodic action)
- Grated, raw celery can be used as a poultice for swollen glands
- Raw, whole celery can be eaten regularly to reduce high blood pressure, and to act as a tonic for the liver

- Celery juice may be drunk, or an infusion of celery seeds, to alleviate sciatica
- Drink celery juice before meals to suppress the appetite and chew celery seeds after a meal as a digestive
- Celery root is said to be an aphrodisiac

)))) *Calcium, Herbalism, Homeopathic Remedies*

## CENTAURY

*Centaurium erythraea*

A Bach flower remedy, centaury is for people who have an excessive desire to please and a willingness to serve. They can be taken for granted and become doormats. Their will to help others is so strong that it undermines their individuality and they find it hard to say no. They can become servants rather than helpers and end up doing more than their fair share. This leads to frustration and a loss of self-confidence, appreciation and expression.

### Key Notes

- People who need centaury lack willpower and they may be tired and exhausted. Inner frustration and anger may sap inner strength. The weaker partner in a co-dependent relationship may benefit from centaury.
- Centaury helps balance the desire to serve by strengthening our willpower and appreciation of ourselves. It helps us make a choice.

)))) *Bach Flower Remedies*

## CERATO

*Ceratostigma willmottiana*

Cerato is a small shrub with bright blue flowers often grown in gardens. It originally came from China and the Himalayas. Cerato is the only Bach flower remedy to be made from a cultivated plant. Cerato is for lack of trust in one's own abilities and judgement. The people who need cerato are intelligent and curious but they lack confidence in themselves, distrust their own intuition and constantly seek the advice and approval of others. They like to be seen to be doing the right thing.

*LEFT: Celery is best eaten raw; not only is it rich in vitamins, but it is believed that it can also calm nerves.*

*RIGHT: Chamomile (pictured) is believed to promote a lengthy and restful sleep.*

### Key Notes

- People who need Cerato often appear weak-willed and silly. They lack constancy and may imitate others, to the extent that they may even join a cult, or become obsessive about a fad.
- Cerato helps to restore confidence, enables us to listen to advice from within and strengthens self-trust.

)))) *Bach Flower Remedies*

## CHAMOMILE

*Chamomilla recutita*

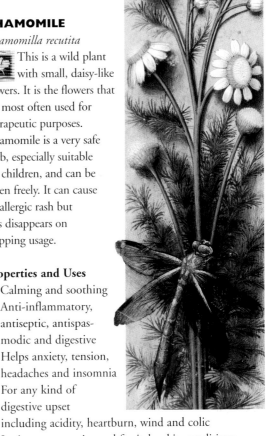

This is a wild plant with small, daisy-like flowers. It is the flowers that are most often used for therapeutic purposes. Chamomile is a very safe herb, especially suitable for children, and can be taken freely. It can cause an allergic rash but this disappears on stopping usage.

### Properties and Uses

- Calming and soothing
- Anti-inflammatory, antiseptic, antispasmodic and digestive
- Helps anxiety, tension, headaches and insomnia
- For any kind of digestive upset including acidity, heartburn, wind and colic
- Lotion or cream is good for itchy skin conditions
- For restless and over-excitable children and most children's complaints including fevers and teething troubles; especially helpful for infants
- Although chamomile is sold in tea bags as a herbal drink for everyday use, it should not be overlooked as a medicinal herb; it is gentle but very powerful

)))) *Aromatherapy*

## CHAMOMILE (ROMAN)

*Chamaemelum nobile*

 Chamomile has a long history of use as a physical and emotional soother. The plant was, apparently, sacred to the ancient Egyptians who dedicated it to the Sun because it cured agues. It is one of the most gentle essential oils available, and particularly suitable for treating young children. Of the many varieties of chamomile available, Roman chamomile is one of the most commonly used in aromatherapy.

Do not use in the first three months of pregnancy and refrain from using chamomile essential oil in the eyes. German chamomile may be used as an alternative to Roman chamomile.

### Properties and Uses

- Calms the nervous system and induces sleep
- It has valuable anti-inflammatory, antiseptic and bactericidal properties; chamomile oil was commonly used until World War II as a natural disinfectant and antiseptic in hospitals and surgeries
- Prevents and eases spasms, relieves pain, settles digestion and acts as a liver tonic
- Children with diarrhoea will respond to gentle massage of the abdomen with this oil
- Can be used to relieve headaches, toothache, period pain, arthritis and neuralgia
- Indigestion, nausea and flatulence can also benefit and all manners of skin problems such as rashes, inflammation, cuts, boils, allergies, insect bites and chilblains can be helped by a chamomile compress or bath; a few drops can be added to a warm bath to reduce weariness and ease pain in any part of the body.
- Inhalations will relieve the pain of headache, migraine, flu, coughs, facial neuralgia and sinusitis; massage a few drops in a light carrier oil around the nose and sinus area for almost immediate relief

- It has a balancing effect on the menstrual cycle, reduces fluid retention and acts as a gentle antidepressant and stress reliever
- Chamomile also helps to reduce fever

⫸ **Aromatherapy, Herbalism**

## CHAMOMILLA

*Matricaria recutita*

Hippocrates was one of the first physicians to understand the medicinal benefits of chamomile. The plant is a member of the daisy family and grows in Europe and America. Homeopathically, the juice is extracted from the whole fresh plant in flower and the remedy is given for those who are sensitive and have a low pain threshold. It is particularly good for children.

Chamomilla works well for those who are sensitive to pain and are unable to deal with their discomfort, being impatient, rude and angry when ill. Often the reaction seems disproportionate to the amount of pain being felt. Even slight pain may cause sweats and fainting in women and children. Children particularly benefit from the remedy. Teething newborns who are feverish and want to be held all the time and infants with earache who will not sit still owing to the pain and may scream can be soothed. Toothache which makes one cheek red and hot can also be alleviated. Other conditions treated include tinnitus, heartburn, heavy, painful periods and diarrhoea with slimy green stools.

The Chamomilla type has a low pain threshold, whines, is impatient, and never satisfied

### Properties and Uses

- Relieves a low tolerance to pain, nervous afflictions, children's ailments
- For people who are angry, irritable, spiteful and oversensitive to people and surroundings
- Worse from 9 p.m. to midnight

- For restlessness
- For teething and toothaches
- For earaches
- Symptoms improve in the warm, wet weather, for not eating and if carried (children), and worsen in heat, fresh air, cold winds, when angry and after coffee

## CHERRY PLUM

*Prunus cerasus*

A small tree with red or yellow fruit, often grown as hedging and windbreaks. It flowers from February onwards.

Cherry plum is for those who fear letting go or losing control. The fearful thoughts may be of a suicidal, compulsive or destructive nature. This mental pain and turmoil may happen during a period of great emotional or physical change when the person is worn out and stressed.

### Key Notes
- People who need Cherry Plum may feel desperate, and fear they may hurt themselves and others. They may have bouts of hysteria.
- Cherry Plum makes it possible to release frustration and restores control and trust of the mind and the emotions.

)))▶ *Bach Flower Remedies*

## CHESTNUT BUD

*Æsculus hippocastanum*

The white chestnut tree is used to make two remedies. To make the chestnut bud remedy, the large, sticky leaf buds are picked when they are just about to open.

This Bach flower remedy is for those who make the same mistake over and over again and who are slow to learn from experience. Chestnut bud is for people who find themselves stuck in the same repeating pattern and who do not seem able to learn the lessons of past experience, events and relationships.

*FAR LEFT: Chamaemelum nobile (Roman chamomile).*

*LEFT: Matricaria recutita (chamomilla).*

*RIGHT: Æsculus hippocastanum (chestnut bud).*

### Key Notes
- The person who needs chestnut bud may be forgetful or absent-minded; may also suffer poor health, chronic conditions may continually flare up or they may suffer from preventable illness
- Chestnut bud helps focus the mind and encourages people to see the correct path and to see it objectively

)))▶ *Bach Flower Remedies*

## CHICORY

*Chicorium intybus*

Chicory is a wayside plant with bright blue flowers. Chicory is related to lettuce, is cultivated as a vegetable and blanched as a bitter plant to add to salads.

Chicory is for those who see love as a transaction incurring duty and as a method of control. They give love in order to receive it. Chicory types are over-anxious to please others. They will love and care publicly, even melodramatically, building up a stock of good works which they expect to be reciprocated, but find that love still does not flow their way.

### Key Notes
- Those who need chicory may be possessive and selfish, fussy, nagging and manipulative; they may be prone to illness if they are not appreciated
- Chicory helps people to see love as a universal force, and to give love selflessly and freely so that it may freely return

)))▶ *Bach Flower Remedies*

- For difficulty in expressing feelings
- For difficulty concentrating
- For headaches, convulsions, dizziness, sallow skin, weak muscles
- Symptoms improve in the warmth, when firm pressure is applied to the affected part and after sleeping, but worsen in the cold or draughts, in the autumn and after sleeping

## CHINA

*China officinalis*

The China remedy is made from Peruvian bark – grown in the tropical rainforests of South America, in India and Southeast Asia – which is stripped and dried. Quinine, an extract of the bark, was the first substance to be tested and proven by Samuel Hahnemann in 1790. He used quinine on himself, noting that large doses caused similar symptoms to malaria, while small doses acted as an antidote. Quinine is still used in conventional medicine today as part of treatment for malaria. Homeopathically, the dried bark of China is used to treat exhaustion.

China aids recovery from nervous exhaustion after debilitating illness and as a result of loss of fluids from vomiting, diarrhoea or sweating. It is also used for digestive conditions such as gastroenteritis, flatulence and gall bladder problems, mental upsets such as lack of concentration, indifference and outbursts that are out of character. Neuralgia, dizziness, tired and twitchy muscles, tinnitus and haemorrhages can also be treated.

The China type tends to be sensitive, intense, artistic and idealistic. They find their own intensity tiring, making them lazy, depressed and even violent. They find it difficult to communicate easily with others, and do so creatively as they have imaginative minds.

### Properties and Uses

- Relieves nervous exhaustion after illness, weakness after vomiting, diarrhoea and excessive sweating
- For the emotionally fragile

## CHINESE HERBALISM

Chinese herbalism is the use of herbs to treat and prevent mental, physical and emotional ill health. Together with acupuncture, it forms the bulk of Chinese medical treatment. Although Westerners tend to think of acupuncture as being more important than herbalism, the number of Chinese doctors who use herbs exclusively is greater than those who only use acupuncture. However, most practitioners combine both therapies to complement each other in the treatment and prevention of illness.

In the Chinese philosophy of the complementary opposites yin and yang, acupuncture is considered yang, because it moves from the outside in, while herbalism is yin because it works from the inside out. Herbalism can be used to support acupuncture treatment, or on its own for certain conditions such as viral infections, and blood disorders like anaemia or menstrual problems, which are perhaps better suited to herbal

*ABOVE LEFT: Jars of traditional Chinese medicine.*
*ABOVE: Chinese herbal medicines.*
*RIGHT: A chiropractic massage treatment is carried out by a trained practitioner who uses his hands to manipulate different parts of the body into their correct positions.*

treatment than to acupuncture. Herbs are also used to strengthen those people who are too weak to have acupuncture. Acupuncture works with the body's own energy, but very weak patients have little energy with which to work, so their response may not be very good. Herbal treatment, on the other hand, actually adds to the body.

The herbalist's knowledge is gleaned from a succession of pharmacopoeias, some centuries old, and clinical handbooks which contain 5, 767 entries, not including Chinese folk herbal medicine. The entries range from plants as common as garlic to minerals and even animal products, such as the gallstones of a cow. In the UK, animal parts cannot be used in medicine.

The World Health Organization (WHO) has published a list of ailments which can benefit from Chinese herbalism. Numerous health problems from arthritis to depression, eczema, hayfever, infertility, sciatica and vaginitis are on that list, with some surprising entries such as cerebral palsy, impotence and stroke.

)))➡ **Traditional Chinese Medicine**

## CHIROPRACTIC

The word chiropractic comes from the Greek *cheir* which means 'hand' and *praktikos* meaning 'done by'. Manipulation of the body has been practised for thousands of years by ancient cultures such as the Greeks, the Egyptians and the Chinese. Even Hippocrates, the father of medicine, suggested that knowledge of the spine was necessary for understanding and treating disease.

Our spinal cord is enclosed by 24 movable vertebrae. Between each vertebra various nerves branch out to every part of the body. If a vertebra is slightly displaced, it can interfere with the spinal cord and the nerves. Chiropractors believe that this slight misalignment may cause problems across the whole body, affecting the way our bodies function.

Chiropractors work to eliminate imbalances causing medical problems by manipulating the spine with their hands to realign the vertebrae. Pain is a message from the body indicating distress or dysfunction on some level. If it is caught early enough, this dysfunction can be treated with chiropractic adjustments that may help the body to heal itself. When pain is ignored, the immune system and parts of the body that control pain become overwhelmed and unable to cope and our body begins to descend into disease and ill-health.

Treatment may involve soft tissue work and then manipulation. They can sometimes feel uncomfortable, but the types of treatment and the amount of pressure used are tailored to the individual. Often very little force is necessary. All treatment is undertaken according to a patient's specific symptoms, level of health, age and build.

Chiropractors treat any kind of pain or condition relating to the muscles and skeleton and the associated nervous system. Treatable conditions include neuritis, sciatica, neuralgia, muscular pains, migraines, headaches, stress and its related disorders (fatigue, insomnia, anxiety and digestive disorders), some asthma conditions, bad posture, sprained muscles and ligaments, accident-related injuries, rheumatism and arthritis.

)))➡ **Manipulative Therapies**

## CHLOROPHYLL

The ancient Greeks utilized green leafy plants for treating wounds and abrasions. The word chlorophyll is derived from the Greek word *chloros* 'green' and *phyllon* 'leaf'. Chlororphyll is the green pigment in plants that harnesses the Sun's energy in photosynthesis. Chlorophyll performs metabolic functions in plants such as respiration and growth. Interestingly, the chlorophyll molecule is chemically similar to that of human blood, except that its central atom is magnesium, whereas that of human blood is iron.

It is used therapeutically for a number of health conditions, including anaemia, circulation problems, breast problems, halitosis (bad breath), cirrhosis, colon disorders, mastitis, pregnancy problems and low vitality. It is also an effective deodorant.

Foods that are rich in chlorophyll include green drinks, such as wheatgrass, barley grass, green algae and kelp.

))))➤ *Wheatgrass*

## CHROMIUM

Chromium is a trace mineral which was discovered in the 1950s. It is an important regulator of blood sugar, and has been used successfully in the control and treatment of diabetes. It is involved in the metabolism of carbohydrates and fats, and is used in the production of insulin in the body.

High levels of sugars in the diet cause chromium to be excreted through the kidneys; it is important that you get enough in your diet if you eat sugary foods. The incidence of diabetes and heart disease decreases with increased levels of chromium in the body.

There is no evidence that chromium is toxic, even in high doses, since any excess is excreted. However, it is not suggested that you take more than 200 mcg daily unless supervised by a doctor.

The best sources of chromium are wholegrain cereals, meat and cheese, brewer's yeast, molasses and egg yolk.

### Properties and Uses

- Aids in the control and production of insulin
- Aids in the metabolism of carbohydrates and fats
- Controls blood cholesterol levels
- Stimulates the synthesis of proteins
- Increases resistance to infection
- Suppresses hunger pains

### Dosage

- There is no Recommended Daily Allowance (RDA), but it is suggested that 25 mcg per day is adequate
- Supplements up to 200 mcg per day may be appropriate

))))➤ *Minerals*

## CINNAMON

*Cinnamomum zeylanicum*

Ancient Ayurvedic practitioners used cinnamon as a treatment for fevers, diarrhoea, and as a flavouring for other less-palatable healing herbs. The Greeks used cinnamon to treat bronchitis. Cinnamon is also used in Chinese medicine, but it is not the same plant. Chinese cinnamon, or cassia, is much more powerful and has different uses.

### Properties and Uses

- Antiseptic, warming
- A pungent, sweet astringent, with stimulating, heating qualities; it acts as a diaphoretic, parasiticide, antispasmodic, aphrodisiac, analgesic and diuretic
- Cinnamon's antiseptic, antibacterial and anti-fungal qualities have been frequently utilized in toothpastes and as a treatment for gum disease
- As an anti-yeast agent, cinnamon has been used to treat candida and other yeast infections

*LEFT: Egg yolks are some of the best sources of chromium.*
*RIGHT: Bales of cinnamon.*

- Because of its strong antibacterial action cinnamon can be used to treat minor scrapes and cuts
- Cinnamon is recommended for respiratory ailments such as colds, sinus congestion and bronchitis
- As a digestive aid, it relieves dyspepsia, intestinal infections and parasites

### Key Notes

- Cinnamon contains the natural anaesthetic oil eugenol, which will help relieve the pain of minor wounds. To treat cuts and scrapes, wash the affected area thoroughly and pat dry. Sprinkle powdered cinnamon lightly over the area, then bind or bandage. Repeat treatment as needed until the area is healed.

### Caution

- Cinnamon aggravates bleeding, can be a skin irritant and a convulsive in high doses
- Cinnamon bark oil in particular can be an irritant and is not recommended for use on the skin
- Cinnamon infusions should not be given to children under two

)))➤ *Home Remedies, Ayurveda, Chinese Herbalism*

## CINNAMON

*Cinnamomum zeylanicum*

The best cinnamon oil is believed to come from Madagascar. The medicinal properties of cinnamon were valued by the ancients and according to legend, it has the ability to enhance psychic ability and acts as an aphrodisiac.

Cinnamon leaf oil may cause skin irritation. Use only in a one per cent dilution and in moderation. Do not confuse with cinnamon bark oil, which is an irritant and should not be used in aromatherapy.

### Properties and Uses

- Cinnamon stimulates a sluggish digestion, relieves flatulence and spasms and combats intestinal infection
- Stimulates respiration and circulation, helping with rheumatic problems and chest infections
- Helps fortify the immune system against chills and infections and has a cooling effect on fevers
- Cinnamon also has antiseptic, anti-microbial and parasiticide properties, making it good for headlice, scabies and other skin infections
- Cinnamon can relieve mental fatigue, improve concentration and nervous exhaustion and help lift depression

)))➤ *Ayurveda, Herbalism*

## CLARY SAGE

*Salvia sclarea*

Also known as 'clear eye', clary sage was used in the Middle Ages for clearing foreign bodies from the eyes. It remains popular in aromatherapy because of its gentle action and pleasant fragrance. Do not use during pregnancy or when drinking alcohol as it can intoxicate, cause drowsiness and nightmares.

### Properties and Uses

- Clary sage is an antidepressant and is sometimes described as a euphoric
- Helps to regulate the nervous system and is most beneficial in treating anxiety, depression and stress-related problems
- Acts as a powerful muscle relaxant, helps ease muscular aches and pains and benefits digestion, relieves indigestion and flatulence
- Its astringent properties make it useful for oily skin and scalp conditions
- Helps to prevent and arrest convulsions
- It is antibacterial and useful for throat and respiratory infections
- It is recommended for absent or scanty periods and PMS, and is a renowned aphrodisiac that can benefit lack of sex drive and impotence

)))➤ *Herbalism*

## CLEMATIS

*Clematis vitalba*

 The wild clematis is a rambling, perennial climber of woods and country hedges.

A popular Bach flower remedy, clematis is for those who are dreamy and not fully awake. Sometimes they daydream or fantasise about a Utopian future. Clematis people prefer to live in the mind or the spirit rather than deal with real issues and the mundane functions of everyday life. Airy and impractical individuals, they customarily 'drift off', are sensitive and often need lots of sleep. Many of them are pale and lack vitality.

### Key Notes

- People who need clematis are dreamy, absent-minded and lack interest in the present; they sometimes have a poor will to live
- They may forget to eat, experience faintness, tiredness and low blood-sugar levels

⟫ *Bach Flower Remedies*

## CLOVE

This pungent, aromatic and warming herb helps to calm the digestive tract, soothing wind and easing nausea. It is beneficial to the lungs and is useful for people who feel cold and are prone to colds. Use clove oil sparingly and only when combined with a carrier oil before use. It can irritate or burn the skin when used directly.

### Properties and Uses

- Acts as an insect repellent and parasiticide
- It is antiseptic and analgesic and can be used locally on swellings and for pains in the gums and teeth
- Used as an air freshener it can both keep a room smelling nice and act as an antiseptic
- Used sparingly in a bath, it can help ease confusion and lethargy

⟫ *Ayurveda, Bach Flower Remedies, Herbalism*

## CLOVES

*Eugenica caryophyllata*

Cloves are the dried buds of a tree, *Syzygium aromaticum*, of the myrtle family. Almost 20 per cent of the clove's weight is essential oil, obtained by distilling and used in perfumes, blends of spices, medications and sweets. Cloves can cause uterine contractions and should not be used in pregnancy.

*LEFT:* Clematis vitalba *helps absent-minded, flighty people find focus and sustain concentration.*
*BELOW LEFT:* Eugenica caryophyllata *(cloves).*
*BELOW:* High concentrations of the trace mineral cobalt are found in leafy, green vegetables like red and green cabbages.

## Properties and Uses

- Antiseptic and analgesic – particularly good for gums and teeth
- Warming, useful for people who are prone to colds
- Anti-inflammatory when used locally on swellings
- Calming on the digestive system
- Eliminates parasites from the body
- A powerful analgesic

## Home Remedies

- Oil of cloves can be chewed or placed directly on a sore tooth or mouth abscess to draw out the infection and ease the pain
- Dab a tiny amount of neat oil on insect bites
- Clove tea is a warming drink and can encourage the body to sweat, which is helpful in cases of high fever or vomiting
- Oil of cloves may be used in a long labour to hasten birth
- Clove tea can be used to soothe wind and ease nausea – particularly travel sickness
- Inhale an infusion of clove to clear the lungs and refresh
- A clove and orange pomander can be used as an insect repellent in cupboards
- Steep cloves in boiling water, simmer, strain and use the remaining liquid as a mild sedative and to soothe an acid stomach
- Clove tea may be used in the treatment of depression – a cup a day can be uplifting.

)))➤ *Herbalism, Aromatherapy, Ayurveda*

## COBALT

Cobalt is an essential trace mineral which is a constituent of vitamin B12. The amount of cobalt you have in your body is dependent on the amount of cobalt in the soil, and therefore in the food we eat. Most of us are not deficient in cobalt, although deficiency is much more common in vegetarians.

The best sources of cobalt are fresh leafy, green vegetables, meat, liver, milk, oysters and clams.

## Properties and Uses

With vitamin B12 cobalt can:

- Prevent pernicious anaemia
- Help in the production of red blood cells
- Aid in the synthesis of DNA and choline
- Encourage a healthy nervous system
- Reduce blood pressure
- Help with the maintenance of myelin, the fatty sheath that protects the nerves

## Dosage

- Cobalt is rarely found in supplement form, but makes up part of a good multivitamin and mineral supplement with the B-complex vitamins; 8 mcg daily appears to be adequate

)))➤ *Minerals, B12*

## CO-ENZYME Q10

Co-enzyme Q10 is a vitamin-like substance found in all cells of the body. It is biologically important since it forms part of the system across which electrons flow in the cells in the process of energy production. When it is deficient, the cell cannot function effectively and the rate at which the muscle cells work is adversely affected. Co-enzyme Q10 is fat-soluble and therefore may be toxic in high doses.

The best source is meat, although co-enzyme Q10 is also made within the body.

### Properties and Uses
- Enhances immunity
- Improves the heart-muscle metabolism
- May prevent coronary insufficiency and heart failure
- Necessary for the healthy functioning of the nervous system and brain cells
))))➤ *Vitamins*

## COFFEA

*Coffea arabica or Coffea cruda*

Coffee is native to Arabia and Ethiopia and is thought to have been first drunk in Persia. Now grown in central America and the West Indies, it has been used widely for medicinal purposes as a diuretic, pain-killer and to ease indigestion. It is also a well-known stimulant. Homeopathically, coffea is made from the raw berries of the coffee tree.

Commonly used to treat excessive mental activity, when the mind seems to be buzzing and where the person is very excitable and hypersensitive, (e.g. toothache or labour pain); when all the senses are so acutely affected that any noise, smell or touch seem unbearable; headaches which are so severe it feels like a nail is being driven into the skull; palpitations when excited or angry; and for acute premenstrual symptoms.

The coffea type tends to be long and lean, perhaps with a stoop. Symptoms may appear after exhaustion, trauma or a failed relationship. A high can descend into gloom and despair. This type has a tendency to burn out.

### Properties and Uses
- For irritability, excitability, mental over-stimulation, sleeplessness
- For heightened senses
- Treats anxiety leading to restlessness, insomnia and buzzing mind
- Good for guilt
- For trembling limbs, headaches, toothaches, palpitations, extremely sensitive skin
- Symptoms improve in the warmth, after lying down and when holding cold water in the mouth, and worsen for extreme emotions such as anger, with touch, smells or noise and in cold, windy weather

## COGNIS (SUPERLEARNING) ESSENCE

This combination flower essence perfectly combines the Australian essences of bush fuchsia, isopogon, paw paw and Sundew to give focus and clarity when speaking, singing, reading or studying. It assists problem-solving by improving access to the Higher Self, which stores all past knowledge and experiences. It balances the intuitive and cognitive processes and helps integrate ideas and information.

### Properties and Uses
- Helps the negative conditions of confusion, being overwhelmed, and daydreaming
- Brings clarity and focus
))))➤ *Australian Bush Flower Essences, Bush Fuchsia*

## COLOCYNTH

*Colocynthis*

The homeopathic remedy colocynth is made from the bitter apple, a fruit that grows in hot, arid conditions. In ancient times, the bitter apple was used by the Greeks as a purgative, to induce abortion and for derangement, dropsy and lethargy. Homeopathically, the fruit is dried and powdered, without the seeds.

It is mainly used to treat symptoms brought on by anger, particularly suppressed anger, such as neuralgia and abdominal pain; stomach pain, facial neuralgia and headaches respond well, as does nerve pain in the ovaries or kidneys; gout, sciatica and rheumatism symptoms can also be helped.

The colocynth type tends to be fair-haired and fair-skinned, reserved and with a strong sense of right and wrong. They dislike being contradicted and they experience physical symptoms when they become angry and indignant.

### Properties and Uses

- Relieves digestive complaints, neuralgia, headaches and stomach pains brought on by anger
- For people who are upset if contradicted
- For those who are keen for justice to be delivered
- For digestive problems and abdominal pain
- For neuralgia and headaches
- Symptoms improve in the warmth, after flatulence or drinking coffee, but worsen after eating, when indignant or angry and in damp, cold weather

### COMFREY

*Symphytum officinale*

A common wild plant with large bristly leaves and clusters of purple flowers. Comfrey root is used for treatment.

### Properties and Uses

- Healing and mucilaginous
- Promotes rapid healing of cuts, wounds, sprains and broken bones
- Taken as a tea or tincture and used in poultices, creams and liniments

*LEFT: Coffee beans, source of coffee.*
*ABOVE: Symphytum officinale (comfrey).*
*RIGHT: A herbal poultice being applied by a herbalist.*

- Use with chamomile and meadowsweet for hiatus hernia and stomach ulcers
- Comfrey ointment is a traditional soothing and healing preparation for sprains and aches and pains

### Key Notes

- Add a few drops of a warming essential oil, such as black pepper, to the infused oil to make a good liniment for arthritis, bunions and aches and pains arising from old injuries.

))▶ *Aromatherapy, Symphytum*

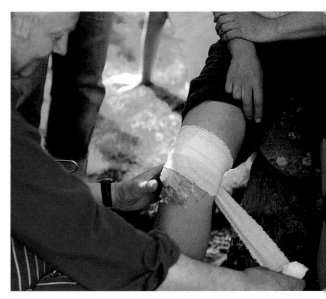

### COMPRESSES AND POULTICES

Compresses and poultices are for external use and can be extremely effective, since the active parts of the herb are able to reach the affected area without being altered by the digestive tract in any way.

A poultice is made up of a plant which has been crushed and then applied whole to the affected areas. You can also boil crushed plant parts for a few minutes to make a pulp, which will act as a poultice, or use a powdered herb and mix with boiling water. Because they are most often applied with heat and use fresh parts of the plant, they are usually more potent than compresses (see over). Poultices are particularly useful for conditions like bruises, wounds and abscesses, helping to soothe and to draw out impurities.

esses are usually made from infusions or
ıs which are used to soak a linen or muslin
cloth. ⅄he cloth is then placed on the affected area,
where it can be held in place by a bandage or plastic
wrap. Compresses can be hot or cold and are generally
milder than poultices.

Cold compresses soothe and draw out heat from
sprains, congestive pain and hot joints. Hot compresses
also warm, relax and encourage circulation for spasm,
stiffness and cold joints.

))))➤ *Aromatherapy, Home Remedies*

## CONFIDENCE ESSENCE

This Australian Bush Flower combination essence
uses the flowers of dog rose, Five Corners,
Southern Cross and Sturt Desert Rose to bring out the
positive qualities of self-esteem and confidence. It allows
us to feel comfortable around other people and be true to
ourselves. It resolves negative subconscious beliefs which
we may hold about ourselves as well as any guilt we may
harbour from past actions and events.

### Properties and Uses
• For low self-esteem, guilt, shyness, lack of conviction
  and a victim mentality
• Encourages confidence and integrity
• Helps people take responsibility for their lives
• Enhances personal power
• Helps people be true to themselves

))))➤ *Australian Bush Flower Essences*

## CONSTITUTIONAL TYPE

Most people, when they are ill, do not only suffer
from the basic symptoms of the disease but other
symptoms that are specific to them. These additional
symptoms are vital for choosing the right remedy. This is
why some patients may receive different remedies for the
same disease.

Many homeopaths noticed that different types of people
reacted strongly to certain remedies and proposed that
people should be placed in different categories, known as
'constitutional types'. This is why a homeopath will say that
someone is a 'sulphur type' or 'obviously a Calc Carb'. This
basically means that people react strongly to these remedies.

The belief is that people of one type share similarities
in terms of body shape, character, personality, and the
type of diseases to which they succumb. For instance,
lycopodium types tend to be tall and stooped with an
anxious expression and a craving for sweets.

Constitutional types are useful, but certainly not the
only criteria for prescribing treatment. Constitutional
treatment means looking at the whole picture of a
person's health, from inherited predisposition, past
illnesses, diet, general reactions to the environment,
intellectual and emotional features, and general attitude
to life. This is constitutional treatment, which differs,
of course, to labelling someone as a constitutional type.

))))➤ *Aromatherapy, Home Remedies*

## CONSULTATION

The consultation is the most important part of
any natural therapy session. This is the first session
with a therapist, and the one in which the most information is exchanged. The first session usually lasts longer
than any subsequent sessions because your therapist will
aim to find out all about you as well as your problem
before any diagnosis can be made. You can expect your
therapist to ask you all about:
• Your physical condition, including past and present
  illnesses, any medication you are taking, any symptoms
  and interesting aspects to them (sharp pains, or
  whether they come on in the morning)
• About your diet, including cravings, appetite, any
  weight problems, alcohol intake
• Your sleeping patterns
• Job and home life, whether or not you have children,
  a partner, or any obvious stresses
• Your exercise patterns
• Your emotional state – are things making you
  unhappy? Have you recently moved, split up
  with a partner, lost someone important, failed an
  important exam?
• Any other treatment you may be undergoing, either
  conventional or complementary
• What you hope to get from treatment

With this information, the therapist can go ahead
and make a diagnosis, which forms the next part of the

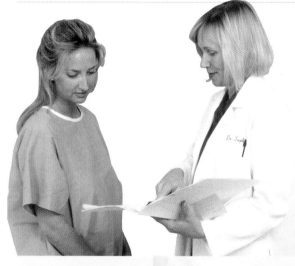

*ABOVE: A consultation between therapist and patient sets the tone for any ensuing natural-therapy sessions and is crucial for establishing trust.*
*BELOW: Concentrations of the essential trace mineral copper are found in nuts.*

consultation. After the consultation, treatment can be undertaken, based on your individual needs. The consultation is one aspect of natural medicine that sets it apart from the conventional approach. Sometimes hours are spent ensuring that the therapist has all the information he or she needs to make an informed diagnosis, and literally get to the bottom of your health problems. The consultation presents a picture of potential causes of the condition, and also provides the therapist with information in order to suggest lifestyle changes.

)))➤ *Diagnosis*

## COPPER

Copper is an essential trace mineral, and is necessary for the act of respiration – iron and copper are required for oxygen to be synthesized in the red blood cells. Copper is also important for the production of collagen, which is responsible for the health of our bones, cartilage and skin.

Copper appears in good multivitamin and mineral supplements, and could be taken alone up to 3 mg. Excessive intake can cause vomiting, diarrhoea, muscular pain and dementia.

The best sources are animal livers, shellfish, nuts, fruit, oyster, kidneys and legumes.

### Properties and Uses
- Protects against cardiovascular disease
- Useful in the treatment of arthritis
- Boosts the immune system
- Acts as an antioxidant

)))➤ *Minerals*

## COUNSELLING

Counselling is a form of treatment for the mind – a form of psychotherapy – and it is not aimed specifically at people who are ill, but at healthy people who wish to deal with a crisis, or improve their lives or relationships. It is, however, often used for relatives of and terminally ill patients, to help them cope with impending death.

The link between the mind and body has been long established on scientific grounds, and a physical illness can give rise to psychological symptoms, while an emotional problem can affect overall health. The clearest example of this is stress, which affects both mind and body. Counselling can help people understand the link between various problems and help them learn how to manage them.

Anyone who feels that they have no one to turn to will benefit from counselling. Similarly, if you are having difficulty coping with life, relationships, or stress, counselling will undoubtedly help. One of the roles of a natural therapist is to act as a counsellor, encouraging

people to express buried emotions and concerns that might be affecting health on all levels. This is one reason why natural medicine is so effective – it addresses the emotional factors with exactly the same emphasis as it does the physical problems.

A counsellor aims to help you to gain insight into your motives and needs, which gives you the confidence to deal more effectively with problems yourself.

## CRAB APPLE

*Malus sylvestris*

A wild apple with small, yellow, very acid fruit, crab apple grows in hedges and in waste ground.

A Bach flower remedy, crab apple is a bitter acid fruit, useful for those who feel bitter towards themselves, expressing self-condemnation and disgust, who feel in need of cleansing or detoxification. This may be a temporary feeling brought on by remorse or guilt over some act of which they are ashamed, or thoughts that are felt to be unclean. Crab apple cleanses the mind and the body.

### Key Notes

- Crab apple is for people who feel unclean on any level. They may feel self-disgust or loathing and may hurt, punish, cut or otherwise abuse themselves. They may have phobias or rituals based around purity or cleanliness.
- This remedy can be used for the physical, emotional and spiritual sides of these problems. It is also used to cleanse the body and spirit after contact with anything contagious or which feels unclean.

))))➡ ***Bach Flower Remedies***

## CRANBERRY

*Vaccinium oxycoccus var. palustris*

Cranberries are small acidic berries that are rich in vitamin C and contain an excellent infection-fighting ingredient. They also contain large amounts of oxalic acid and should not be eaten raw.

### Properties and Uses

- Improves the health of the circulatory system
- Aids in the treatment of kidney stones
- Cranberries contain a substance which affects the acidity of the urine and acts as a bactericide; a daily glass of cranberry juice will prevent and treat cystitis and discourage kidney stones
- Crushed cranberries, boiled in distilled water and skinned, can be added to a cup of warm water to overcome an asthma attack; there is an ingredient in the berries which contain an active ingredient similar to the drugs used to control asthma

))))➡ ***Herbalism, Vitamin C***

## CRANIAL OSTEOPATHY

The philosophy of osteopathic medicine is based on the theory that the human body constitutes an ecologically and biologically unified whole. All body systems are united through the neuro-endocrine and circulatory systems. Therefore, when looking at disease and other health problems, osteopaths address the whole body, not just the symptoms. The name osteopathy stems from the Latin words *osteon* and *pathos* which translates to 'suffering of the bone'. This name has caused some confusion, for it suggests that osteopaths treat only conditions involving bones. However, the name was chosen because Dr Andrew Still, the American founder of osteopathy, recognized that a well-balanced, properly functioning body relies on both the muscular and skeletal systems being healthy.

Cranial osteopathy was developed in the 1930s by American osteopath, William Garner Sutherland, a disciple of Andrew Still. His training taught him that the bones of the skull, which are separate at birth, grew together into a fixed structure and so could not move. He also noticed, however, that the bones of the skull retained some potential for movement even into adulthood. If they could move, they could also be susceptible to dysfunction. Dr Still had taught his students that cerebrospinal fluid (the clear watery fluid which surrounds the brain and spinal cord) was 'the highest known element in the human body'. Sutherland discovered that the fluid had detectable rhythms which he called 'the breath of life', as the rhythms appeared to be influenced by the rate and depth of breathing. By gently manipulating the skull he found he could alter the rhythm of this fluid flow and suggested that it might stimulate the body's self-healing ability and help to heal conditions which appeared unrelated to the cranium.

The human skull is made up of some 26 bones which are not fixed but can move slightly. Inside the skull the brain is surrounded by cerebrospinal fluid. The fluid is secreted in the brain and from there flows out of the skull and down the spine, enveloping the spinal cord and the base of the spinal nerves. Practitioners believe that cerebrospinal fluid is pumped through the spinal canal by means of a pulsation, which has its own rhythm, unrelated to the heartbeat or the breathing mechanism. When the bones of the skull move normally the cranial rhythm remains balanced, but any disturbance to the cranial bones can disturb the normal motion of the bones and consequently alter the cranial rhythm. This affects the functioning of other parts of the body.

A trained osteopath can feel the rhythm of the cranial pulse anywhere in the body, but principally at the skull and the sacrum. By holding and exerting very gentle pressure on the skull the practitioner can feel the rhythm of the cranial pulse and detect irregularities. The technical approach used involves extremely gentle, but specifically applied adjustments to the movement of body tissues.

*LEFT: Cranberries are a rich source of Vitamin C and can guard against infection.*
*RIGHT: A rose quartz crystal.*

Cranial osteopathy is both gentle and non-invasive, making it a very safe method of diagnosis and treatment for even newborn babies.

There are many conditions that have been successfully treated by cranial osteopathy, including asthma, co-ordination difficulties, dental problems, digestive problems, dyslexia, glue ear, hyperactivity, colic, sleeping problems, migraines and headaches, digestive disorders, speech problems and also scoliosis (abnormal curvature of the spine).

))))➤ *Osteopathy*

## CRYSTALS

A crystal is defined as a mineral that has a definite atomic structure, with smooth, flat faces arranged in a geometric pattern. Every crystal is believed to be a perfect example of organized matter. Tuning into the perfection of the crystal is believed to bring the individual closer to perfection.

Crystals and gemstones are believed to exert positive healing energies that can help to rebalance us because they match the energy of the human aura very well. Crystals can generate, store and give off electromagnetic energy. Each crystal has its own particular energy which vibrates at a level that can have specific healing effects on mind, body and spirit. The electrical qualities of quartz, for example, are believed to help us to think more clearly and speed up healing. Amber has a calming energy that helps ward off depression and moonstone can help maintain emotional and hormonal balance.

))))➤ *Crystal Therapy*

## CRYSTAL THERAPY

For thousands of years crystals have been credited with mystical and healing powers. They were used by ancient astrologers, diviners and priests and have long been revered for their beauty and power. Today, crystals are used for their unique healing powers, and crystal therapy has become a popular form of treatment.

Like many other therapies, crystals work on an energy level, or a 'vibrational' basis. Everything in our physical environment is comprised of energy; in fact, humans are simply dense bodies of energy. This energy can be depleted or become imbalanced by numerous external and internal influences, from thinking negatively to eating the wrong foods and absorbing radiation from computer screens.

Crystals vibrate with energy that has the potential to alter our energy flow, and they work in a similar way to flower essences. A crystal therapist will adapt their own treatment, depending on your individual requirements.

They may place crystals around your chair or couch to surround you with healing energy, or they may give you a crystal to hold. Some therapists will place crystals on the body's seven energy centres, known as chakras. If you have physical pain, the therapist may place a crystal over the site of the pain. Energy from the crystal then passes through the body to the point of pain or imbalance. The crystals can be left in place for a few seconds or for several minutes, it varies enormously depending on the site and intensity of the pain. The choice of the crystal or crystals depends on what the therapist believes to be your own particular needs.

Healers believe that crystals can help with every level of healing, from strengthening the spirit to reducing stress and even healing wounds. There has been considerable success with conditions such as back pain and arthritis.

)))⧫ *Crystals*

*ABOVE: A crystal sphere and an amethyst crystal represent only a fraction of the tools which may be used in the practice of crystal therapy.*
*RIGHT: Cucumbers originate from a vine plant and have been widely used in folk medicine.*
*FAR RIGHT: Healing progresses outwards from the more important organs towards the lesser ones and symptoms should disappear in the reverse order to which they appeared.*

## CUCUMBER
*Cucumis sativis*

The cucumber, *Cucumis sativus*, is a vine fruit that can be eaten fresh or pickled. Cucumber has been widely used in folk medicine to reduce heat and inflammation. It is a rich source of vitamin C and can be used externally to cool and cleanse.

### Properties and Uses
- Diuretic, cooling, cleansing, particularly for skin disorders
- Used in the treatment of gout and arthritis
- Anti-inflammatory – soothes inflamed skin
- May help to treat lung and chest disorders
- Drink cucumber juice or eat fresh cucumber to soothe heartburn or an acid stomach; drink 100–150 ml every two hours for a gastric or duodenal ulcer
- Place a cucumber slice over strained or inflamed eyes to reduce swelling and soothe
- Apply fresh cucumber or cucumber juice to sunburn to cool
- Ground dried cucumber seeds are used to treat tapeworm
- Cucumber juice, drunk daily, may help to control eczema, arthritis and gout
- Cucumber juice acts as a kidney tonic

## CULPEPER, NICHOLAS

Nicholas Culpeper (1616–54) is the best known of the famous English herbalists. He was the first person to translate the *Pharmacopoeia* of the London College of Physicians from Latin into English. The secret doctors' knowledge was thus made available to the ordinary person in his own language. He was the first person to produce a truly English herbal guide, based on plants that could be found in any English garden. Because herbal medicines were the only treatments of the day, and herbs from the garden cost next to nothing, the book was an immediate success. This book, entitled *The English Physician* (also known as the *Culpeper Herbal*), has been published continuously, worldwide, since the seventeenth century.

## CURE

The aim of all medicine, whether conventional or natural, is to effect a cure. Natural therapists claim that the conventional medical system has become

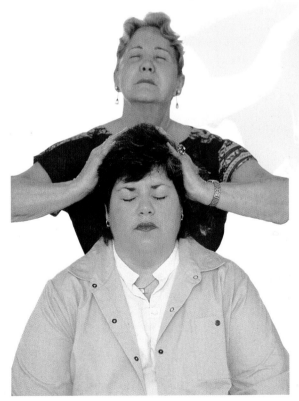

obsessed with treating, and in many cases, suppressing and masking symptoms, rather than looking to cure the cause of a health problem.

Many natural therapies have a rigorous set of principles and systems set up to define a health problem and then to cure it. In homeopathy, for example, the 'law of cure' was developed to pinpoint the steps of the healing process, to ensure that cure was eventually attained. They are:

- The body seeks to externalize disease – keeping it to more external locations
- Healing progresses from more important organs to less important ones
- Symptoms should disappear in reverse order to their original appearance
- Healing progresses from the top of the body downwards (especially in the case of skin rashes)
- You can use this law to help you evaluate the success of any form of treatment you are receiving

))))➤ *Homeopathy*

## CYMATICS

Cymatics was developed in the 1960s by British medical doctor and osteopath Dr Peter Manners. The therapy grew out of early research into electromagnetic energy and the concept that every living thing – person, animal, plant or organism – is surrounded by an energy field which resonate at its own particular frequency.

Cymatics comes from the Greek word *kyma,* meaning 'a great wave'. Cymatic therapy is a form of sound therapy, based on the principle that every cell in the body, of which there are believed to be 60 million, is controlled by an electromagnetic field which resonates at its own particular sound frequency. When we are well this frequency is constant, but dysfunction or disease upsets the harmony of the body and the area affected generates an increased resonance. The practitioner uses the cymatic machinery to generate a frequency identical to that of healthy cells. His aim is to support what the cell is trying to do naturally, therefore empowering the healing process and restoring the body to health and harmony.

))))➤ *Sound Therapy*

## CYSTEINE

The amino acid cysteine contains sulphur, which is said to work as an antioxidant, protecting and preserving the cells in our body. It is also said to protect the body against pollutants, but much work has still to be done to properly understand the effects of the amino acid, cysteine.

Diabetics should not take cysteine supplements unless supervised by their doctor. Cysteine may also cause kidney stones but a high vitamin C intake should prevent this from occurring.

The best source of cyskine are eggs, meat, dairy products and some cereals.

### Properties and Uses

- May protect against copper toxicity
- Protects the body against free radicals
- May help to reverse damage done by smoking and alcohol abuse
- Offers protection against X-rays and nuclear radiation
- May help to treat arthritis
- Helps to repair DNA, preventing the effects of ageing

### Dosage

- Take with vitamin C for best effect (three times as much vitamin C as Cysteine); doses up to 1 g are considered to be safe, but consult your doctor first

))))➡ *Amino Acids*

## DAGGER HAKEA

*Hakea teretifolia*

For people who feel resentment and bitterness and hold grudges against those with whom they have been very close e.g. family members and old lovers. This resentment is rarely openly displayed. The plant gets its name from the needle-like barb that grows on its leaves.

### Properties and Uses

- For resentment and bitterness towards close family, friends, lovers
- Brings forgiveness and open expression of feelings

))))➡ *Australian Bush Flower Essences*

## DANCE THERAPY

Dance therapy uses movement and dance to explore how a patient's emotional disturbance is linked to their bodily experiences. A dance therapist observes and analyses how you express yourself through the use of your body, assesses your strengths and identifies areas in which you might benefit from therapy. The therapist may also work with you on an individual basis, using movements designed to help you build a stronger sense of your own identity.

Movement can also be used to help resolve issues that may have occurred before you learnt to speak, when movement was your natural means of expression. In group work the therapist notes how members share emotional expression, assesses how the group works together and judges when to intervene. For example, introducing the concept of leading and following may help to draw someone out of their self-preoccupied isolation.

A therapist will have various pieces of equipment such as balls, beanbags and stretch cloths in the room, which can be used by the group to explore particular themes. Members of the group, for example, can pull and release cloths while exploring the theme of trust.

*ABOVE: Students take part in a dance therapy class, at which a therapist will closely observe body movements to assess and redress emotional imbalances and disturbances.*
*CENTRE RIGHT: Taraxacum officinalis (dandelion).*
*FAR RIGHT: An illustration of a medieval herbalist selling a decoction.*

## DANDELION

*Taraxacum officinalis*

The leaves, flowers and the roots of the common dandelion are a mainstay of herbal medicine, and are best known for their tonic and diuretic properties. The fresh leaves are very nourishing.

### Properties and Uses

- An excellent diuretic and kidney tonic
- Cleansing, by neutralizing the acids in the blood
- Dandelion-root coffee is an excellent liver tonic, and can be used in chronic and acute liver conditions
- Dandelion root may be decocted and used to treat and prevent gallstones
- The fresh white sap of the stalks will eliminate warts when used regularly

)))) *Homeopathic Remedies*

## DECOCTIONS

The roots, twigs, berries, seeds and barks of a plant are used to make a decoction – they are boiled in water to extract the plants' ingredients. The liquid is strained and taken with a bit of honey or brown sugar as prescribed. Decoctions should be refrigerated and will last about three days.

)))) *Aromatherapy, Infusion*

## DETOXIFICATION

Our bodies are designed to cope with a certain number of toxins – those naturally occurring in our foods, for example. Toxins are neutralized, transformed or eliminated by our bodies. The liver helps to transform toxic substances into harmless ones, the intestines break down protein, carbohydrates and fats, while the kidneys filter waste from the bloodstream. We also eliminate toxins through our skin, when we sweat, and our lymphatic system clears debris from our blood. The immune system is also involved – fighting off bacteria and other invaders.

Too much junk food, pollution and everyday stress can mean that the process is impaired. What happens is a condition called 'toxic overload', where we have taken in more toxins than we can eliminate. Uneliminated toxins are stored in our tissues and they can harm our overall health on a daily basis, and sow the seeds of future illness. Every chemical with which we come into contact has to be dealt with – or detoxified – by the body. If we use drugs to control eczema, or asthma, for example, they place a strain on the body, as do carbon monoxide, scented shampoos and soaps, cleaning products, perfumes, radiation from televisions, computers, mobile telephones, electricity masts, pollution, smoke and even ordinary household dirt and dust.

As increasing demands are placed on your body, an increasing amount of energy is required to deal with them. This is the same energy required for other body functions, such as breathing, digestion, fighting off infection, thinking, moving, developing and growing. Toxins build up, and body systems start to work less effectively. This is one of the most common causes of low-grade niggling diseases on a daily basis (insomnia, fatigue, irritability, headaches, digestive disorders, skin problems, poor concentration and susceptibility to common ailments, for example). In the long-term toxic build-up can be responsible for large-scale immune-system failure and a host of debilitating diseases.

Many therapies initiate a process of detoxification, which means that toxins are forced out of the body, through the use of natural remedies, such as oils, herbs, nutrients and even specific foods. Hydrotherapy and massage can also encourage detoxification. When this happens, you may suffer from symptoms such as head aches, dizziness, bad skin, rashes, diarrhoea, nausea and discharge. These symptoms clear to leave a state of enhanced mental and physical health.

## DIAGNOSIS

Many therapists use a variety of diagnostic techniques alongside the information the patient provides. For example, an Oriental (Chinese, for example) therapist will use personal touch and observation, including:

- Pulse-taking (there is more than one pulse in Chinese medicine)

*LEFT: A variety of diagnostic techniques are used to profile patients and prescribe suitable treatments.*
*RIGHT: A balanced diet when we are young helps us prepare to lead better, healthier lives when we are older.*
*BELOW RIGHT: Fibre-rich foods, such as fruit and vegetables, encourage digestion and promote an optimum uptake of nutrients within the body.*

- Abdominal touch
- Posture, movement and skin texture diagnosis
- Tongue diagnosis
- Possible urine analysis

Other therapists may use some of these techniques:
- Dowsing: a pendulum is held over the body's energy centres or *chakras* to indicate strengths and weak-nesses in the energy system. It may also be used to give yes/no answers (by swinging clockwise or anti-clockwise) to specific questions about the person's health status and requirements.
- Radionics: using instruments to measure different aspects of your child's energy state from a 'witness' – a hair clipping or drop of blood – to provide a diagnosis of overall health.
- Aura reading: many healers appear to be able to read people's auras or energy fields by clairvoyance, touch, or an in-built instinct. Most healers effectively scan the energy field with their hands, sensing areas of heat, cold, pain or tingling which indicate problems. Some therapists actually see and interpret the colours of the aura, and can pick up the effects of past traumas and potential future problems.
- Kirlian photography: developed by a Russian engineer, Kirlian photographs show the energy radiations emitted by living things, including plants and animals. A healthy person emits strong radiations while weak radiations are believed to show imbalances that need to be treated.
- Muscle-testing or applied kinesiology
- Iridology: the iris of the eye represents a map of the glands, organs, and systems of the whole human body. Problems show up on the iris as spots, flecks, white or dark streaks and texture and colour indicate the person's general state of health.

- Reflexology
- Hair analysis: chemical analysis of hair is often used to reveal nutritional deficiencies in the body, particularly of minerals.
- X-rays.

))⯈ **Kinesiology, Kirlian Photography, Reflexology**

## DIET

Diet is an essential part of every single natural therapy, as it forms the foundation of our overall health. Everything we eat has the power to enhance or detract from our health. We now know, for example, that 80 per cent of all cancers are linked to diet. So are fertility, heart disease, immune function, mental prowess, weight, the health of our bones and teeth, allergies, and, of course, well-being.

In the West, we have adopted a diet based around pre-packaged, easy-to-cook or 'instant' convenience foods. Not only are these poor in the essential nutrients required for growth and the functioning of every system in our bodies, but they contain a host of chemicals that put a strain on our bodies and act as anti-nutrients, meaning they actually use up what little nutrition we do get in order to process the 'junk'.

A healthy diet is easy to achieve, and should be based around whole foods in their natural state. In other words, wholegrain breads are far superior to white processed breads, and brown rice is better than white. The key is to replace processed foods with natural foods and obviously to improve our children's diets – replacing processed foods with natural, unrefined alternatives. We need to eat more fruit and vegetables, whole grains, pulses, lean meats and low-fat dairy produce.

Reduce or remove anything with artificial chemicals, in the form of additives, preservatives, flavours and anything else. All of these put strain on the body, in particular the liver, which is so crucial for the stress response.

Aim for the following:

- Lots of healthy proteins, including very lean meats, fish, poultry, cheese, yoghurt, nuts, soya products (including tofu), pulses such as lentils, seeds (three to five servings a day).
- Plenty of fruit and vegetables and their juices. Anything goes. Remember that the more colourful the vegetable, the more nutritious it tends to be. (Five to seven servings a day.)
- Lots of carbohydrates for energy. Anything wholegrain or unrefined, including pastas, bread, brown rice, grains (such as rye, barley, corn, buckwheat), pulses, potatoes and whole-grain, sugar-free cereals. (Four to nine servings a day.)
- As much fluid as you can drink. Water is the most important. Between 500–4000 ml is recommended, depending on age and weather.
- Fibre-rich foods, to help encourage digestion and optimum uptake of nutrients in the food we eat.
- Eat organic when you can. There is still considerable debate about whether or not it is more nutritious, but there is no doubt that it is lower in chemicals that place a strain on your system.
- Cut down on sweets, crisps, soft drinks and fast or junk foods of any nature. These not only tend to take the place of healthier alternatives in our diet but they are also a key source of damaging chemicals, fat and anti-nutrients.
- Watch the sugar! Given that stress causes the immune system to become less effective, it is important to take steps to ensure that it is being boosted in every other possible way. Sugar is one of the worst culprits in terms of immunity.

As long as your diet is 80 per cent healthy, you can do what you like with the other 20 per cent!

## DIETARY FIBRE

Dietary fibre, also known as bulk or roughage, is an essential element in the diet even though it provides no nutrients. The chewing it requires stimulates saliva flow and the bulk it adds in the stomach and intestines during digestion provides more time for absorption of nutrients.

The best sources of dietary fibre are fruits, vegetables, wholegrain breads, and products made from nuts and legumes.

### Properties and Uses

- Reduces the production of cholesterol
- Helps to control diabetes
- Helps to control weight
- Can be used to treat intestinal disorders such as diverticulosis
- Protects against cancers of the colon

### Key Notes

- A diet overly abundant in dietary fibre can cut down on the absorption of important trace minerals during digestion. Take a good multivitamin and mineral tablet if you increase your fibre intake significantly.

## DIMETHYLGLYCINE (DMG)

Dimethylglycine is a derivative of glycine, the simplest of the amino acids. It acts as a building block for many important substances, including a number of important hormones, neurotransmitters and DNA.

Low levels of DMG are present in meats, seeds and grains. No deficiency symptoms are associated with a lack of DMG in the diet, but taking supplemental DMG can have a wide range of therapeutic benefits, including helping the body to maintain high energy levels and boosting mental acuity. DMG has also been found to enhance the immune system, and to reduce elevated blood cholesterol. It helps to normalize blood pressure and blood-sugar levels and improves the functioning of many organs.

Choose supplements produced by a reputable supplier, and follow the instructions on the label. Do not exceed the recommended dose.

)))➤ *Amino Acids*

## DISEASE

Disease is, literally, a state of 'dis-ease', when the body is unbalanced and its systems are not working in harmony. One of the main differences between conventional and natural medicine is the approach to health. Conventional practitioners treat illness as a biological or chemical malfunction of the body. The main premise of conventional medicine is that curing disease will lead to good health, ignoring the fact that pathology is individual to the sufferer, and that

*LEFT: Although lacking in nutrients, the dietary fibre (or roughage) found in fruit, vegetables and nuts adds bulk to our digestion and stimulates healthy bowel action.*

*ABOVE RIGHT: Doctors who practise conventional medicine believe curing disease will lead to good health, but neglect the many elements of health: the mind, body and spirit.*

*FAR RIGHT: Chinese angelica or dong quai capsules.*

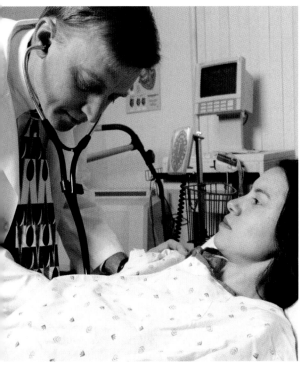

each one of us is unique. For example, tonsillitis would be treated with antibiotics in most cases; asthma with Ventolin, steroids or the equivalent; eczema with hydrocortisone cream or another suppressive remedy.

Natural practitioners believe that there is something more afoot than simply a physical diagnosis of disease. Indeed, the many elements of health – the mind, body and spirit – are taken into consideration when treating children suffering from virtually any health condition, at any level. But more than that, there is a belief in a vital or life force.

There are well-known physical processes that keep our bodies alive, including the immune system, the brain and nervous system and the endocrine system. These are important on a physical level, and are crucial to maintaining the body's equilibrium. However, they are not the only level of functioning. Equally important is the guiding mechanism. Some complementary medical disciplines believe that energy flows through our bodies, and that illness or 'dis-ease' is caused by blockages and imbalance. Others believe that it is simply a governing force that can be weakened by environmental

factors (diet, trauma, stress, pollution, or lack of sleep, for example), so that it can no longer keep the whole body (that is, mind, body and spirit) balanced.

## DONG QUAI

Chinese angelica, or *dong quai*, has been used in Asia for thousands of years, and is enjoying renewed popularity as a gynaecological aid. Ayurvedic practitioners prescribe the herb for menstrual problems, as well as arthritis, abdominal pains, and flu.

Do not use with hypertension or heart disease, or while pregnant. Chinese angelica can be used as an inhalant, nose drops, diffuser, tea, tincture and massage oil.

### Properties and Uses

- *Dong quai* increases the effects of ovarian and testicular hormones
- It is used in the treatment of female problems, such as hot flushes and other menopausal symptoms, premenstrual syndrome and vaginal dryness

⫸ *Traditional Chinese Medicine*

## DOUCHE

Many herbs and essential oils can be used in the vagina, to treat infections and imbalances. They are administered in the form of a douche, which can be purchased from a chemist. Remember that the lining of the vagina is extremely delicate, and regular douching can play havoc with the bacterial balance (healthy/unhealthy) as well as the vagina's own secretions, which offer natural protection.

⫸ *Aromatherapy*

## DROSERA

*Drosera rotundifolia*

 The sundew is a carnivorous plant from which the homeopathic remedy drosera is made. Sundew was used in the Middle Ages to treat the plague and sixteenth-century physicians used it for tuberculosis. Homeopathically, the whole fresh plant is used, mainly to treat coughs and complaints such as whooping cough, characterized by a violent, spasmodic, hollow-sounding cough, triggered by a tickling sensation in the throat. The cough worsens after midnight and at the acute stage is accompanied by retching and vomiting, cold sweats and nosebleeds, after which the patient becomes talkative. This remedy also helps the tingling pain associated with growing pains, stiffness and a hoarse voice.

The drosera type is restless and obstinate when ill, cannot concentrate, dislikes being left alone and tends to be worried about being given bad news.

### Properties and Uses

- Relieves severe, spasmodic coughing, breathing difficulties, retching or vomiting of mucus, growing pains
- Helps with difficulty in concentrating
- For those who cannot settle and become stubborn
- For barking, hollow cough
- For tingling in leg bones
- Symptoms improve when walking, in fresh air, with pressure, when sitting up and when quiet, and worsen after midnight, after cold food and drinking, when lying down, and if the bed is too warm

## DYNAMIS ESSENCE

This combination essence contains the flowers of Old Man Banksia, Macrocarpa, Crowea, Wild Potato Bush and Banksia Robur, which renew enthusiasm and a joy for life. It is for those who feel 'not quite right', drained, jaded, disheartened or burdened by their physical body. It also helps with feelings of physical restriction and limitation.

### Properties and Uses

- For temporary loss of drive and enthusiasm
- Harmonizes vital forces

))))➡ ***Australian Bush Flower Essences***

## ECHINACEA

*Echinacea angustifolia* and *Echinacea purpurea*

Echinacea is known as the purple cone flower, and is native to North America. It has become a bastion of natural healthcare, with its powerful and now well-proven ability to improve immunity.

### Properties and Uses

- Anti-microbial, immunomodulator, anti-catarrhal, alterative
- One of the primary remedies for helping the body rid itself of microbial infections it is often effective against both bacterial and viral attacks, and may be used in conditions such as boils, septicaemia and similar infections

### Key Notes

- Especially useful for infections of the upper respiratory tract such as laryngitis, tonsillitis and for catarrhal conditions of the nose and sinus

- May be used as an external lotion to help septic sores and cuts
- Activates the body to destroy both cancerous cells and pathogens, increases the level of white blood cells and boosts the immune system in general

## Notes and Dosages
- Decoction: put one to two teaspoonfuls of the root in one cup of water and bring it slowly to boil. Let it simmer for 10–15 minutes. This should be drunk three times a day.
- Tincture: take 1–4 ml of the tincture three times a day. Echinacea is often – inappropriately – used as a daily immune-system support.
- Daily intake should only take place during the cold and flu season but for chronic infections such as chronic hepatitis, echinacea may be used continuously for several months. However, for the maintenance of a healthy immune system echinacea is most wisely used periodically – a few weeks on, and a few weeks off, throughout the year.

))))➤ *Immunity*

# ELDERFLOWER AND ELDERBERRIES
*Sambucus nigra*

Elderflower is a popular herb in natural remedies and is one of the main diaphoretic herbs (it encourages perspiration and the elimination of toxins). They are nutritious and work as a laxative among other things. In some cases, the bark is used therapeutically.

## Properties and Uses
- Bark: purgative, emetic, diuretic
- Leaves: externally emollient, internally as purgative, expectorant, diuretic and diaphoretic
- Flowers: diaphoretic, anti-catarrhal, antispasmodic
- Berries: diaphoretic, diuretic, laxative
- The elder tree is a medicine chest in itself. The leaves are used for bruises, sprains, wounds and chilblains. It

*FAR LEFT: Drosera rotundifolia (sundew).*

*NEAR LEFT: Echinacea purpurea.*

*RIGHT: Preparing a Sambucus nigra (elderflower) tincture.*

has been reported that elder leaves may be useful in an ointment for tumours. Elderflowers are ideal for the treatment of colds and flu. They are indicated in any catarrhal inflammation of the upper respiratory tract such as hayfever and sinusitis. Catarrhal deafness responds well to elderflowers. Elderberries have similar properties to the flowers with the addition of their usefulness in rheumatism.

## Dosages
- Infusion: one cup of boiling water on to two teaspoonfuls of the dried or fresh blossoms and infuse for 10 minutes. Drink hot three times a day.
- Juice: boil fresh berries in water for two to three minutes, then express the juice. To preserve, bring to the boil with one part honey to 10 parts of juice. Take one glass diluted with hot water twice a day.
- Ointment: take three parts of fresh elder leaves and heat them with six parts of melted Vaseline until the leaves are crisp. Strain and store.
- Tincture: take 2–4 ml of the tincture (made from the flowers) three times a day.

## ELM

*Ulmus procera*

This Bach flower remedy is made from the stately English elm tree. Elm is for temporary feelings of inadequacy. People who benefit from elm do good work and are proud of themselves and their calling. They hope to do something important and to be of service and benefit to all humanity. They seek and aim for perfection. This goal can sometimes feel unattainable and become overwhelming. Elm is for brief faltering moments of despair and the lack of confidence, when the task seems too much. Elm restores faith in one's own judgement.

### Key Notes

- People who need elm are usually confident and capable, but are temporarily overwhelmed with the scope, weight and burden of their work. They may be tired, with the exhaustion leading to mild depression.
- Elm helps us find the strength to balance idealism with the practical needs of everyday reality and carry on.

)))➡ ***Bach Flower Remedies***

## EMERGENCY ESSENCE

This flower-essence combination is made from the essences of fringed violet, grey spider flower, sundew, waratah and crowea. It will help ease distress, fear, panic, etc. If a person needs specialized medical help, this essence will provide comfort until treatment is available. Administer this remedy every hour, or more frequently if necessary, until the person feels better. It can also be used topically or mixed into a cream.

### Properties and Uses

- Eases panic, distress and fear
- Increases your ability to cope

)))➡ ***Australian Bush Flower Essences***

## EMOTIONAL HEALTH

In natural medicine, emotional health is considered to be as important as physical health, and is one of the key elements of well-being. Illness is more than just a series of physical symptoms. There is a great deal more involved in ill-health than what is going on in the body. It is important to understand that emotional health, spiritual health and physical health go hand-in-hand – that is the underlying premise of the holistic revolution. We are more than the sum of our physical parts and optimum well-being is based on three distinct elements: mind, body and spirit.

As adults, we can often sense when we are becoming ill and tend to become irritable, emotional or tearful. We will also succumb to illness more readily during periods of stress, or following a trauma, such as a bereavement or a divorce. The mind-body relationship is not the paragon of alternative medicine alone; there are literally hundreds of scientific studies that show how closely the two are linked.

When there is an emotional imbalance, physical health can be affected. Similarly, physical health can impact on

emotional health. These factors are inextricably inter-twined and as we need to learn to recognize changes in our emotional health in order to see the whole picture.

)))➤ *Homeopathy*

## ENERGY

Natural practitioners believe that there is something more afoot than simply a physical diagnosis of disease. Indeed, the many elements of health – the mind, body and spirit – are taken into consideration when treating children suffering from virtually any health condition, at any level. But more than that, there is a belief in a vital or life force.

Different therapies and disciplines have a variety of names for this force: spirit or energy, for example. But the concept remains the same. It is the body's controlling energy. It vitalizes the physical body, and it is the link between the body, soul and mind. The vital force is not a material substance, such as water or air, but it is equally indispensable for life. Its presence distinguishes living things from inanimate matter. When illness occurs, it appears first as a disturbance in this natural energy long before it manifests itself as physical symptoms. This is why we appear grumpy, tired or out of sorts for some time before symptoms actually appear.

Many of the most ancient therapies are based on the existence of a vital energy flow. Western medicine was, until fairly recently, in agreement that there is an animating force, but as the focus became more scientific, the idea of a vital energy was largely dispensed with. However, the huge wealth of material amassed by scientists into the functioning of the human body is all true and correct, and they do not by any means contradict the idea of the vital force. Physical and chemical mechanisms are merely tools of the vital force, which act upon the physical plane of the body.

Natural remedies work on energy level, focusing our energy and vitality towards healing so that we overcome

the problem naturally. They do not heal, in the same way that we might expect if we took a conventional drug, and they do not pretend to do so. Instead, natural remedies encourage the body to heal itself, by operating on a level that is above the physical.

)))➤ *Flower Essences, Homeopathy, Vibrational Medicine*

## ENZYMES

Dr Edward Howell called enzymes the 'sparks of life'. These energized protein molecules play a necessary role in virtually all the biochemical activities that go on inside the body. They are essential for digesting food, for stimulating the brain, for providing cellular energy, and for repairing all tissues, organs and cells.

Enzymes are catalysts, which accelerate and precipitate the hundreds of thousands of biochemical reactions in the body that control the processes of life. Each enzyme has a specific function in the body that no other enzyme can fulfil. There are two groups of enzymes, digestive enzymes and metabolic enzymes.

The body manufactures a supply of enzymes, and can also obtain some from food, but really only in its raw form. Good sources include avocados, papayas, pine-apples, bananas, sprouts, barley grass, broccoli, cabbage and most green plants. Digestive enzymes are also available in supplement form.

*ABOVE LEFT: The Bach elm flower remedy.*

*CENTRE LEFT: Being energetic is an indication of good health and internal balance.*

*TOP RIGHT: The enzymes contained in avocadoes act as catalysts across a host of vital biochemical processes occurring inside the body.*

## EPHEDRA

Ephedra is also known as *Ma huang*, and is used in both Western and Chinese herbalism.

### Properties and Uses
- Acts as a decongestant and aids in the elimination of fluids
- Relieves bronchial spasm and stimulates the central nervous system
- May decrease appetite and elevate mood
- Useful for allergies, asthma, colds and other respiratory complaints, as well as for depression and obesity

### Key Notes
- Do not use if you have an anxiety disorder, glaucoma, heart disease or high blood pressure, or if you take MAOI antidepressants
- Follow instructions on the packet label and do not exceed recommended dose.

*Traditional Chinese Medicine*

## ESSENTIAL FATTY ACIDS

Essential fatty acids are not only crucial to health, but they are a form of healthy fat, which our obsession with a fat-free diet has nearly eliminated. Essential fatty acids are converted into substances that keep our blood thin, lower blood pressure, decrease inflammation, improve the function of our nervous and immune systems, help insulin to work, affect our vision, co-ordination and mood, encourage healthy metabolism and maintain the balance of water in our bodies. There is also exciting new research showing that it can affect behaviour and the ability to learn. Children with a low fatty acid intake seem to be more at risk of attention deficit disorders. Fatty acids fall into two main categories: omega-3 and omega-6 oils.
- Omega-3 oils are found in leafy green vegetables, pumpkin seeds, flaxseed oil, walnuts and oily fish (including salmon, herring, sardines, mackerel, pilchards and fresh tuna)
- Omega-6 oils are found in vegetables and seed oils (including corn, soya, sesame, sunflower and safflower oils) and in peanuts, peanut oils and olive oils

### Key Notes:
- Choose cold-pressed olive oil for cooking, which does not become unstable when heated
- Add flaxseed oil (available as capsules or as an oil on its own), which has the highest concentration of omega-3 oils, to your diet; it should not be heated, but you can drizzle a little in salads, or add it to yoghurts, or warm foods just before serving.

))))▶ *Evening Primrose, Fish Oils, Flaxseed Oil*

## ESSENTIAL OILS

Essential oils are extracted from the aromatic essences of certain plants, trees, fruit, flowers, herbs and spices. They are natural, volatile oils with identifiable chemical and medicinal properties. Over 150 essential oils have been extracted, each one with its own scent and unique healing properties. Oils are sourced from plants as commonplace as parsley and as exquisite as jasmine. For optimum benefits essential oils must be extracted from natural raw ingredients and remain as pure as possible.

The oils and their actions are extremely complex. All the oils are antiseptic, but each one also has individual properties; for example they may be analgesic, fungicidal, diuretic or expectorant. The collective components of each oil also work together to give the oil a dominant characteristic. It can be relaxing as in the case of chamomile, refreshing like grapefruit or stimulating like rosemary.

Essential oils also have notable physiological effects. Certain oils have an affinity with particular areas of the body. For example, rose has an affinity with the female reproductive system, while spice oils tend to benefit the digestive system. The oil may also sedate an overactive system, or stimulate a different part of the body that is sluggish. Some oils such as lavender are known as adaptogens, meaning they do whatever the body requires of them at the time. The psychological response is triggered by the effect of the aromatic molecules on the brain.

Essential oils can be used alone or blended together. Oils are blended for two reasons: to create a more sophisticated fragrance or to enhance or change the medicinal actions of the oils. Blending changes the molecular structure of essential oils and when blended well, therapists can create a synergistic blend, where the oils work in harmony and to great effect.

## EUCALYPTUS

*Eucalyptus globulus*

Several of the 700 species of eucalyptus are used to distil medicinal-quality essential oil, but the Australian 'blue gum' is by far the most widely used. Eucalyptus is a traditional remedy in Australia and a familiar ingredient in numerous chest rubs and decongestants. The first works on the antiseptic and anti-bacterial properties of the oil were published in the nineteenth century by German doctors.

Do not take eucalyptus when using homeopathic remedies. Do not use for more than a few days at a time because of risk of toxicity. Do not use on babies or very young children.

## Properties and Uses

- Eucalyptus is a powerful antiseptic and renowned decongestant, used mostly for coughs, colds, chest infections, and sinusitis

- The oil is also used to reduce fevers and treat skin infections, cuts and blisters, genital and oral herpes, chickenpox and shingles
- It alleviates inflammation generally, and is helpful in treating rheumatism, muscular aches and pains and fibrositis
- It is a diuretic and a deodorant, with strong antiviral and immune-stimulating properties and is an effective local painkiller, especially for nerve pain
- Urinary tract problems such as cystitis respond well to regular use of the oil

))⟩⟩ *Herbalism*

*LEFT Ephedra or* Ma huang, *used in both Chinese and Western herbalism.*
*CENTRE LEFT: The essential oil Chamomile is best known for its ability to make us relax.*
*ABOVE: Making a decoction of Eucalyptus globulus.*

## EUPHRASIA

Herbalists use eyebright (*Euphrasia*) either internally or externally. It can work as a tea to help strengthen eye muscles and can also help with problems associated with the upper respiratory tract.

### Properties and Uses

- Used as an eye wash
- Prevents secretion of fluids and relieves discomfort from eye-strain or minor irritation
- Good for allergies, itchy and/or watery eyes, and runny nose
- Used to combat hayfever
- Good for congested catarrhal conditions and as an antiseptic for glue ear and sinusitis

### Dosage

- Use 1 ml tincture diluted in water, or one teaspoon of the herb infused in a cup of boiling water
- For external use two to three drops of tincture in an egg cup of freshly boiled cooled water

## EUPHRASIA

*Euphrasia Officinalis*

Eyebright – as its name suggests – has been used for centuries to treat eye problems. Homeopathically, the whole fresh plant is used when in flower to make a remedy for sore, irritated eyes and eye injuries.

*Euphrasia* is useful for any eye irritation or inflammation, such as conjunctivitis, inflammation of the eyelid or

iris and small blisters on the cornea. Effective for dimmed vision, dislike of bright lights; watery, irritated eyes associated with hayfever sufferers, but accompanied by only bland nasal discharge; colds accompanied by flushed face and runny catarrh; eye injuries; dry eyes associated with the menopause. Also useful for constipation, exploding headaches, short painful periods, the early stages of measles and, in men, inflammation of the prostate gland.

## Properties and Uses

- Relieves stinging, watery eye discharge, inflammation or injury to eyes, running eyes associated with hayfever
- For intolerance of bright light
- For hot cheeks
- For bursting headaches
- Symptoms improve after lying down in a darkened room and with drinking coffee, and worsen in bright light, in the evening, in enclosed spaces and during warm, windy weather

## EVENING PRIMROSE (GLAs)

Native Americans were the first to recognize the potential of evening primrose oil as a healer, and they decocted (boiled) the seeds to make a liquid for healing wounds. Evening primrose oil is a rich source of gamma linolenic acid, which is better known as GLA. The body makes GLA from essential fatty acids (EFAs). EFAs have numerous functions in the body – one of which is to manufacture hormone-like substances called protaglandins, which have very important effects on the body, such as toning blood vessels, balancing water levels, aiding the action of the digestive system and brain functioning. Prostaglandins also have a beneficial effect on the immune system.

## Properties and Uses

- Reduces scaling and redness, prevents itching and encourages healing in cases of eczema; it is also used in the treatment of psoriasis
- Discourages dry skin and ensures that the cellular membranes that make up the skin are stable and strong; there is some evidence that the oil retards the ageing process
- Evening primrose oil may help to prevent multiple sclerosis (MS) and appears to be particularly useful for children suffering from the condition
- May help in cases of liver damage caused by alcohol (cirrhosis of the liver), hyperactivity in children and cystic fibrosis

- May have a stimulating effect on the body, encouraging it to convert fat into energy, making it an excellent treatment for obesity
- Hormonal imbalances, perhaps causing conditions like PMS, and symptoms of the menopause may be eased by reducing symptoms of bloating, water retention, irritability and depression
- Reduces the inflammation of rheumatoid arthritis
- May have an immuno-suppressive effect on the body

## Dosage

- Evening primrose oil is most often take in the form of capsules, but it is also available as an oil (sometimes flavoured), and it can be applied to the skin to treat skin conditions. Take 500 mg each day for two months, and then for the 10 days preceding each period if you suffer from PMS.
- In menopause, 2000–4000 mg should be taken daily for four weeks and then 500–1000 mg daily thereafter.
- For asthma, take two 500 mg tablets, three times daily for three to four months, and then one tablet three times daily. If you are taking steroids, this treatment will not work because steroids interfere with the action of evening primrose oil.

)))➤ *Herbalism*

*FAR LEFT:* Euphrasia officinalis *(eyebright).*
*CENTRE LEFT:* Euphrasia *(pictured) is used by herbalists to strengthen eye muscles, help allergies and decongest catarrhal conditions.*
*ABOVE: Evening primrose.*

## EXERCISE

Exercise is a crucial part of overall health and well-being, and is therefore an important aspect of a healthy lifestyle. All natural therapists will encourage moderate exercise. Studies show that exercise brings the following benefits:

- Strengthens the cardiovascular system and increases heart mass.
- Dilates the blood vessels so that the heart can pump more easily to supply blood to the rest of the body, thus reducing blood pressure.

- Reduces stress. One study claims that regular exercise can reduce stress dramatically. During periods of high stress, those who reported exercising less frequently had 37 per cent more physical symptoms than their counterparts who exercised more often. In addition, highly stressed people who get less exercise report 21 per cent more anxiety than those who exercise more frequently. Exercise works by using up the adrenaline that is created by stress and stressful situations. It also creates endorphins, the feel-good hormones that improve mood, motivation and even tolerance to pain and other stimuli.
- A 1997 study showed that physical activity may play a role in deterring cancer, particularly colonic cancer, probably by reducing the amount of time that potential cancer-causing agents take to move through the intestinal system.
- Aerobic exercise is effective in helping to maintain bone strength.
- Good for the brain. Aerobic exercise helps to increase the number of brain chemicals called neurotransmitters, so that messages can be carried more quickly over brain cells. This increases mental flexibility and agility over longer periods of time.
- Regular exercise can promote good, regular sleeping habits.
- Long-term aerobic exercise programmes result in improved maximal aerobic power and enhanced physical performance, resulting in improved exercise tolerance and less non-specific fatigue.
- Preliminary evidence suggests that exercise helps to increase insulin sensitivity and resistance to diabetes.
- Exercise increases health on many levels, and one side-effect is an improved resistance to disease. Regular exercise produces muscle strength, gains in aerobic fitness, feelings of control over a person's environment and positive feedback from friends, which can make us feel better about ourselves.

*LEFT: Regular exercise is an essential part of a healthy lifestyle regime.*
*ABOVE RIGHT: Meditation exercises, such as those taught during yoga sessions, can help give the individual the spiritual focus necessary to undertake lengthy fasts.*
*FAR RIGHT: Foeniculum vulgare (fennel); the berries, roots and stems.*

## FASTING

 Fasting forms a part of naturopathy and a variety of other natural therapies. It serves several purposes; principally it gives the digestive system a rest, detoxifies the system and stimulates the metabolism to get the body up and running so that healing and renewal take place. Naturopaths recommend that most of us should undertake to fast one day a month, even when perfectly healthy.

There are various types of fast, some moderate, some extreme. The Guelpa fast, for example, is a saline fast that lasts for three days and is often prescribed for rheumatic problems. The Schroth cure is also reputed to be good for rheumatic conditions. It is a three-day fast that alternates dry days (where you eat mainly dry foods) with liquid days (where you drink, but do not eat) for two or three weeks. Fasting is not recommended for children, the elderly or people with diabetes. Always ensure that fasts are undertaken with supervision.

)))➡ *Naturopathy*

## FEMIN ESSENCE

 Harmonizes any imbalances during menstruation and menopause. It allows a woman to discover and feel good about her own body and beauty.

### Properties and Uses

- Helps with mood swings, weariness and physical dislike
- Restores female balance
- Restores calm and stability
- Helps one cope with change

)))➡ *Australian Bush Flower Essences*

## FENNEL

*Foeniculum vulgare*

 The berries, roots and stems of this familiar cooking herb are used in therapeutic treatment.

### Properties and Uses

- Warming, carminative, antispasmodic, antidepressant and promotes milk flow in nursing mothers
- Eases colic, wind and irritable bowel syndrome (IBS)
- Alleviates anxiety, depression and disturbed spirits
- Relieves arthritis and water retention
- Aids griping in infants; give the tea in teaspoon doses, as much as they will take, or add two teaspoons to milk formulas

### Dosage

- Fennel-seed tea bags are easily available. Use one teaspoon of crushed seed to a cup of boiling water and infuse for 10 minutes. Take three times daily.

# FENNEL OIL

*Foeniculum vulgare*

In folklore fennel was believed to convey courage and strength and contribute to a long life. It also has a history of use as an antidote to poisons. The essential oil, distilled from the crushed seeds, is still valued for its detoxifying abilities.

## Properties and Uses

- Fennel appears to have a re-balancing effect on hormones, probably due to an oestrogenic-like plant hormone
- It is a good diuretic, anti-microbial and antiseptic which can help with premenstrual water retention and urinary tract infections
- It helps to eliminate toxic wastes from the body, making it valuable in treating arthritis and cellulite
- It reduces digestive spasms, calms and tones the stomach and digestive system and has a slightly laxative effect, benefiting nausea, indigestion, constipation and stomach cramps
- Fennel makes a good mouthwash for gum disease or infections

## Caution

- Use only sweet fennel (also known as Roman or French fennel), as bitter fennel should not be used on the skin. Do not use during pregnancy. It is not suitable for epileptics or children under the age of six. It is a narcotic in large doses.

# FERRUM PHOS

*Ferrum phosphoricum*

The Ferrum Phos remedy is made from iron phosphate which is a chemical combination of iron sulphate, sodium phosphate and sodium acetate. It is one of the 12 biochemic tissue salts. It has a variety of different uses, including the first stages of inflammation or infection, when more blood is flowing to the affected areas, causing congestion before the onset of other symptoms. Ferrum Phos is also good for slow-starting colds accompanied by nosebleeds and fevers, accompanied by hacking coughs, headaches which are helped by cool water, rheumatic pain, gastritis including vomiting undigested food, indigestion with sour-tasting burps, haemorrhages in women, intermittent, painful, periods, stress, incontinence; first stages of dysentery with bloody stools.

The Ferrum Phos type is pale and anaemic-looking, prone to sudden facial flushes, and driven by ideas. They tend to complain a lot, but are good-natured. They tend to suffer from respiratory and gastrointestinal complaints.

## Properties and Uses

- Relieves early stages of inflammation or infection and slow-onset coughs and colds
- For headaches and head colds
- For dry, hacking cough, laryngitis, hoarseness
- For shooting rheumatic pains
- For facial flushing and rapid pulse
- For chills starting in the early afternoon
- Symptoms improve with gentle exercise and cold compresses, and worsen in the heat, with movement, when touched, lying on the right side, between 4 a.m. and 6 a.m., when sweating is suppressed

⮞ *Biochemic Tissue, Salts*

# FEVERFEW

*Tanacetum parthenium*

A small-flowered daisy, easily grown in gardens and window boxes.

## Properties and Uses

- As an anti-inflammatory, antispasmodic, emmenagogue
- For migraine and arthritis; combined with valerian for migraine linked with anxiety and tension

## Dosage and Uses

- The best preparation is the tincture made from the fresh plant. Use one teaspoon in a little water at the first signs of a migraine, repeat in two hours if necessary. For repeated attacks and as a treatment for arthritis take one teaspoon every morning.
- If you have a plant, two or three medium-sized leaves equals one teaspoon of tincture.

## FISH OILS

A source of essential fatty acids (EFAs), fish oils contain two long-chain fatty acids called eicosopentaenoic acid (EPA) and docosahexaenoic acid (DHA) which affect the synthesis of prostaglandins, which have a regulatory effect on the body. There are numerous claims for fish oils, which are now believed to improve overall health and treat many conditions. Fish oils, however, may be harmful to diabetics by causing an increase in blood-sugar levels and a decline in insulin secretion.

The best sources of fish oils are herring, salmon, tuna, cod and prawns.

## Properties and Uses

- May be useful in the treatment of kidney disease, and can counteract the effects of some immuno-suppressive drugs
- May help to prevent cancer, in particular breast cancer

*LEFT: Fennel oil, once distilled as an extract from the seeds of the plant (pictured), is believed to help re-balance hormones.*
*ABOVE: Tanacetum parthenium (feverfew).*
*BELOW: Cod liver oil is a source of essential fatty acids (EFAs).*

- Stops the progression of arthritis
- May help to protect against high blood pressure
- Helps to prevent cardiovascular disease
- May help to prevent and treat psoriasis

## Dosage

- People suffering from arthritis or psoriasis can take up to 4 g daily, but for most people it is most suitable to increase your intake of fish and seafood in order to achieve the benefits of the fish oils in the natural form. Maximum suggested dosage for supplements, without the supervision of your doctor, is 900 mg per day.

➤ *Essential Fatty Acids*

SEVEN SEAS
*Lemon Flavour*
PURE
COD LIVER
OIL

## FLAXSEED OIL

*Linum usitatissimum*

The seeds of the flax plant contain a remarkable healing oil which can be used both internally and externally. Flaxseed is also known as linseed, but should not be confused with the boiled linseed oil available from building merchants. As far back as Hippocrates, flaxseed tea has been used to treat sore throats, hoarseness and the spasms of bronchitis. Flaxseed is a rich source of essential fatty acids (EFAs), and supplementing with flaxseed is one of the best ways to ensure an oil balance in your diet.

### Properties and Uses

- Mildly laxative
- Tonic for the kidneys and encourages their action
- Encourages healing
- Analgesic
- Antispasmodic

- Apply the oil to sprains to reduce inflammation and ease the pain
- Mix with lime water to reduce the pain of burns
- Flaxseed (linseed) tea can be used for mild constipation, and to encourage kidney function; the tea also works to ease kidney pains and cramping
- The tea can be drunk during bouts of bronchitis to reduce the inflammation of the lungs and prevent spasm
- Take the supplement for all the health benefits associated with EFAs

))))➤ *Essential Fatty Acids*

## FLOWER ESSENCES

Flower essences, or flower remedies, as they are more commonly known, are used therapeutically to harmonize the body, mind and spirit. The bottled flower essences are said to contain vibrations of the Sun's energy, absorbed by the flowers' petals when immersed in Sun-warmed water. The remedies use the vibrational essence of the flowers to balance the negative emotions which lead to, and are symptoms of, disease. They are a simple natural method of establishing personal equilibrium and harmony.

Therapists believe the remedies contain the energy or 'memory' of the plant from which it was made and work in a way that is similar to homeopathic remedies – on a vibrational basis. Some of the remedies are known as 'type remedies'. Your type remedy is effectively the remedy that is most compatible with your personality or basic character, and it can be taken when the negative side of your character threatens the positive.

Flower remedies are ideal for home use as they are simple to make and use. They are made in water, preserved with alcohol and employ the ability of flowers to change and enhance mood, and to balance the negative emotions which contribute to disease.

Flower essences work to reverse negative emotions, which depress the mind and immune system, repress activity and contribute to ill-health, improving well-being on an emotional level that transmits to good physical health. They can be used to prevent and treat illness by working on an emotional level.

))))➤ *Bach Flower Remedies*

*LEFT: Linum usitasissimum (flaxseed).*

*ABOVE: Flower essences are thought to contain the vibrations absorbed from the Sun's energy by the plants themselves, which then exercise beneficial effects on the mind and body.*

*RIGHT: Olibanum (frankincense).*

## FLUORINE

Fluorine is a trace mineral found naturally in soil, water, plants and animal tissues. Its electrically charged form is fluoride, which is how we usually refer to it. Although it has not yet been officially recognized as an essential nutrient, studies show that it is important in many processes, and may play a major role in the prevention of many modern killers, such as heart disease.

The major source of fluorine is from drinking water, which is normally fluoridated or has enough naturally occurring fluoride to make fluoridation unnecessary. It is important that fluoride supplements are always taken with calcium.

An excess of fluoride causes fluorosis, characterized by irregular patches on tooth enamel, and depresses the appetite. Eventually the spine calcifies.

The best sources of fluorine are seafood, animal meat, fluoridated drinking water and tea.

### Properties and Uses
- Protects against dental caries
- Protects against and treats osteoporosis
- May help to prevent heart disease
- May help to prevent calcification of organs and musculo-skeletal structures.

### Dosage
- Its major source is drinking water, and the typical daily intake is 1–2 mg. Tablets and drops are available from pharmacies, but should be limited to 1 mg daily in adults and 0.25–0.5 mg for children. Do not supplement fluoride without the advice of your dentist.

)))⯈ *Minerals*

## FRANKINCENSE

Frankincense, also known as *olibanum*, is distilled from the resin produced by the bark of a small North African tree. Since ancient times it has been considered a spiritual oil, used by many to encourage meditation, and it is enormously calming. Frankincense is safe to use during pregnancy but do not take internally and keep out of children's reach.

### Properties and Uses
- Frankincense slows the breathing and calms the nervous and digestive systems, relieving anxiety, depression, nervous tension, emotional upsets and stress-related digestive problems
- As an immune stimulant and an expectorant it can help respiratory and catarrhal conditions such as asthma, colds, sinusitis, chest infections, and chronic bronchitis
- Frankincense has wound-healing, astringent, antiseptic and anti-inflammatory properties, making it ideal for treating cuts, scars, blemishes and inflammation and it is recommended for firming ageing skin
- Frankincense is helpful for cystitis as it has an affinity with the genito-urinary system
- Irregular or heavy periods and nosebleeds can also benefit from its healing properties

## FRINGED VIOLET

*Thysanotus tuberosus*

Fringed violet can be used for treating damage to the aura where there has been shock, grief or distress e.g. from abuse or assault. This remedy maintains psychic protection, especially for those working in psychic areas. When used in combination with flannel flower or wisteria it is beneficial for those who have suffered abuse.

### Properties and Uses
- For damage to aura, distress and lack of psychic protection
- Helps with the removal of effects of recent or past distressing events
- For psychic protection

)))⯈ *Australian Bush Flower Essences*

## GARLES

Although essential oils should not be swallowed, using them as mouth washes and gargles is an excellent way to treat mouth ulcers, gum disease, throat infections and bad breath.

Many herbs can also be prepared in the form of a gargle, which has the same therapeutic benefits as an essential-oil gargle. Simply use an infusion, decoction or mix a few drops of tincture in cooled, boiled water and gargle. Most herbs can be safely swallowed.

### Dosage

Dilute four to five drops of essential oil in a teaspoon of brandy. Mix into a glass of warm water and swish around the mouth or use as a gargle. Do not swallow.

))))➤ *Aromatherapy, Essential Oils*

## GARLIC

*Allium sativum*

Garlic belongs to the onion family, and is one of the best-known and most-used medicinal herbs. It has a strong odour, which many people find off-putting, but its health-giving and preventative properties make it well worth suffering the effects. Garlic has been shown to lower total serum cholesterol as well as LDL cholesterol in human clinical trials. Effective herbal preparations of garlic can be used at less cost and with fewer side effects than most pharmaceutical drugs and its use has recently been applauded by the conventional medical establishment.

### Properties and Uses

- Cleanses the blood and helps to create and maintain healthy bacteria (flora) in the gut
- Helps to bring down fever
- As an antiseptic with antibiotic and anti-fungal actions
- Tones the heart and circulatory system
- Boosts the immune system
- May help to reduce high blood pressure
- May prevent some cancers, stomach cancer in particular
- Treats infections of the stomach and respiratory system
- Prevents heart disease and reduces the risk of atherosclerosis
- Antioxidant
- Decongestant
- Fresh garlic, eaten daily, can reduce chronic acidity of the stomach
- May help to reduce attacks of allergic asthma and hayfever
- Infused oil can be used as a chest rub for respiratory or digestive ailments, or in the ear to reduce inflammation
- Fresh garlic, eaten regularly, will reduce the need for antibiotics
- Garlic syrup can be used to treat bronchitis, lung infections and digestive disorders
- Fresh garlic juice is anti-fungal, and can be applied neat to fungal infections, such as athlete's foot
- Chewing whole roasted garlic cloves improves circulation
- The intestinal tract can be cleansed by adding several mashed, raw garlic cloves to salads; excellent in combination with red onion

))))➤ *Ayurveda, Immunity*

## GELSEMIUM

*Gelsemium sempervirens*

The jasmine plant, from which this homeopathic remedy is made, was used as a treatment for fevers in herbalism before being proven in homeopathy.

Conditions which affect the nervous system respond well, such as the nerves and muscles, respond well to the remedy. Headaches which worsen with movement or light, muscle pain which accompanies fever, nervous disorders such as multiple sclerosis, nerve inflammation,

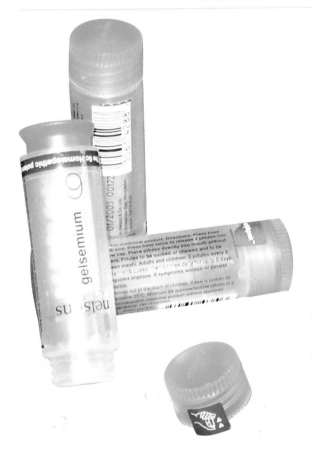

*FAR LEFT:* Allium sativum *(garlic).*

*LEFT:* Gelsemium sempervirens.

*BELOW: Gemstones are considered to be full of vibrational energy and are used in gem therapy like 'gem essences', capable of transmitting the positive energy of the Sun on to a recipient.*

- For headaches causing tightness
- For faintness
- For facial flushing
- For visual disturbances
- For muscle pain and trembling
- Symptoms improve after urinating and perspiring, after alcohol or stimulants, and when bending forward, and worsen after physical exertion, in heat, humidity, damp or fog, with excitement, worry or stress about their symptoms

## GEM THERAPY

Gemstones such as emeralds, garnet and jade vibrate with energy. They are used like other crystals, but are also used to create gem essences. These work in a similar way to flower essences. The stones are immersed in purified water and left in the sunshine, so that the Sun's rays transmit the energy from the gem to the water. The same effect is sometimes achieved using a pyramid, pendulum or the energy of a healer. The energized water is then poured into small bottles, which you can use by either holding in your hand for several minutes or by placing a few drops under the tongue. Not all gems are suitable for essences as some, such as turquoise and malachite, contain copper and are poisonous.

More than 200 gem and mineral essences have been created in the belief that they will assist the healing of specific mental and emotional states.

)))) *Crystals*

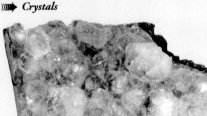

right-eye pain, heavy, drooping eyelids, inflamed tonsils and summer colds can all be helped. Also fevers, including flushing, an unpleasant taste in the mouth, twitchy muscles and chills. It can help alleviate fears and shock accompanied by shaking or trembling. Visual disturbances and blurred vision can also be treated.

The gelsemium type tends to be dull and heavy looking with a blue tinge to the skin, of below average intelligence, and possibly a heavy smoker. They tend to be rather cowardly and mentally weak.

### Properties and Uses
- Relieves complaints of the nervous system, fears and phobias, colds and flu, visual disturbances
- For fears and phobias, accompanied by trembling and the need to urinate
- For dull and lethargic feelings
- For nervousness and feelings of inadequacy

## GENTIAN

*Gentianella amarella*

Gentian flower essence is one of the Bach flower remedies. It can be used in cases of despondency and depression due to circumstances. Gentian types are prone to negativity and therefore are easily discouraged. When everything is going well they are happy but they can be easily disheartened and can slip back into a pessimistic outlook. They tend to look on the black side and in response may doubt all aspects of themselves, their worth and the purpose of life. Doubt and lack of faith are important elements. Gentian restores the courage to understand that life is not a competition and that there is no failure when trying our best.

### Key Notes

- People who benefit from gentian are easily discouraged and despondent; they may be pessimistic and take things personally.
- In extreme cases they may be too despondent to care for themselves properly.
- Gentian helps us take responsibility for our own life and thoughts, to put setbacks and disappointments into perspective and develop a positive attitude.

)))➡ ***Bach Flower Remedies***

*ABOVE: Gentianella amarella (gentian)*
*RIGHT: The geranium family.*
*FAR RIGHT: Ginger has long been used by Ayurvedics as an internal and external cleanser, as well as an aid to digestion.*

# GERANIUM

*Pelargonium graveolens*

This lovely aromatherapy oil is traditionally regarded as a feminine oil, a powerful healer and a valuable insect repellent. Do not use during the first three months of pregnancy and not at all if there is a history of miscarriage.

## Properties and Uses
- Geranium is mentally uplifting and refreshing
- It has a balancing effect on the nervous system, helping to alleviate apathy, anxiety, stress, hyper-activity and depression
- The anti-inflammatory, soothing and astringent properties of geranium account for its success in treating arthritis, acne, nappy rash, burns, blisters, eczema, cuts and congested pores
- Antiseptic properties make it useful for cuts and infections, sore throats and mouth ulcers
- It is also a diuretic, used to relieve swollen breasts and fluid retention and to stimulate sluggish lymph and blood circulation
- Geranium helps to stop bleeding and acts as a tonic for the liver and kidneys
- It is used to treat premenstrual syndrome (PMS) and menopausal problems and has a balancing effect on mind and body

)))▶ *Essential Oils*

# GINGER

Ginger is native to India, where the ancient Ayurvedics used it to preserve food, as a digestive aid, and as a spiritual and physical cleanser.

## Properties and Uses
- Ginger is a pungent, sweet herb with warming and drying qualities
- It acts as a stimulant, a diaphoretic, an antidepressant, and expectorant; ginger stimulates all tissues of the body and is highly recommended in cases where the illness is due to poor assimilation
- Ginger is a muscle relaxant, and soothes menstrual cramps
- Relieves nausea, particulary during pregnancy, and travel sickness

- Relieves wind, colic and irritable bowel syndrome (IBS)
- For chills, colds and poor circulation; for fevers add to elderflower or yarrow tea.

## Key Notes and Dosage
- May be added to most remedies to improve absorption and activity.
- Half a teaspoon of powder added to a cup of boiling water may be taken freely.
- Tincture, 5–20 drops in any herb tea.

)))▶ *Ayurveda, Chinese Herbalism*

# GINGER OIL

*Zingiber officinale*

Originally from India and China, warm spicy ginger is now grown commercially throughout the tropics. It has been used in both food and medicine for thousands of years, particularly by the Chinese. The essential oil distilled from the root smells similar to fresh root ginger. Use sparingly as high concentrations of ginger can cause irritation in sensitive people, and do not use in excessively hot or inflamed conditions.

## Properties and Uses
- Ginger is a rubefascient which can effectively ease painful conditions such as arthritis, rheumatism or muscle pain and improve poor circulation
- Massaged around the stomach and abdomen diluted ginger calms the digestion, tones and soothes the stomach and stimulates appetite
- Helps to alleviate nausea, travel sickness, indigestion, pain and diarrhoea
- Ginger is pain-relieving, antiseptic and antioxidant, valuable for preventing and treating colds, sore throats and catarrhal congestion; it also eases coughing and because it promotes sweating it can be useful for flu
- When inhaled, warming ginger eases mental confusion and relieves fatigue and nervous exhaustion.

)))▶ *Ayurveda, Chinese Herbalism*

## GINKGO BILOBA

*Ginkgo biloba* is one of the most widely sold herbs in Europe, typically taken for cognitive enhancement, circulatory disorders, and as a powerful antioxidant. An ever-increasing range of research is being undertaken into its therapeutic qualities, and the results have been nothing short of amazing.

*Ginkgo* has been one of the most commonly pre-scribed herbs in the Chinese *materia medica* for over 5,000 years, and it has been used to treat a huge range of conditions, including age-related circulation and memory loss, cancer, asthma, pulmonary diseases, impaired hearing and sexual dysfunction.

### Properties and Uses

- Improves blood flow, strengthens blood vessels, is anti-inflammatory and relaxes the lungs
- Aids poor circulation, thrombosis, varicose veins, cramp which comes on walking, white finger and spontaneous bruising
- Especially helpful for failing circulation to the brain in elderly people
- Strengthens memory
- Often improves deafness, tinnitis, vertigo and early senile dementia
- Helpful in treating asthma

### Dosage

- The tea is best taken in large doses: at least three cups a day for some months. Tablets are also available: always follow dose on the packet.

⟫➤ *Traditional Chinese Medicine, Herbalism*

## GINSENG

*Panax ginseng* and *Eleutherococcus senticosus*

Siberian ginseng belongs to a different botanical family than American and Korean ginseng, but the properties and uses of all three are similar and all are generally referred to as ginseng. This is an extremely popular herb, with a wide range of therapeutic uses.

### Properties and Uses

- Replenishes vital energy and strengthens the immune system, adaptogenic, increases concentration
- Strengthens the adrenal and reproductive glands
- Promotes lung functioning and stimulates the appetite
- Useful for bronchitis, circulatory problems, diabetes, infertility, lack of energy and stress
- For convalescence, exhaustion, lack of concentration, weakness in old age
- With other strengthening herbs for persistent infections
- For loss of sex drive in men
- Helps the body to cope with the side effects of chemotherapy for cancer
- For jet lag

### Key Notes and Dosage

- Dose: 1g of powdered root, 3 g of cut root in decoction or 20–30 drops of the tincture twice daily. Many preparations are available in the shops: follow the dose on the packet.
- Do not use if you have hypoglycaemia or high blood pressure.

⟫➤ *Herbalism, Traditional Chinese Medicine*

## GLUCOSAMINE

This is one of a number of substances classified as an amino sugar. Unlike other forms of sugar in the body, amino sugars are components of carbohydrates that are incorporated into the structure of body tissues, rather than being used as a source of energy. Glucosamine is involved in the formation of the nails, tendons, skin, eyes, bones, ligaments and heart valves. It also plays a role in the mucous secretions of the digestive, respiratory and urinary tracts.

### Properties and Uses

- Supplemental glucosamine can be helpful for asthma, bursitis, candidiasis, food allergies, osteoporosis, respiratory allergies, tendinitis, vaginitis and various skin problems

- Because it is important for the formation of bones, tendons, ligaments, cartilage and synovial fluid, glucosamine has been enormously effective in treating arthritis, including infectious arthritis

## GLUTAMINE

Glutamine is a derivative of glutamic acid, which is believed to help reduce cravings for alcohol. Studies are inconclusive as to the real benefits of taking this amino acid, and it is not recommended that you take more than 1 g daily unless you are supervised by a doctor.

### Properties and Uses

- To help reduce craving for alcohol
- To speed the healing of peptic ulcers
- For depression
- To help energize the mind
- May help to treat and prevent colitis

### Dosage

- Up to 1 g daily is believed to be safe, but do so only with the supervision of your doctor.

)))➡ *Amino Acids*

## GLYCINE

Glycine is considered to be the simplest of the amino acids, with a variety of properties that are still being studied.

### Properties and Uses

- For low pituitary gland function
- Used in the treatment of spastic movement – particularly in patients suffering from multiple sclerosis
- To treat progressive muscular dystrophy
- Used in the treatment of hypoglycaemia

### Dosage

- It is not recommended that you take this amino acid as a supplement unless supervised by your doctor. Doses below 1 g are thought to be safe, but research is ongoing.

)))➡ *Amino Acids*

*FAR LEFT: Gingko biloba.*
*ABOVE LEFT: Korean ginseng for sale in the Namdaemun market in Seoul.*
*ABOVE: Glocosamine when taken in supplement form can be useful for those suffering from asthma.*

## GOLDENSEAL

*Hydrastis canadenis*

This is a powerful anti-microbial and antiseptic herb that has been used in traditional herbal medicine for centuries. Use goldenseal with caution as it can raise blood pressure and may be harsh on the digestive tract. Blend it with other soothing herbs and avoid using it for prolonged periods or during pregnancy. It is not appropriate for those with diabetes, heart disease or glaucoma.

### Properties and Uses

- Acts as a uterine tonic by increasing circulation to the uterus; can be given for heavy periods and is useful during labour
- Acts as an antibiotic, cleanses the body and has anti-inflammatory and antibacterial properties
- Increases the effectiveness of insulin and strengthens the immune system
- Cleanses mucous membranes, counters infection, improves digestion and regulates periods
- Good for piles and varicose veins, particularly when they are inflamed and bleeding
- Used for catarrhal or infected conditions of the respiratory tract, such as bronchitis, or sinusitis
- It is a bitter herb which stimulates the liver and digestive system and can be used for loss of appetite, indigestion and constipation
- Used at the first sign of symptoms it can stop colds, flu and sore throats from developing

## GORSE

*Ulex europaeus*

This Bach flower remedy is for severe hopelessness and despair. The person who needs Gorse has tried everything, they may seek help in order to please others, but underneath they know that nothing more can be done for them. They have lost the heart to strive, perhaps in response to a life event, an accident, a medical diagnosis or to a long-standing illness or fear. They are trapped by negative feelings and unwilling to try again. Gorse gives the courage to try, renews hope and the heart to continue the fight towards recovery.

### Key Notes

- Gorse can help give people the heart to stay with a course of treatment. It is useful when a long period of retraining is necessary, for example after a stroke, loss of limbs or major accident. It can help to ease hope-lessness and despair after a long struggle.
- Gorse helps open a door to possibilities, encourages an objective attitude and strengthens the heart to face them.

))))▶ *Bach Flower Remedies*

## GOTU KOLA

*Centella asiatica*

The natives of Sri Lanka were the first to use gotu kola. In Ayurvedic medicine, gotu kola was used for many skin diseases, including leprosy. Today it is used to aid a variety of conditions.

## Properties and Uses

- Aids in the elimination of excess fluids, decreases fatigue and depression
- Increases sex drive, shrinks tissues and the central nervous system
- May neutralize blood acids and lower body temperature
- Aids heart and liver function
- Useful for cardiovascular and circulatory disorders, fatigue, connective tissue disorders, kidney stones, poor appetite and sleep disorders

### Key Notes

- Some individuals may experience minor irritation or a skin rash when taking gotu kola. Others have experienced headaches. Should such side-effects occur, lessen or discontinue use.
- Use as a massage oil, shampoo, poultice, tea or skin cream.

)))**➤ *Ayurveda***

## GRAPEFRUIT

*Citrus paradisi*

Like all citrus fruit, grapefruit is rich in vitamin C and potassium. Pink grapefruit is rich in vitamin A, and acts as a natural antioxidant. Grapefruit is an excellent cleanser for the digestive and urinary systems, and the peel has many therapeutic properties. Grapefruit essential oil is popular in aromatherapy.

*LEFT: Ulex europaeus (gorse).*
*BELOW LEFT: Centella asiatica (gotu kola).*
*BELOW: Yellow grapefruits are rich in vitamin C and potassium, although pink grapefruit contains a higher concentration of vitamin A.*

## Properties and Uses

- Cleanses the digestive and urinary systems – often recommended by naturopaths
- Reduces appetite
- Aids in the breakdown of fats in the body
- Strengthens the respiratory system, and aids respiration
- Invigorating – used as a tonic
- Relieves symptoms of colds and flu
- May help in the treatment of osteoarthritis.
- Balances the nervous system
- Grapefruit seeds can be eaten to rid the body of worms
- Grapefruit pith and membranes lower cholesterol in the blood
- Drinking grapefruit juice can encourage healthy skin – used in the treatment of acne for its mild exfoliating properties
- Grapefruit juice cleanses the kidneys and rids the body of toxins
- Massage is invigorating and uplifting, and may help to treat depression
- Local massage with a few drops of essential oil in a carrier oil will relieve headaches
- Drinking grapefruit juice with iron supplements, or foods rich in iron, increases the absorption of iron in the body
- Detoxifies the liver, can ease chronic liver conditions and may help to reduce the severity of a hangover
- Massage stimulates the immune system, which is particularly useful when suffering from infections

)))**➤ *Aromatherapy, Essential Oils***

## GRAPEFRUIT OIL

Refreshing grapefruit oil is expressed from the peel of the fruit cultivated mainly in California, Brazil, Florida and Israel. It has a fresh, tangy citrussy scent that enlivens the mind and disperses feelings of gloom.

Never ingest grapefruit oil orally and keep out of the eyes.

### Properties and Uses

- Grapefruit is diuretic, detoxifying and cleansing to the kidneys; it also has a stimulating effect on the lymphatic system; because of these properties it helps relieve fluid retention and eliminates the toxins that cause cellulite
- It is also beneficial in a massage blend to ease stiff muscles after exercise
- Grapefruit tones an oily skin and scalp, is helpful in treating acne and congested pores and can be applied neat to cold sores
- It also stimulates digestion and improves immunity to infection
- As an antidepressant grapefruit oil enlivens the mind, relieves anxiety and combats nervous exhaustion

⟫⟫ *Homeopathic Remedies*

## GREY SPIDER FLOWER

*Grevillea buxifolia*

This essence helps calm extreme terror, especially terror experienced in life-threatening situations or psychic attack. It deals with panic and nightmares. The essence will restore faith and trust.

### Properties and Uses

- For terror, fear of supernatural and psychic attack
- Brings calm and courage
- Grey spider flower brings lightness, faith and the certainty that we are loved by the world
- Ideal for children terrorized by bad dreams

## HAHNEMANN, DR SAMUEL

The founder of homeopathy, Dr Samuel Hahnemann (1755–1843) lived and taught in Germany, later establishing a practice in Paris at the age of 79. Between 1790 and 1805 Hahnemann tested 60 drugs from a variety of sources on himself and a small group of students. This method of 'proving' substances to discover the range of symptoms they were capable of causing enabled Hahnemann to find out what they could also cure.

In Hahnemann's time diseases were treated with large doses of toxic substances, and many patients were literally poisoned by 'medicines' such as arsenic and mercury. Hahnemann was careful to test these substances for their homeopathic effects in a very dilute form. Paradoxically, he found that the effectiveness of the remedy actually increased as it became more dilute – doing away with the problem of side-effects at the same time. Hahnemann developed a system of successive dilution and succussion, in which the remedy is shaken vigorously to release the healing potential of substances.

The word homeopathy, invented by Hahnemann to describe his system of medicine, is derived from the Greek for 'similar suffering'.

## HEALING

Healing, also known as spiritual healing, is the channelling of healing energy from its spiritual source to someone who needs it. The channel is usually a person whom we call a healer and the healing energy is usually transferred to the patient through the hands of the healer. The important distinction here is that healing does not come *from* the healer, but *through* him. The word spiritual does not refer to belief in any organized religion, rather it refers to the divine nature of the energy, which healers agree comes from one external, invisible, intelligent source. The healing energy from this source is available to everyone, irrespective of their religious beliefs.

Healers see the body, mind and spirit as one inter-dependent unit and believe all three must work in

*LEFT: Samuel Hahnemann, founder of homepathic medicine.*
*ABOVE: Spiritual healing involves channelling energy through a healer to a recipient. This method of treatment is becoming increasingly popular in the US.*
*RIGHT: Calluna vulgaris (heather).*

harmony to maintain health. A problem at any level, be it a broken leg or a feeling of hopelessness, needs healing to restore the balance of the whole person. Sickness often begins in the mind or at the deeper level of the spirit and it is often here that healing begins.

When a healer lays his hand on you, he acts as a conductor or channel for the healing energy which he believes has the 'intelligence' to go where it is needed. Healers say that we all have the power to heal, if we choose to develop it. They claim the motivating force behind all healing is unconditional love and the only requirement is that the healer is open to receiving and channelling healing energy. However, some people do seem to have a gift for healing.

## HEATHER
*Calluna vulgaris*

Heather, a Bach flower remedy, is ideal for people who are caught up with themselves and their own interests. They are poor listeners and do not like to be alone. It is hard for them to share and they tend to be reactive, using other people and their views and responses to shape and define themselves. They may concentrate on fulfilling personal needs in order to avoid loneliness.

### Key Notes
- People who need heather can be self-centred and self-obsessed. They may intrude into other people's personal space, cling or be aggressively talkative. They can also be weepy and hypochondriac. Because they are demanding, friends will often avoid them, causing loneliness.
- Heather helps us to look after ourselves without being obsessed with our own personality needs. It gives us the space to listen to others and experience genuine love and companionship.
  ➤ *Bach Flower Remedies*

## HEPAR SULPH

*Hepar sulphuris*

This homeopathic remedy is made from heating the calcareous inner layer of oyster shells with flowers of sulphur, and is used to treat skin infections and ailments accompanied by a discharge.

It is commonly used to treat infections in which there is discharge, such as conjunctivitis, sinusitis, cold sores and mouth ulcers, as well as general infections such as earache, tonsillitis, phlegm-filled chests and flu. It is also used for infections to aid expelling pus, such as acne, where the spots are sensitive to touch. Other conditions helped include colds accompanied by a tickly cough and dry, hoarse coughs accompanied by phlegm.

The Hepar Sulph type tends to be flabby or overweight, pale-looking, lethargic and listless, with excessive likes and dislikes. They tend to be anxious and bad-tempered, easily offended and fail to think things through properly.

### Properties and Uses

- Relieves pus-producing infections, skin infections and conditions accompanied by sensitivity to touch
- For those who have a tendency to be depressed
- Relieves sluggishness
- For sensitivity to pain, cold air or noise
- For sour-smelling secretions
- Alleviates moist and sensitive skin
- Good for those with a low pain threshold
- For seeping ailments, such as ulcers, cold sores, acne, boils
- For coughs, colds, sore throats, flu
- Symptoms improve in warmth, after applying warm compresses and after eating, and worsen in the morning, in the cold, when touching or lying on the affected parts

*RIGHT: Herbalism has been around as a respected practice since the Middle Ages. This is a fifteenth-century manuscript showing a doctor prescribing a herbal infusion to his patient.*
*RIGHT: A family of herbs: comfrey (left), rosemary (centre) and sage (right). Any parts of a flower, tree or plant can be used in herbal remedies or tisanes.*
*BELOW RIGHT: A bottle containing an oil-based infusion of St John's wort.*

## HERBALISM

Herbalism embraces the use of plants, in particular herbs, for healing. While herbs are used in many cultures, most specifically China and India, the tradition of Western medical herbalism is a rich and varied one, calling upon folk remedies, ancient customs and practical experience, and combined with new research, clinical training and diagnostic skills.

Herbal medicine is based on a holistic approach to health, like many other complementary medicines, and treatment will be undertaken after an assessment of your individual symptoms as well as your lifestyle and overall health, on both a physical and spiritual level.

Herbal medicine is designed to be gentle, stimulating our bodies to return to health by strengthening their systems as well as attacking the cause of the illness itself. Probably the most important principle of herbal medicine is that extracts are taken from the whole plant (or the whole of a part of the plant, like the leaves or the roots), not isolated or synthesized to perform specific functions.

Advice and treatment is always tailored to individual needs and because of this there is far less chance of having an adverse reaction to treatment. The aim of herbalism is to help the body heal itself and to restore balanced health, not just to relieve the symptoms of the disorder being treated.

Herbalism is not a miracle cure and, like any other therapy, works best for specific conditions. Having said that, almost anyone can benefit from the prudent use of herbs as a form of restorative and preventative medicine. Herbs are a rich source of vitamins and minerals, aside from having healing properties, and can be an important part of your daily diet, eaten fresh, or perhaps drunk as a tisane. A herbal tonic is useful, for example, in the winter months, when fresh fruit and green vegetables are not a regular part of our diets. Echinacea or garlic, for instance, can be taken daily to improve the general efficiency of the immune system.

Some of the most common conditions that respond to herbal treatment include: hayfever, colds and respiratory disorders, digestive disorders (like constipation and ulcers), cardiovascular disease, headaches, anxiety, depression, chronic infections, rheumatism, arthritis, skin problems, anaemia and many hormonal, menstrual, menopausal and pregnancy problems.

Other than purchasing herbal teas at your local health-food shop, it is wise to consult a registered medical herbalist before taking herbs for medicinal purposes. The majority of herbs are safe for most people, but there are also many contra-indications – especially if you are pregnant, very old or very young, or suffer from a long-term or chronic condition. Always remember that herbs can be a powerful form of healing and must be taken in moderation.

))))➤ *Herbs, Minerals, Vitamins*

## HERBS

A herb is any part of a flower, tree or other plant. Herbage, like foliage, refers to plants with green leaves but in herbal remedies more than leaves are used. Any part of a plant can be used, for example:

- Flowers – chamomile, marigold, linden, St John's wort
- Leaves – peppermint, sage, thyme, comfrey

- Bark – willow, oak, cinnamon
- Buds – cloves
- Seeds – fennel, cardamom
- Fruits – cayenne, rose hips
- Root – dandelion, marshmallow
- Inner sap or gel – aloe
- Bulb – garlic
- Wood – Pau d'arco
- Resin – myrrh, frankincense
- Essential oil – rose, rosemary, lavender
- Fixed oil – olive oil, St John's wort

The chemical make-up of plants is extraordinarily complicated, with each element having specific roles within the body outside the active ingredient itself. For example, aspirin – one of the most common drugs to be related to the active ingredient of a plant (in this case white willow) – is very irritating to the stomach, often causing bleeding and gastric ulcers. Meadowsweet, another herb with aspirin-like components, has anti-inflammatory as well as analgesic properties. In fact, it is often used to soothe damaged digestive systems, reducing the acidity of the stomach. As a whole, meadowsweet would be a much more effective treatment than aspirin, offering pain relief and preventing the irritating effects that it causes.

The actions of the herbs are widespread within the body, not just addressing the condition at hand, but increasing vitality and replacing deficiencies that could cause problems in the future.

))))➤ *Nutrition*

## HIBBERTIA

*Hibbertia pendunculata*

For people who are strict and regimented or even fanatical with themselves, or for whose who use their knowledge to gain an upper hand. They constantly devour information and philosophies purely to make themselves better people, but often without truly integrating it. In the positive mode these people will be accepting of themselves and their own innate knowledge and experiences, without wanting to be superior to others.

### Properties and Uses

- For people who are fanatical about self-improvement, driven to acquire knowledge and have excessive self-discipline
- For people with feelings of superiority
- Helps us to be content with our own knowledge, brings acceptance
- For ownership and utilization of own knowledge

))))➤ *Australian Bush Flower Essences*

## HIPPOCRATES

Hippocrates (460–377 BC) is universally referred to as the 'Father of Medicine'. References to him written during his lifetime refer to Hippocrates as a member of an Aesclepiad, a term indicating a group of doctors. He used and wrote about a great number of plant medicines, and regarded the body as a whole, not just a collection of parts. His work has influenced Western conventional medicine, as well as the study of aromatherapy, herbalism and nutrition. Most important of all was Hippocrates' contribution to medical theory, philosophy and ethics. The Hippocratic Oath, still taken by many medical students today, was not composed by Hippocrates but by his pupils or followers. He lived and taught high moral standards which still act as guidelines for practitioners in all disciplines today. He once wrote 'Let food be thy medicine', which is now the basis for almost all natural therapies.

))))➤ *Nutrition*

## HISTADINE

Histadine is one of the lesser-known amino acids, and its role in our bodies is not yet fully understood. Research is ongoing into the possible effects of histadine supplementation.

### Properties and Uses

- Used in the treatment of arthritis and for those who have an abnormally low level of this amino acid in their blood
- May boost the activity of suppresser T-cells, which could be useful in the fight against AIDS and auto-immune conditions.

### Dosage

- Do not take more than 1.5 grams daily unless supervised by your doctor.

))))➤ *Amino Acids*

## HOLLY

*Ilex aquifolium*

This Bach flower remedy is for those who are attacked by feelings of hatred, envy, jealousy, suspicion, and revenge. People who need holly have intense, negative feelings. They also have other intense emotional feelings but they are too frightened to express these fully. The free flow of emotion and love is then blocked or expressed unclearly, leading to tension, unclear communications, frustration, anger and emotional outbursts.

*LEFT: Hippocrates, the Greek physician, known as 'the Father of Medicine'.*
*RIGHT: Homeopathic remedies have been diluted many times from their original concentrations, making them safe, free from side-effects and allowing the body to heal itself.*

## Key Notes

- Negative emotions may be spiteful and nagging with intense feeling and outbursts of temper. People requiring holly may be suspicious or mildly paranoid, perhaps with a victim mentality.
- This is a useful remedy for the temper tantrums of two-year-olds, and for children who are overly dependent upon the word 'no'.
- Holly makes it possible to recognize that these feelings are the negative expression of our caring interaction with others.

)))➡ *Bach Flower Remedies*

## HOMEOPATHIC REMEDIES

A homeopathic remedy is an extremely pure, natural substance that has been diluted many times. In large quantities these substances would cause the same symptoms that the patient is trying to cure. In small, diluted doses, it is not only safe and free from side-effects, but it will trigger the body to heal itself.

Many scientists have claimed that a study of the remedies themselves has proved that there is little or even no trace of the original substance in the tablet. This is the basis of the scientific assertion that homeopathy effects cure through positive thinking alone. Do not be fooled by these claims. Homeopathy is an extremely subtle medicine, based on the concept of 'vibrational medicine'. Because the remedies are so diluted, they often contain only a vibration of the original substance, and it is this

vibration that works on the body's natural energy field. It is like a radio signal rather than an overt substance, but it is that subtle signal which effects a cure.

Homeopathic remedies are classified into three levels of potency; X, C and M refer to 10, 100 and 1,000 in terms of the amount of dilution. The more a tincture is diluted, the more potent it becomes. So, while a C is more dilute than an X, the C is more powerful. M-classified remedies are extremely potent and are normally prescribed by homeopathic practitioners on a constitutional basis.

If you plan to use homeopathic remedies, you will need to learn to take into account many factors apart from overt symptoms. Choosing the correct remedy involves matching the symptom picture of the remedy as closely as you can to your symptoms. Symptom pictures, or descriptions of symptoms, take into account the condition of the whole person, not just one symptom. If two remedies seem to be very close and it is difficult to decide between them, pick the one that best matches your most prevalent symptom.

## Key Notes

- Remedies come in tablet form, or as granules for young children. Tinctures and creams are also available.
- The number printed on the label of any homeopathic medicine you buy indicates how many times it has been diluted and succussed. A 6 potency has been diluted six times, while a 30 has been diluted 30 times.
- One tablet (or a few granules) is enough for one dose. Dissolve the tablet under your tongue without water. Crush tablets in paper for small children or babies, and try to avoid touching it with your own hands.
- Children can have a tablet dissolved in a small quantity of water, but again, do not touch the remedy with your own hands.
- Do not eat, drink, clean your teeth or smoke for at least 20 minutes before or afterwards, in case any strong substances in your mouth spoil the effectiveness of the remedy.
- Store the remedies in their original containers away from direct light, heat and strong-smelling substances.
- In case of accidentally taking a number of remedies – do not panic. Taking dozens of tablets is no different to taking just one.

## HOMEOPATHY

Homeopathy is a system of medicine that supports the body's own healing mechanism, using specially prepared remedies. It is 'energy' medicine, in that it works with the body's vital force to encourage healing and to ensure that all body systems are working at optimum level. Homeopathy is often confused with herbalism, partly, perhaps, because some of the remedies are made from herbs. However, herbalists use material concentrations of plants, while homeopathic remedies use plants, minerals and even some animal products as a base. They are prepared through a process known as potentization to bring out their subtle healing properties.

We know from modern physics that our seemingly solid bodies are just dense fields of energy. A disturbance in our energy field can give rise to disease, and a potent form of energy can rebalance us. Homeopathy uses potentized remedies to rebalance our body's subtle energy system. Once this is back in balance the immune system and all the other interconnected systems in our body start functioning better.

The term homeopathy comes from the Greek language, meaning 'similar suffering'. It reflects the key principle behind the

homeopathic method – that a substance can cure the symptoms in an ill person that it is capable of causing in a healthy person.

Samuel Hahnemann believed that symptoms and signs of an illness are in fact attempts on the part of the body to heal itself, so that when a substance capable of producing a similar symptom 'picture' to that of the disease is used, it encourages a powerful strengthening of the defence mechanism. A homeopath, therefore, must study the entire symptoms picture in order to get a full picture of the disease and prescribe the correct remedy. Often it is the symptoms that seem almost

incidental, strange or rare that are the most valuable to the homeopathic practitioner, for they give the disease its own particular character and thus suggest the remedy.

Homeopathy can be used to treat everyone from babies through to the elderly. It is completely safe for people of all ages. It is particularly useful for the following health conditions: effects of stress, post-traumatic stress syndrome, phobias, psychological problems and depression, myalgic encephalomyelitis (ME) and glandular fever, hepatitis, epilepsy, allergies, repeated infections, PMS, hormonal problems associated with the periods, fertility or menopause, acne, herpes, chronic thrush and cystitis, migraines, irritable bowel syndrome (IBS), colitis, arthritis, complaints associated with pregnancy, to aid childbirth, infections and ailments of infants and children, behavioural problems and

*BELOW LEFT: A homeopathic pharmacist doses a remedy. Homeopathy works in conjunction with the body's energy levels and healing abilities.*
*LEFT: Apis Mel is just one of a whole selection of homepathic remedies now readily available at natural pharmacies.*
*RIGHT: Different types of honey are produced by bees from the nectar of different flowers.*

hyperactivity. Used correctly homeopathy can treat almost any condition successfully.

Homeopathy is completely safe if you follow some simple guidelines:

- Do not attempt to treat yourself at home if you have serious health problems.
- Do not use self-help remedies instead of seeing your doctor for a diagnosis – or take yourself off medication without advice.
- Do not take lots of different remedies at the same time.
- Do not keep taking homeopathic remedies indefinitely, as this can aggravate your symptoms if the remedy is not appropriate for you.
- Do not take high potencies (200 and over) of remedies unless prescribed by a registered homeopath. These potencies work on an emotional as well as physical level and your symptoms may require only physical treatment. You may bring on a whole host of unwanted effects by choosing too high a potency.

))))▶ *Herbalism, Homeopathic Remedies*

## HONEY

Honey is the sweet liquid produced by bees from the nectar of flowers. The source of the nectar from which the honey is made, determines its colour and flavour. For centuries honey has been used as an antiseptic, for external and internal conditions, and as a tonic for overall good health. Each country has a distinctive type of honey, dependent on the local flowers upon which the bees feed. All honeys are complex mixtures of the sugars fructose and glucose with water, organic acids, and mineral and vitamin traces, as well as some plant pigments.

Unpasteurized honey should not be eaten by pregnant women, and only sparingly by children. However, ensure that you buy cold-pressed honey because heated honey contains additives and loses its healing effect.

### Properties and Uses

- Soothes raw tissues
- Helps to retain calcium in the body
- Helps to balance acid accumulations in the body (because of the significant amount of potassium it contains)
- Sedative, anti-fungal and nourishing
- Antibacterial, for external and internal infections; there are active antibiotic properties in unpasteurized honey
- Honey water can be used as an eye lotion (particularly good for conjunctivitis and other infective conditions)
- Gargle with honey water to soothe a sore throat and ease respiratory problems
- Honey and lemon are a traditional remedy for coughs
- Mix with apple cider vinegar as a tonic or 'rebalancer'; this concoction may also help to relieve the symptoms of arthritis, and reduce arthritic deposits
- Honey ointment can soothe and encourage healing of sores in the mouth or vagina
- Honey is an excellent moisturiser and can be rubbed into the skin as a revitalizing mask
- Eating a little local honey will sensitize you to pollens in the area – acting as a natural remedy for hay fever and all its symptoms

## HONEYSUCKLE

*Lonicera caprifolium*

Honeysuckle, a Bach flower remedy, is for those who dwell too much on memories of the past, and who do not expect to experience such happiness and companionship again. The past seems rosy and familiar, the future seems dark, bleak, forbidding and unknown. Honey-suckle is for nostalgia, a far-away sense of regret or loss, often tinged with pessimism.

### Key Notes

- This is the ideal remedy for people who live in the past. There may be homesickness or deep regrets about the past. It is also useful for grief and bereavement.
- Honeysuckle integrates past experiences and gives strength to face new challenges.

))**➤** *Bach Flower Remedies*

## HORNBEAM

*Carpinus betulus*

A Bach flower remedy, hornbeam is for those who feel that they do not possess enough strength to fulfil the responsibilities of daily life. This feeling often comes from boredom or some basic dis-satisfaction with the work they are doing. The person might feel that they are in the wrong job, or in some way not fully expressing their creative potential. Hornbeam restores confidence and optimism, and helps us find the satisfaction in the mundane aspects of our lives.

### Key Notes

- People who need hornbeam feel exhausted at the thought of working. They may feel in a rut.
- Hornbeam is usually for a temporary feeling. If the weakness is a regular occurrence the person may be exhausting themselves in the wrong direction and other remedies may be needed.

))**➤** *Bach Flower Remedies*

## HYDROTHERAPY

Hydrotherapy, or water therapy, can be used to improve circulation and increase vitality so that the vital force can work more efficiently. It can also be used to ease pain. Hot, cold and alternate hot and cold water is used to achieve specific effects. Hot water is initially stimulating but has a secondary relaxing effect. Cold water is also stimulating with an invigorating and tonic effect. Alternate hot and cold baths or showers stimulate blood and lymph circulation, help to remove congestion and have a tonic effect on body tissues.

Naturopaths use many forms of water therapy, such as cold compresses which are used to boost the elimination of toxins, cold baths, hot baths, saunas, and sitz baths. Sitz baths are hip baths where you sit alternately in hot and cold water. They are believed to be particularly helpful in pelvic disorders such as fibroids, constipation and haemorrhoids. Epsom salts baths are commonly recommended by naturopaths and are valued for the cleansing effect they have on the body.

Internal uses of hydrotherapy such as enemas and colonic irrigation are sometimes used, but their use is a cause of some debate, even among naturopaths.

))**➤** *Naturopathy*

## HYPERICUM

*Hypericum perforatum*

The St John's wort shrub is native to Asia and Europe, but is now grown worldwide. In homeopathy, the whole fresh plant is used when in flower and it is most commonly given to treat nerve pain following injury, due to its effective action on the central nervous system.

Hypericum works well on any area affected by nerve pain and injury, but particularly on injuries to the body where there are many nerve endings, such as the spine, head, fingers, toes and lips. It can also help concussion, neuralgia, back pain, pain that shoots upwards, pain after dentistry, small wounds such as bites or splinters, nausea, asthma which worsens in fog, painful piles and rectal nerve pain. In women, late periods accompanied by headaches can also be alleviated.

## Properties and Uses

- Relieves nerve pain after injury, head injuries, shooting pains
- For depression
- For sleepiness
- Reduces neuralgia
- For concussion
- Relieves toothache
- For severe shooting pains that travel upwards
- Reduces cravings for hot drinks and wine
- Symptoms improve when the head is tilted backwards, but worsen in warm, stuffy rooms, in damp, cold or foggy weather, when touched or when the affected part is exposed

⫸ *Herbalism, St John's Wort*

## HYSSOP

*Hyssopus officinalis*

Revered as a sacred cleansing herb by the Hebrews and the ancient Greeks, hyssop has also long been valued by herbalists for its medicinal

*ABOVE LEFT: Lonicera caprifolium (honeysuckle).*
*BELOW LEFT: Carpinus betulus (hornbeam).*
*BELOW: Hyssopus officilanis (hyssop).*

properties. Both the leaves and the small blue or mauve flowers are distilled for their essential oil.

Dilute well and use for no more than a few days at a time because there is some risk of toxicity. Do not use during pregnancy. Do not use if you are epileptic. For people with high blood pressure hyssop should only be used by a qualified aromatherapist.

## Properties and Uses

- Hyssop is an expectorant with antispasmodic, bactericidal and antiseptic properties, which can be helpful for coughing, whooping cough, catarrh, sore throats and chest infections.
- It can be used in skincare for cuts, bruises, and inflammation.
- Hyssop has hypertensive properties making it useful in the treatment of low blood pressure and it has a general tonic effect on circulation
- As an emmenagogue it can be used for scanty or missing periods; the oil can also soothe indigestion and relieve colicky cramps
- Hyssop's sedative and tonic properties can benefit stress or anxiety related problems; it helps to clarify thinking, relieve fatigue and increase alertness

⫸ *Essential Oils*

## IGNATIA

*Ignatia amara*

The seeds of the *Ignatia amara* tree have been used through the centuries for their healing properties. Homeopathically, the seeds are separated from their pods and powdered. The remedy is used to treat emotional upsets, such as shock and grief, as the strychnine acts on the central nervous system.

Ignatia is commonly used to treat conditions which occur as a result of emotional upheaval. Shock, anger and grief, for instance, over the break-up of a relationship, or suppression of these feelings can be treated, as can bereavement characterized by changes of mood, insomnia and hysteria. Conditions such as nervous headaches, fainting, sweating, choking, or a tickly cough which are a result of emotional upset also respond well. Ailments which are changeable or symptoms which seem contradictory, for instance, a sore throat which feels better after eating solids, are helped. In women, lack of periods or uterine spasms during periods, constipation, piles and shooting pain in a prolapsed rectum are relieved.

The Ignatia type is normally female, thin and dark-haired. They tend to be tired, strained-looking, emotionally sensitive, artistic and nervous. Unpredictable, they have high expectations, but blame themselves when things go wrong. They have trouble expressing emotions, and dislike fruit, sweet foods and alcohol. Ignatia children tend to be bright, excitable, highly-strung and sensitive to noise; they do not cope well with stress, becoming angry and scared. They tend to suffer nervous headaches and are prone to nervous coughing and laryngitis.

### Properties and Uses

- Relieves emotional trauma, bereavement, depression, headaches, changeable ailments
- For those who fear being emotionally hurt
- For those who dislike losing control, enclosed spaces or crowds
- For people who have difficulty in expressing emotions
- For people who are often contradictory
- Reduces sensitivity to pain
- For people who are moody
- For those who blink, yawn or sigh repeatedly
- Useful for those with a weak nervous system
- Reduces intense headaches
- Diminishes cravings for sour or acidic foods
- Symptoms improve after eating, urinating, with firm pressure or lying on the affected side, heat, and worsen in the cold, when touched, after emotional upset, when taking coffee or smoking, when exposed to strong odours

## IMMUNITY

The body has an impressive array of defences to block, trap and kill outside organisms it considers a threat – with a memory to prevent them attacking again. Without this defence system (known as the immune system) most people would constantly fall ill from the wide range of threats to the body.

The immune system consists of the blood supply, the lymph system, and small sets of organs known as the tonsils, thymus gland, and the spleen. Defence against disease is essentially a function of white cells in the blood (leukocytes), and it is one of the jobs of this group of organs to produce these cells.

The immune system is the physical defence mechanism of the body. It is important that it is working at optimum level to protect from infections and infestations, and to ensure quick and efficient recovery when you do succumb to illness.

Some of the factors that affect immunity are:
- Poor or inadequate sleep
- Poor diet
- Stress (emotional, physical or environmental)
- Overuse of antibiotics

- Some drugs (including, according to a new study, the overuse of paracetamol)
- Exposure to toxins, which include cigarette smoke, car exhaust fumes, household chemicals and anything else that requires the body to work harder
- Emotional factors (including depression, unhappiness, fear, jealousy and any other negative emotional states)
- Injuries
- Chronic illness
- Digestive disorders, such as candida, enzyme deficiencies and chronic constipation
- Surgery
- Over-exertion

The immune system and, indeed, every other system in your body, works more effectively when external factors are under control. The majority of natural remedies and therapies are designed to boost immunity, and even the healthiest of us will benefit from their prudent use. The idea is not to work on immunity when you become ill, but to ensure that your immune system is strong and healthy enough to resist illness, and to fight it off quickly when you do become ill. This is one of the most important aspects of preventative medicine, which is the cornerstone of the natural health revolution.

Signs of a weakened immune system include:
- Fatigue
- Listlessness
- Repeated infections (healthy adults have an average of two colds a year; children, particularly at school age, will suffer from many more than this, but if your child has more than about four a year, his or her immune system could use a boost)

- Inflammation
- Allergic reactions
- Slow wound healing
- Chronic diarrhoea
- Infections that represent an overgrowth of some normally present organisms, such as oral thrush, candidiasis or, in girls, vaginal yeast infections

))➤ *Homeopathy*

*LEFT:* Ignatia amara.
*ABOVE: Immunity levels are bolstered by regular consumption of fresh fruit and vegetables.*
*RIGHT: A healthy, well-balanced diet is important to enable the immune system to work at its optimum level.*

## IMPATIENS

*Impatiens glandulifera*

This Bach flower remedy is for those people who are quick in thought and action and who are always on the go. They know their mind and want things to be done at speed. They become irritable at hindrance, hesitation and delay, and impatiently blame others. They can alienate people by being brusque and unsympathetic and by speaking their mind quickly and without thought. They refuse to slow down even when illness overtakes them. Impatiens restores acceptance of the natural pace of life, rather than fighting against it.

### Key Notes

- For people who suffer from impatience and irritability with everything and everyone and the desire to do everything quickly
- People who will benefit from impatiens may fidget, find it hard to sit still and therefore suffer from indigestion and nervous tension
- People who have learned the lesson of impatiens have patience, they are capable and decisive, knowing how to get things done and turn the pace of life to their advantage

))))➤ *Bach Flower Remedies*

## INFUSED OILS

An infused oil differs from an essential oil both in its qualities and in the method by which it is made. An essential oil is extracted directly from the plant, while an infused oil is made by placing the plant (usually the leaves of petals, but sometimes the stalks) in a container of bland unperfumed oil. This is kept in a warm place for two or three weeks, or until the base oil has absorbed the perfume or properties of the plant. The oil is strained and ready for use. This method has been in use for many thousands of years.

))))➤ *Massage*

## INFUSIONS

Effectively another word for tea, an infusion uses dried herbs, or in some instances fresh, which are steeped in boiled water for about 10 minutes. You can make your own infusion. Infusions are most suitable for plants from which the leaves and flowers are used, since their properties are more easily extracted by gentle boiling. Tisanes are mild infusions, usually prepackaged and sold in the form of a teabag, which can be boiled for a much shorter period of time than an infusion. The chamomile tea available at the supermarket would be considered a tisane.

## IODINE

Iodine is a mineral, first discovered in 1812 in kelp. Iodine was extracted and given its name because of its violet colour. Iodine occurs naturally and is a crucial part of the thyroid hormones which monitor our energy levels.

The best sources of iodine are seafood and seaweed and most table salt is fortified with iodine. Optimally iodine should be taken as potassium iodide and under the supervision of a doctor or nutritionist. Iodine is toxic in high doses and may aggravate or cause acne as large doses can interfere with hormone activity.

### Properties and Uses
- Determines the level of metabolism and energy in the body
- Prevents against toxic effects from radioactive materials
- Prevents thyroid disorders
- Acts as a natural antiseptic

))))➤ *Minerals*

## IPECAC

*Ipecacuanha*

Ipecacuanha is a small, perennial shrub, grown in the tropical rainforests of southern and central America. Homeopathically, the root, collected when the plant is in flower and then dried, is used to treat nausea, vomiting and the accompanying sweats and clamminess.

Ipecac is also good for stomach complaints, accompanied by salivating, lack of thirst, weak pulse and fainting, conditions causing breathing difficulties, such as asthma and coughing; coughing and vomiting at the same time. It can also be used to treat persistent nausea.

### Properties and Uses
- Relieves persistent nausea and breathing difficulties
- Can be used to treat contemptuousness
- For anxiety, including fear of death and moroseness
- For fainting, clamminess, cold or hot sweats

*LEFT: A fourteenth-century manuscript showing a medical practitioner giving a herbal infusion to a patient. Infusions use fresh or dried herbs steeped in boiled water for several minutes.*

*RIGHT: The iris of the eye represents a kind of map of the whole human body in microcosm: this is the principal tenet upon which the practice of iridology is founded.*

- For bleeding or haemorrhaging
- To improve a weak pulse
- Symptoms improve in fresh air and worsen in warmth, in winter, when moving or lying down and when under stress or embarrassed

))))➤ *Herbalism*

## IRIDOLOGY

According to iridologists, the iris of the eye represents a kind of map of the human glands, organs, and systems of the whole human body. Problems show up on the iris as spots, flecks, and white or dark streaks. Texture and colour indicate the person's general state of health.

Some iridologists claim tendencies towards inherited disease and possible future problems are also found and some even address emotional and spiritual health problems this way.

Iridology was developed in the nineteenth century by the Hungarian Dr Ignatiz von Peckzely who, as a boy, noticed changes in the eye of an owl with a broken leg. He published his theories in 1881 and soon after, a Swedish doctor, Nils Lilinquist, added his own observations. But iridology did not become widely popular until Dr Bernard Jensen pioneered the use of iridology in the US, eventually, in 1950, publishing a chart that he said showed the location of every gland and organ reflected in each eye.

The left eye, he said, corresponds with the left-hand side of the body, the right with the right-hand side. Generally speaking the upper organs (e.g. the brain) are at the top of the iris and the lower ones (e.g. the kidneys) at the bottom. The bodily systems – digestion, blood and lymph, glands and organs, muscles, skeleton and skin – appear in six rings around the pupil.

Some practitioners examine the iris with a torch and magnifying glass. Others take colour photographs or trans-parencies (slides) that are magnified and read. Iridology, or iris diagnosis as it is also known, is widely used by many natural therapists to aid assessment, particularly in the US, Germany and Australia.

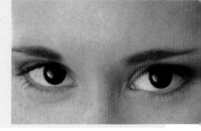

))))➤ *Diagnosis*

## IRON

Iron is a trace mineral which is essential for human health. Anaemia, which is the condition most commonly associated with deficiency, was described by Egyptian physicists as long ago as 1500 BC. Today, 10 per cent of all women in the Western world suffer from iron-deficiency anaemia.

We now know that iron is present in our bodies as haemoglobin, the red pigment of blood. Iron is required for muscle protein and is stored in the liver, spleen, bone marrow and muscles. Iron absorption is highest in childhood and reduces with age. Our bodies need vitamin C for iron to be efficiently absorbed.

The best sources of iron are shellfish, brewer's yeast, wheat bran, offal, cocoa powder, dried fruit and cereals.

### Properties and Uses
- Improves physical performance
- Anti-carcinogenic
- Prevents learning problems in children
- Prevents and cures iron-deficiency anaemia
- Improves immunity
- Boosts energy levels
- Encourages restful sleep and maintains energy levels

### Key Notes and Dosage
- Pregnant, breastfeeding and menstruating women, infants, children, athletes and vegetarians may require increased levels of iron. Iron supplements will be prescribed by your doctor if necessary.
- Maximum dosage is 15 mg daily, unless under supervision.
- Excess iron can cause constipation, diarrhoea and rarely, in high doses, death. Be very cautious when giving children iron supplements – even doses as little as 3 g can cause death.

))⟩ *Minerals*

## JACARANDA
*Jacaranda mimosaefolia*

An essence for people who dither, never completing things because they are constantly changing them. There is a fine distinction between sundew and jacaranda. Sundew deals with dreamers, whilst jacaranda is for those who dither, are 'all over the place' and are always changing their mind.

### Key Notes
- For people who are scattered, changeable, dithering and always rushing
- Brings decisiveness, quick thinking, being centred

))⟩ *Australian Bush Flower Essences*

## JASMINE
*Jasminum officinale*

Jasmine is known as the king of essential oils, largely because it takes so many flowers to produce a small quantity of this expensive oil, and because just a little oil offers profound therapeutic benefits. Very rarely jasmine may cause an allergic reaction.

### Properties and Uses
- Jasmine has a reputation as an aphrodisiac, reducing impotence in men and frigidity in women
- It is also a uterine tonic which can help with period pain and disorders of the uterus; its pain-relieving properties and ability to strengthen contractions make it one of the best oils to use during childbirth; it is also believed to strengthen male sex organs and has been used for prostate problems
- Its relaxing and antidepressant effect helps with post-natal depression. It is excellent for stress relief and is uplifting during times of lethargy

## JUNIPER

*Juniperus communis*

Used in ancient Greece and Egypt to combat the spread of disease, Juniper was still being used in French hospitals during World War I. Do not use Juniper if pregnant. It is not suitable for people with kidney disease.

### Properties and Uses

- Physically and emotionally cleansing, juniper helps to detoxify the body of harmful waste products that contribute to problems such as rheumatoid arthritis and cellulite, and clears the mind of confusion and exhaustion
- Juniper is also diuretic, has an affinity with the genitourinary system and is excellent for treating cystitis
- Skin problems, especially weepy eczema and acne, respond well to its toning, astringent and antiseptic properties
- Juniper is also good for haemorrhoids and hair loss and assists with wound healing
- It stimulates appetite, relieves nervous tension and is an excellent disinfectant

))))▶ *Essential Oils*

## JUNIPER

The berries of this popular plant are most often used in herbalism. They contain a variety of therapeutic properties, including essential oils, but may interfere with the absorption of iron and other minerals when taken internally.

### Properties and Uses

- Acts as a diuretic, helps to regulate blood sugar levels and relieves inflammation and congestion
- Helpful in the treatment of asthma, bladder infection, fluid retention, gout, kidney problems, obesity and prostate disorders

*LEFT: It is important not to forget to eat iron-rich foods; there is a tendency to think that by eating mainly fruit and vegatables that we are maintaning a balanced diet, yet 10 per cent of women suffer from anaemia in the Western world.*
*ABOVE: Jasminum officinale (jasmine).*
*RIGHT: Juniperus communis (juniper).*

- Jasmine has a soothing, warming and anti-inflammatory effect on joints and a rejuvenating effect on dry, wrinkled or ageing skin
- Its antiseptic and expectorant properties also make it applicable for catarrh, chest and throat infections

))))▶ *Herbalism*

## KALI BICH
*Kali bichromicum*

This homeopathic remedy is useful for any condition which affects the mucous membranes, leading to a stringy, yellow or white discharge. It can help alleviate problems such as sinusitis, glue ear, coughs and colds accompanied by catarrh or where the affected areas feel congested and under pressure. Vomiting, where the cause is a digestive disorder and yellow mucus is ejected, can also be helped, as can rheumatic pain in joints when the pain tends to move about and becomes worse in hot weather. Migraines which begin at night, feel worse when bending, but get better when pressure is applied to the base of the nose can also be treated with kali bich.

The kali bich type is down-to-earth and straightforward, with high morals. They may be small-minded and self-absorbed, conservative and pay great attention to detail.

### Properties and Uses
- Relieves all forms of mucus or discharge, pain that moves about
- For those who are preoccupied with details
- For those who dislike hot weather
- For those who are chilly and sensitive to cold when ill
- Alleviates discharge from nose, throat, stomach, vagina
- For catarrhal coughs, heavy colds and blocked ears
- For migraines
- Symptoms improve in the warmth, after eating, vomiting or moving, and worsen in cold, wet weather, after drinking and on waking, between 3 a.m. and 5 a.m., in hot summer heat and when cold

## KALI CARB
*Kali carbonicum*

This remedy is used when the potassium/sodium balance of the body is upset. Stabbing pains are an indication that this imbalance is present. It is useful for catarrhal, congestive headaches, dry coughs with some phlegm which become worse after eating and drinking. It also good for chronic bronchitis, wheeziness and flatulence.

The Kali Carb type is exhausted, touchy and irritable. They want company, but tend not to get on with anyone. They are normally fearful of the future and of death.

### Properties and Uses
- Reduces sensitivity to draught or movement
- Alleviates stitching pains
- For dry hacking, barking coughs, particularly in cold air
- For swelling between eyelids and eyebrows

## KALI MUR
*Kali muriaticum*

This remedy is one of the biochemic tissue salts and works very well in a low potency in acute situations. Its good for earache with blocked Eustachian tubes, and for indigestion and diarrhoea caused by too much rich and fatty food. It is also helpful in the secondary stages of inflammatory complaints.

### Properties and Uses
- For thick white discharges
- For ulcerated throat
- Unblocks sinuses
- Alleviates dark menstrual flow
- Alleviates constipation
- Soothes blister-like eruptions
- Symptoms are worse when exposed to open air, draughts and damp, but no better when lying in a warm bed

)))⟩ *Biochemic Tissue Salts*

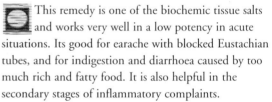

*LEFT*: Kali bichromicum.
*ABOVE RIGHT*: Kali phosphoricum, *one of the 12 tissue salts identified by Dr Wilhelm Schussler.*
*RIGHT*: Anigozanthos manglesii *(kangaroo paw).*

## KALI PHOS

*Kali phosphoricum*

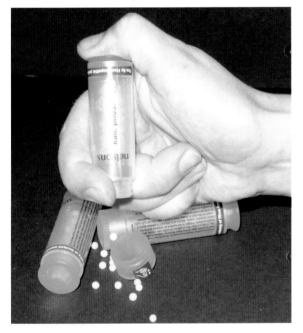 Kali Phos is also one of the 12 tissue salts identified by the German doctor, Wilhelm Schussler. Homeopathically, it is prepared by adding dilute phosphoric acid to a solution of potassium carbonate (also known as potash). Used to treat mental and physical exhaustion, particularly when the nerves

become so frayed the patient is on edge and sensitive to any disturbance or distraction. Sufferers wish to be left alone and become introverted. Conditions such as sensitivity to cold, pus or yellow vaginal discharge, discharge from the lungs or in the stools, muscle fatigue, early morning awakening and chronic fatigue syndrome can all be alleviated.

The Kali Phos type tends to be conservative but out-going, clear-sighted and easily upset by bad or distressing news. Stress and overwork tires them out easily.

### Properties and Uses
- Relieves physical and mental exhaustion, disorders of the nervous system
- Relieves worry and stress
- For those who are easily exhausted by hard work
- For those who are sensitive to disturbances and cold
- For discharge from bladder, vagina or lungs
- For muscular weakness
- Symptoms improve in the warmth, after eating or gentle movement and in cloudy weather, and worsen in cold, dry conditions, in winter, after cold drinks, after physical exertion or talking and when exposed to noise

))))➤ *Biochemic Tissue Salts*

## KANGAROO PAW

*Anigozanthos manglesii*

This Australian bush flower essence is for people who are socially inept. They do not know how to interact properly with other people. They can be very insensitive because they are so focused on themselves that they miss the cues and needs of other people around them. They can be very self-centred.

### Properties and Uses

- For people who are gauche, unaware, insensitive, inept and clumsy
- The remedy brings kindness, sensitivity, *savoir-faire*, enjoyment of people and relaxation

))))➤ *Australian Bush Flower Essence*

## KAVA KAVA

The roots of this powerful herb are used in herbal medicine to induce physical and mental relaxation.

### Properties and Uses
- Mentally and physically relaxing
- Acts as a diuretic and genito-urinary antiseptic
- Helpful for anxiety, depression, insomnia, stress-related disorders and urinary tract infections

### Key Notes
- Can cause drowsines; if this occurs, discontinue or reduce the dosage.
- Take as directed on the label and do not exceed dose

## KELP

Kelp is a type of seaweed which is a rich source of vitamins, particularly B vitamins, and many valuable minerals and trace elements.

### Properties and Uses

- Beneficial to the brain tissue, the membranes surrounding the brain, the sensory nerves and the spinal cord
- Helps with the health of the nails and blood vessels
- Used in the treatment of thyroid problems because of its high iodine content
- Useful for other conditions, such as hair loss, obesity and ulcers
- Protects against the effects of radiation and softens stools

### Key Notes

- Available in a wide variety of forms including raw, dried, granulated, powdered or even liquid
- Can be taken as a daily dietary supplement, particularly in people with mineral deficiencies

⟫⟫ *Iodine, Minerals*

## KINESIOLOGY

Kinesiology is a combination of Western technology and the Oriental principles of energy flow. Each of the major organs and systems of the body is fuelled by an invisible channel of energy called a meridian. These channels work together to form a network of energy that powers the mind, all the major functions, organs and muscles of the body. When we are healthy, energy flows freely through the channels, but blocked energy can lead to weakness in the corresponding organ and will register in the muscle that relates to that organ. For example, the quadriceps in the front of the thigh are linked by energy to the small intestine and the hamstrings are similarly linked to the large intestine. If you were sensitive to wheat and you

*BELOW: Kelp, or bladderwrack, is a type of seaweed beneficial for brain function and nerve cell transmission.*
*LEFT: An example of Kirlian photography (c. 1960s) which captures the quality of energy possessed by particular objects (pictured, a leaf).*
*BELOW RIGHT: Drunk as an infusion or smeared on the skin as a type of ointment, kombucha mushrooms have been proven to cure mild to severe cases of eczema.*

ate a piece of bread, the intolerance would register first in the intestines and then in the corresponding muscles in your legs. A kinesiologist would test the strength of the relevant muscle and from there work backwards to find the cause of the problem. This system works for physical, mental and emotional problems.

Kinesiology is a gentle non-invasive therapy, with no side-effects. It is perfectly safe for people of all ages and states of health, even babies and pregnant women.

))))➤ *Allergy Testing, Diagnosis*

## KIRLIAN PHOTOGRAPHY

Kirlian photography was developed in 1939 by the Russian electrician, Semyon Kirlian, and his wife, Valentina. The technique is a way of photographing the quality of the energy of a person or object. It is based on the belief that we are electrical beings and that human electrical energy can be photographed and analysed. The feet and hands are the parts most commonly photographed.

The participant places a hand or a foot on a machine with photographic plates that emits a high-frequency electrical signal. The image produced indicates the quality of your energy by showing your capacity to resonate with the frequency that is emitted through the plate. The image varies depending on how you feel. The therapist looks at the splines, and at the continuity of the outline of the image, for information about the quality of your energy.

))))➤ *Diagnosis*

## KOMBUCHA MUSHROOMS

The kombucha or Manchurian mushroom has been used for centuries. The mushroom itself is not eaten, but is made into a tea, created by fermenting the mushroom for about a week, and blending it with water, sugar and green or black tea with apple cider. In this mixture, the mushroom reproduces, and can then be used to produce more tea.

Kombucha is actually not a mushroom, but a combination of different elements, including lichen, bacteria and yeast. The tea contains a variety of different nutrients and other health-promoting substances.

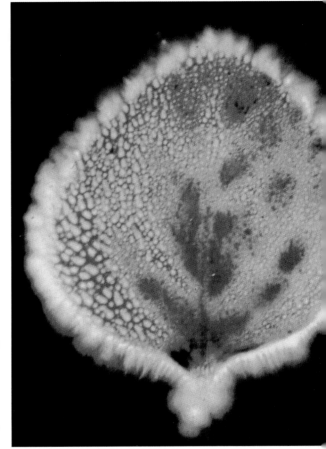

### Properties and Uses

- A natural energy booster and detoxifier that may help to slow down or reverse the ageing process and fight serious diseases, such as AIDS and cancer
- A strong immuno-stimulant

))))➤ *Immunity*

## LACHESIS

*Trigonocephalus lachesis*

The South American bushmaster snake, whose venom forms the basis of this homeopathic remedy, is extremely poisonous, and affects the heart and central nervous system. The remedy uses fresh venom and treats wounds that are slow to heal or wounds that bleed profusely.

Lachesis is helpful for premenstrual problems such as erratic pain, relieved by blood flow and problems associated with the menopause, such as hot flushes and dizziness. It works well for any problems connected with blood flow and circulation, such as varicose veins, irregular pulse, angina and palpitations. Problems which occur on the left side, such as earache, headaches and sore throats can be alleviated; wounds that are not healing well, such as bleeding piles, ulcers and cuts are also helped. Other conditions that can be treated include nervous disorders such as fainting and *petit mal* epileptic attacks; blue wounds; purplish, bloated face; fever; sweats; pulsations; waking up feeling as if choking and swollen glands.

The lachesis type tends to be redheaded, freckled, pale skinned and puffy or bloated looking. They are egocentric with no regard for others, while at the same time being intuitive, creative, aspiring, selfish, devious or jealous. They dislike commitment and being restricted and are strong ideologists. They are usually gloomy and quiet, preferring sour and starchy foods and alcohol and cannot tolerate hot drinks and wheat. Children tend to be hyperactive and difficult to control, prone to jealousy and possessive of friends.

### Properties and Uses

- Relieves premenstrual and menopausal complaints, circulatory and vascular problems, left-sided complaints, slow-healing wounds
- Helps control fears about burglars, poisoning, water, suffocating, death
- Pacifies those who are disgruntled on waking

*RIGHT: Larix decidua (larch).*
*CENTRE RIGHT: Fields of lavender.*
*FAR RIGHT: Lavendula augustifolia (lavender).*

- For people with strong ideas and philosophies
- For those who are suspicious of people and jealous
- Alleviates nightmares
- For those who are prone to post-menopausal depression
- Improves a short temper
- For blueness around skin problems
- For bloating
- For restlessness
- For those who are oversensitive to touch and noise

### Key Notes

- Weak areas include left side of the body, circulation, nervous system and female reproductive organs.
- Symptoms improve after discharges, such as menstruation, nosebleeds or bowel movement, in fresh air and after a cold drink, and are worse on the left side, with sleep, when touched, with motion, in heat, and after hot drinks.

## LARCH

*Larix decidua*

The Bach flower remedy larch is for those who lack confidence in themselves and fear failure; those who feel that they are not as capable as those around them.

At times lack of confidence may completely immobilize them and prevent them from even trying. They do not think that they are capable or worthy of success. Feelings of total uselessness can also lead to great unhappiness, despair and isolation. Larch increases confidence and strengthens personal will.

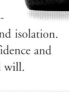

## Properties and Uses

- For those who lack confidence and self-esteem, are passive, have a fear of trying, have a poor self-image and feelings of inferiority
- Suitable for children starting a new school or a new job who feel timid, shy and inferior
- Feelings of worthlessness may hide deeper problems or a pattern of abuse
- Larch strengthens confidence and helps us appreciate our real worth and value our personal contribution to the planet

))))➤ *Bach Flower Remedies*

## LAVENDER

*Lavendula augustifolia*

This fragrant herb has a wide range of uses. As an infusion and a tea it acts by carrying blood away from the head and relaxes the nervous system.

## Properties and Uses

- Relaxes the nervous system, making it good for pains, cramps and burns
- Helpful for insomnia and tension headaches
- Antiseptic and therefore useful for urinary tract infections
- Good as an infusion to wash the face and hair
- Has a soothing, cleansing and healing effect on delicate skin

## Dosage

- Infuse one teaspoon of the herb in a cup of boiling water and drink three times a day. Or dilute 1–2 ml of tincture in water and take three times a day.

))))➤ *Aromatherapy*

## LAVENDER

*Lavendula augustifolia*

Lavender has been used since ancient times for both its perfume and its medicinal qualities. Lavender is the most versatile and most widely therapeutic of all essential oils and has a huge range of therapeutic properties.

Lavender is usually safe to use for all age groups, but some hayfever or asthma sufferers may be allergic to it. Lavandin is often sold as lavender because it is cheaper to produce, but be aware that it will not work.

## Properties and Uses

- Calming, soothing, antidepressant and emotionally balancing
- Its antiseptic, antibacterial and painkilling properties make it valuable in treating cuts, wounds, burns, bruises, spots, allergies, insect bites and throat infections
- Lavender is the oil most associated with burns and healing of the skin, and can be applied neat to a burn to prevent infection and encourage speedy healing
- Because it is a decongestant it is also effective against colds, flu and catarrhal conditions
- Lavender lowers blood pressure, prevents and eases digestive spasms, nausea and indigestion
- It is anti-rheumatic and a tonic; problems of the nervous system such as tension, depression, insomnia, headaches, stress and hypertension respond particularly well to its soothing properties

))))➤ *Essential Oils, Herbalism*

## LECITHIN

Lecithin has for some time been a popular supplement, used for a variety of health conditions. It is comprised of choline, insoitol, fatty acids and phosphorus and is available as a liquid or as dry granules. It is widely used in foods to maintain consistency, and is probably one of the only nutritious food additives. Lecithin in large quantities may cause depression in some people. Very high doses may even cause nausea, vomiting and dizziness.

The best sources are egg yolks, soya beans, liver, meats, fish, cauliflower and cabbage.

### Properties and Uses

- Protects against cardiovascular disease
- Helps to reduce high blood pressure
- Used to treat memory loss and nervous conditions such as dementia and Alzheimer's disease
- May help in the treatment of mental disorders such as manic depression
- Has some anti-viral activity
- May have some anti-ageing properties
- May prevent and treat gallstones
- May help to treat viral hepatitis, repairing the membranes of the liver cells

### Dosage

- Doses of up to 1 g daily are acceptable, but see your doctor to discuss your individual needs. Lecithin appears in a wide range of foods and it is probably best to increase your intake of these instead of supplementing.

## LEDUM

*Ledum palustre*

Wild rosemary has been used for its antiseptic qualities for centuries. Homeopathically, ledum is made from the whole fresh plant in flower, which is dried and powdered.

Ledum is a useful first-aid remedy and helps prevent infection in cuts and wounds. Complaints that need immediate treatment, such as stings, cuts, grazes, eye injuries and puncture wounds respond well, especially if there is accompanying bruising and the area becomes painful, swollen and puffy. It can also help to alleviate rheumatic pain which starts in the feet and moves up, painful or injured joints which may look pale or bluish and where the affected part feels cold to the touch but the person feels hot.

### Properties and Uses

- Relieves cuts, grazes, stings, pain that moves about
- Prevents wounds becoming infected
- For the timid, but impatient
- For people who are morose and want to be left alone
- For anger and hate
- For stiff joints
- For puffy, bluish skin
- Alleviates night sweats
- For black eyes
- Symptoms improve when cold compresses are applied to the affected part and if left uncovered; symptoms worsen if warm, if touched, in bed and at night

## LEMON

*Citrus limon*

Lemons are the most widely grown acid species belonging to the citrus group of fruits. They rank third in tonnage among all citrus fruit produced and have, for generations, been used for their wide range of therapeutic properties and uses. Lemons are a rich source of vitamin C, and have a cleansing effect on the digestive system. They are the mainstay of any good 'home remedy' chest. The leaves and the whole fruit may be used according to requirements.

- To help cure cold sores put a few drops of undiluted lemon juice on the affected area and repeat several times a day until the sore disappears

))))➤ *Aromatherapy*

## LEMON

*Citrus limon*

Lemons have been used for thousands of years for their therapeutic properties. The essential oil is obtained from the oily rind of the fruit. It can, however, irritate sensitive skin. Do not use before sunbathing, dilute well for massage and bath blends, and do not use for more than a few days at a time.

### Properties and Uses

- Lemon can stimulate the body's defences to fight all kinds of infection; it is beneficial in treating inflamed or diseased gums, mouth ulcers, sore throats and acne
- It helps to clear colds, flu and bronchitis and can be used to remove warts and verrucae and to clear herpes blisters
- The oil has a tonic effect on the circulation and is often used to treat varicose veins, poor circulation, high blood pressure and fluid retention
- Lemon is both a diuretic and a laxative and has the ability to stop bleeding in minor cuts and nosebleeds
- As an astringent it benefits greasy skin and can also be used to reduce a fever; because it also counteracts acidity in the body, lemon helps to relieve acid indigestion, arthritis and rheumatism
- Lemon is refreshing and can help to ease the symptoms of depression

))))➤ *Homeopathic Remedies*

### Properties and Uses

- Blood purifier, improves the body's ability to expel toxins and useful for skin problems e.g. acne and boils
- Rich in vitamins B and C
- Anti-fungal, antacid, antiseptic, digestive aid
- One of the most powerful natural styptics; use on cuts and grazes to stop bleeding
- Antibacterial and antiviral properties; excellent for halting the progression of infections
- Controls bladder and kidney infections
- The high potassium content of lemons will encourage the heart action and lemons are a useful tonic for anyone with heart problems
- Lemons are a natural insecticide and will discourage mosquitoes, black flies and house flies
- Drink fresh lemon juice (lemon in hot water will do) to cleanse the system
- Lemon strengthens the immune system, helps relieve the symptoms of colds and flu and can also be beneficial in the treatment of other infections
- Use pure lemon juice on wasp stings to relieve pain
- Regular intake of fresh lemons may be useful in the treatment of haemorrhoids, kidney stones and varicose veins
- Lemon juice mixed with olive oil may help to dissolve gallstones

*LEFT: Lecithin is found in leafy green vegetables like cabbage.*
*ABOVE: Citrus lemon slices.*

## LEMON BALM

*Melissa officinalis*

A common plant in Britain, Europe, Western Asia and North Africa, lemon balm (also called balm or melissa) is used fresh, if in season, or the leaves can be dried for remedies.

### Properties and Uses

- Carminative, nervine, antispasmodic, antidepressive, diaphoretic, anti-microbial and hepatic
- Balm is an excellent carminative herb that relieves spasms in the digestive tract and is used in flatulent dyspepsia; because of its mild antidepressive properties, it is primarily used where there is dyspepsia associated with anxiety or depression, as the gently sedative oils relieve tension and stress reactions, thus acting to lighten depression
- It may be used in migraines that are associated with tension, neuralgia, anxiety-induced palpitations and insomnia
- Balm has a tonic effect on the heart and circulatory system which can lower blood pressure; it can be used in feverish conditions such as flu

### Dosage

- Infusion: pour a cup of boiling water on to two or three teaspoonfuls of the dried herb or four to six fresh leaves and leave to infuse for 10–15 minutes, well covered until drunk. A cup of this tea should be taken in the morning and the evening, or when needed.
- Tincture: take 2–6 ml three times a day.

))))➤ *Aromatherapy, Melissa*

## LEMONGRASS

*Cymbopogon citratus*

Lemongrass is used as a flavouring in Thai cuisine and has been used in traditional Indian medicine for centuries. The essential oil is distilled from the grass leaves. It has a strong refreshing citrus smell that has numerous aromatherapy and domestic uses.

Dilute well as lemongrass may cause skin irritation in some people. Do not use on babies or children and do not use around the eyes.

### Properties and Uses

- Lemongrass has a tonic effect on the nervous system and the body in general
- Use as a painkiller and antidepressant; good for headaches, lethargy, symptoms of stress and beneficial for muscular pain and poor muscle tone
- It has fever-reducing properties and helps the immune system fight infections
- As a deodorant lemongrass can be used for excessive perspiration and sweaty feet and its astringent properties make lemongrass an effective skin toner which helps to close open pores
- Lemongrass is also an effective flea, lice and tick repellent; use it in a vaporizer to keep flies out of the kitchen in summer and to get rid of pet smells from the home

))))➤ *Herbalism*

## LIQUORICE

*Glycyrrhiza glabra*

Native to the Mediterranean region and parts of Asia, liquorice, a pretty blue flower, is cultivated worldwide. The sweet substance is obtained mainly from

*LEFT:* Melissa officinalis *(lemon balm).*
*ABOVE:* Cymbopogon citratus *(lemongrass).*
*ABOVE RIGHT:* Glycyrrhiza glabra *(liquorice).*

the roots, and is used medicinally and as a flavouring. It is cultivated chiefly in the Middle East.

There is a small possibility of affecting electrolyte balance with extended use of large doses of liquorice. The whole herb has constituents that counter this, but it is best to avoid liquorice if you have hypertension, kidney disease or during pregnancy.

## Properties and Uses

- Liquorice is expectorant, demulcent, anti-inflammatory, antispasmodic and a mild laxative
- Can be effective in the treatment of chronic hepatitis and cirrhosis
- Liquorice is used in allopathic medicine as a treatment for peptic ulceration; a similar use to its herbal use in gastritis and ulcers, and it can be used in the relief of abdominal colic
- Detoxifies the body
- Raises blood pressure and can be used in the treatment of low blood pressure
- Stimulates the kidneys and bowels

## LYCOPODIUM

*Lycopodium clavatum*

This plant has long been used to treat stomach complaints and urinary disorders. For homeopathic use the pollen dust is shaken out of the spikes of the fresh plant.

This remedy is commonly used to treat digestive complaints, such as vomiting, indigestion, distended abdomen with flatulence, constipation, bleeding piles and hunger which turns to discomfort after eating. Other problems that can be alleviated include swelling in the ankles, feet or hands (oedema); burst blood vessels in the eye; chronic catarrh; psoriasis on the hands and pneumonia.

The lycopodium type is tall and lean, but not strong. Deep frown lines are common, as is the tendency to become prematurely bald or grey. They appear detached and poised, and tend to hold distinguished positions. Insecurity leads to gross exaggerations. They dislike change and challenges, but enjoy company. Children tend to be thin and sallow, are shy and lack confidence, prefer reading to outdoor activities, have a slightly distended abdomen, and although well behaved at school are bossy at home.

## Properties and Uses

- Relieves stomach disorders, digestive conditions, bladder and kidney complaints, problems on the right side, emotional problems and anxiety caused by insecurity
- Relieves fear of being alone, enclosed spaces, crowds, death
- Helps eliminate thoughts of failure
- Alleviates a dislike of the dark
- Reduces intolerance of weakness in others and illness
- For weakness on right side of body
- For sensitive areas including the digestive organs, brain, lungs, skin, liver, kidneys and bladder
- For fatigue
- Symptoms improve when in cool, fresh air, when wearing loose clothing, after hot food and drinks and at night, and are on the right side, in stuffy rooms, wearing tight clothing, after over-eating or not eating, between 4 a.m. to 8 a.m. and 4 p.m. to 8 p.m.

## LYSINE

Lysine is an essential amino acid, which means that it is necessary for life. It is needed for growth, tissue repair, and for the production of antibodies, hormones and enzymes. It should be obtained from the diet, although supplements are available. Lysine is not suitable for children.

The best sources of lysine are fish, milk, lima beans, meat, cheese, yeast, eggs and all proteins.

### Properties and Uses
- Inhibits herpes – high doses are now believed to be effective in reducing the recurrence of outbreaks
- May help to build muscle mass
- Helps to prevent fertility problems
- Improves concentration

### Dosage
- Up to 500 g daily is believed to be safe, although some experts recommend 1 g daily at mealtimes
- Take on an empty stomach, with some juice or water; do not mix with other proteins
- Take with an equal quantity of arginine if you want to increase muscle mass

⫸ *Amino Acids, Arginine*

## MACROBIOTICS

The term macrobiotics comes from the Greek words which mean 'large' and 'life', and macrobiotics is based on the fundamental belief that everyone should be healthy enough to enjoy life to the full. Macrobiotics has a rich and lively heritage, harking back to early Tibet and China, where the philosophy was largely inspired by three books – the *Nei Ching*, the *I Ching* and the *Tao Te Ching*. The overwhelming emphasis of these books was the idea that humanity is part of the environment and the cosmos, and

that health and judgement is a reflection of our appreciation, connection and intake from the world around us.

In the 1880s, a Japanese doctor, Sagen Ishizuka, discovered that many health problems could be treated with dietary changes, usually involving wholegrains and vegetables, cutting out refined carbohydrates and white rice. His work was published in two volumes, and was later drawn upon by George Ohsawa, who, by 1945, had synthesized all the beliefs and coined the term 'macrobiotics'.

In the 1960s, Michio Kushi, one of Ohsawa's students, began teaching in America and Europe, where he broadened the dietary guidelines and developed Ohsawa's ideas further. The result of his ideas and ideals is modern-day macrobiotics, which has evolved from being a fairly strict regime to include all the essential elements of basic nutrition. The idea is that we can live life to its full potential, assisted by a diet which promotes physical, mental, emotional and spiritual health.

Macrobiotics is based on the Chinese philosophy of yin and yang, which are two qualities which balance one another, and which exist in every natural object and cycle. Yin is the flexible, fluid and cool side of nature, while yang is the strong, dynamic and hot side. There are yin and yang elements to everything, including people, and macrobiotics is a philosophy aimed at balancing them to promote health.

Yin qualities are peacefulness, calm, creativity, sociability and relaxed attitude and behaviour. Yang qualities are activity, alertness, energy and precision, among others. Most people are a balance of these two qualities, however, when one becomes stronger than the other, a state of imbalance can occur, which can result in illness. Too much yin can lead to depression, fatigue and sleeping problems; too much yang can cause tension, irritability, hyperactivity and insomnia.

The macrobiotic attempts to right that balance, by suggesting an increased intake of yin foods for someone suffering from too much yang, and the opposite for someone with too much yin. There are many other factors involved in this theory, including exercise, which is broken into yin and yang (yoga is yin; aerobics is yang), and temperature and climate.

The diet is similar to that of the traditional Japanese peasant, which consists of:

- 50 per cent cooked whole cereal grains, pasta, bread, porridge, stir-fried rice or noodles
- 25 per cent local seasonal vegetables, cooked in a variety of ways (for example, raw, pickled, steamed, sautéed, boiled, etc.)
- 10 per cent protein, drawn from local fish, beans and soya bean products, like tofu or tempeh
- 5 per cent sea vegetables, used in soups, stews and condiments
- 5 per cent soups, including miso soup, fish soup, bean soup and vegetable soup, among others
- 5 per cent desserts and teas, including simple teas and grain coffees, and desserts using fruits and fermented rice (*amaskae*), *agar agar* (sea vegetable), seeds and nuts

Foods which are not suggested on the diet include sugar, spices and alcohol (which are said to be too yin), and meat, eggs and cheese (which are said to be too yang). These foods are generally believed to be too strong for human consumption, unbalancing the system and causing illness.
)))⯈ *Diet*

*FAR LEFT: A macrobiotic diet and regular exercise (low-impact aerobics, pictured) can help you get fit and improve your quality of life.*
*CENTRE LEFT: The Chinese philosophy of yin and yang, the two directly opposed male and female qualities which make up the universe.*
*ABOVE: Throbbing headaches and neuralgia can be alleviated by treatment with the homeopathic remedy* Magnesia phosphorica *(Mag Phos).*

## MAG PHOS
*Magnesia phosphorica*

Magnesium phosphate is one of the homeo-pathically prepared biochemic tissue salts. The homeopathic remedy is made chemically from magnesium sulphate and sodium phosphate and has an antispasmodic effect.

It is a useful remedy for any type of cramp, from infant colic and abdominal cramp to menstrual pains and writer's cramp, with the sufferer doubled up in pain. Abdominal cramps are sharp and intense, with the pain jumping from one part to another and may improve when bending, with heat and hard pressure and worsen in the cold, draughts and at night. Headaches and neuralgia, when the head throbs, the face is flushed and pain suddenly comes and goes, improves in the warmth and if the head is bound. Symptoms worsen in the cold, in draughty conditions and at night. Pains tend to be on the right side of the body.

The Mag Phos type tends to be thin, weak, sensitive and artistic, as well as being intense and rather intellectual.

### Properties and Uses
- Relieves cramps, neuralgia, pains on the right side
- For people who are impulsive and dislike mental effort
- For those who stammer
- For those who are forgetful
- For the complaint of a cold spine
- For headaches and dizziness
- Alleviates jerky movements
- Symptoms improve in the warmth, with pressure, hot compresses and bending double, and are worse on the right side, when cool, when touched and at night

)))⯈ *Biochemic Tissue Salts*

## MAGNESIUM

Magnesium is a mineral which is absolutely essential for every biochemical process in our bodies, including metabolism and the synthesis of nucleic acids and protein.

Magnesium deficiency is very common, particularly in the elderly, heavy drinkers, pregnant women and regular, strenuous exercisers, and it has been proven that even a very slight deficiency can cause a disruption of the heartbeat. Other symptoms of deficiency include weakness, fatigue, vertigo, nervousness, muscle cramps and hyperactivity in children.

Magnesium is toxic to people with renal problems or atrioventricular blocks. High doses are believed to cause flushing of the skin, thirst, low blood pressure and loss of reflexes in some people, although this is rare.

The best sources of magnesium are brown rice, soya beans, nuts, brewer's yeast, wholewheat flour and legumes.

### Properties and Uses
- Necessary for many body functions, including energy production and cell replication
- Essential for the transmission of nerve impulses
- Helps to prevent kidney and gallstones
- Useful in treatment of prostate problems
- Repairs and maintains body cells
- Required for hormonal activity
- Useful in treatment of high blood pressure
- Protects against cardiovascular disease
- Helps to treat PMS

### Dosage
- Dietary intake is thought to be inadequate in the average Western diet; supplements of 200–400 mg are recommended daily

⟫⟫ *Minerals*

*ABOVE: Magnesium is present in nuts, and helps regulate our body's metabolism.*
*ABOVE RIGHT: Calendula officinalis (marigold) harvesting.*
*RIGHT: Reflexologists treating visitors at the London Festival of Mind, Body and Spirit. Manipulative therapies make use of physical manipulation of parts of the body to bring about a therapeutic effect.*

## MANGANESE

Manganese is an essential trace element which is necessary for the normal functioning of the brain, and effective in the treatment of many nervous disorders, including Alzheimer's disease and schizophrenia. Deficiency is usually related to a poor diet – particularly one where foods are processed and refined.

Our understanding of manganese is still incomplete but it may prove to be one of the most important nutrients in human pathology. It is likely that manganese is one of the antioxidant minerals.

There is some evidence that diabetes, heart disease and schizophrenia are linked to manganese deficiency.

Toxic levels are usually quite rare, but symptoms of excess manganese may include lethargy, involuntary movements, posture problems and coma.

The best sources are cereals, tea, green leaf vegetables, wholemeal bread, pulses and nuts.

### Properties and Uses
- Maintains a healthy nervous systems
- Necessary for female sex hormones
- Necessary for the synthesis of structural proteins of body cells
- Necessary for normal bone structure
- Important in the formation of thyroxin in the thyroid gland
- Necessary for the functioning of the brain
- Used in the treatment of some nervous disorders
- Necessary for glucose metabolism

### Dosage
- 2–5 mg is considered adequate, but doses up to 10 mg are thought to be safe

⟫⟫ *Minerals*

## MANIPULATIVE THERAPIES

Manipulative therapies are natural therapies that rely on physical manipulation of the body to create a therapeutic effect. The best-known examples are osteopathy, chiropractic, massage and reflexology. Some of these therapies involve manipulating the whole body (as in chiropractic), while others focus on smaller parts of the body, such as the hands and feet (as in reflexology). Each

of these disciplines has their own theory as to how treatment works, but in all, the healing power of touch is relevant to the benefits.

))))➤ *Massage, Natural Therapies, Osteopathy, Reflexology, Chiropractic*

## MARIGOLD (CALENDULA)

*Calendula officinalis*

Known as marigold, or calendula, the whole flower tops or petals of the common garden plant are used therapeutically.

### Properties and Uses

- Anti-inflammatory, antispasmodic, lymphatic, astringent, emmenagogue, anti-microbial
- Calendula is one of the best herbs for treating local skin problems; it may be used safely wherever there is an inflammation on the skin, whether due to infection or physical damage
- It may be used for any external bleeding or wound, bruising or strains; it will also be of benefit in slow-healing wounds and skin ulcers
- Ideal for first-aid treatment of minor burns and scalds
- Internally it acts as a valuable herb for digestive inflammation and thus it may be used in the treatment of gastric and duodenal ulcers

- As a cholagogue it will aid in the relief of gall-bladder problems and also through this process help indigestion
- Calendula has marked anti-fungal activity and may be used both internally and externally to combat such infections
- Also used in the treatment of delayed menstruation and painful periods

### Dosage

- Infusion: pour a cup of boiling water on to one or two teaspoons of the florets and leave to infuse for 10–15 minutes. This should be drunk three times a day. External use as a lotion or ointment for cuts, bruises, diaper rash, sore nipples, burns and scalds.
- Tincture: 1–4 ml three times a day.

))))➤ *Calendula*

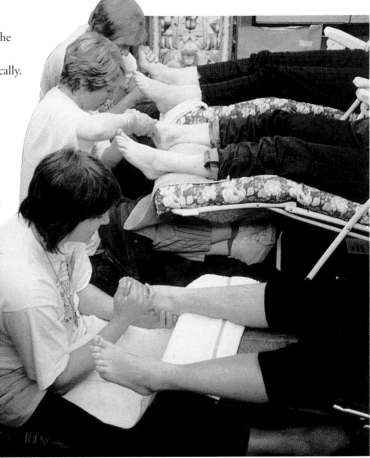

## MARJORAM

*Origanum marjorana*

In ancient times marjoram was reputed to promote longevity, a belief that encouraged the ancient Greeks to include it in perfumes, cosmetics and medicine. The essential oil is used to relieve agitation, dispel grief and restore calm. Do not use marjoram during pregnancy.

### Properties and Uses

- Marjoram is warming and pain-relieving; it also has antispasmodic properties, making it good for muscle spasms and strains
- It is a sedative and a nerve tonic which works to relieve nervous tension and promote restful sleep
- Inhaling marjoram can help to relieve headaches and migraine
- Antiviral and bactericidal properties help to fend off colds and infections, and its expectorant properties make it a useful oil to include in a steam inhalation for chest infections
- Massaged into the chest or throat marjoram can also relieve painful coughs
- The oil is a vasodilator which is beneficial in treating high blood pressure and improving circulation
- It also calms digestion, strengthens intestinal peristalsis and eases period pain

## MASSAGE

The therapeutic effects of massage are well-documented and although sceptics insist that any health benefits derived from treatment are the result of an improved sense of well-being, rather than any biological response by the body, there is no doubt that massage works on many levels to improve overall health.

Massage is one of the oldest, simplest forms of therapy and is a system of stroking, pressing and kneading different areas of the body to relieve pain, relax, stimulate and tone the body. Massage does much more than make you feel good, it also works on the soft tissues (the muscles, tendons and ligaments) to improve muscle tone. Although it largely affects those muscles just under the skin, it is believed that it also reaches the deeper layers of muscles and possibly even the organs themselves. Massage also stimulates blood circulation and assists the lymphatic system (which runs parallel to the circulatory system), improving elimination of toxic waste throughout the body.

### Key Notes

- Massage is known to increase the circulation of blood and the flow of lymph. The direct mechanical effect of rhythmically applied manual pressure and movement used in massage can dramatically increase the rate of blood flow. Also, the stimulation of nerve receptors causes the blood vessels (by relaxation) to dilate, which also encourages blood flow.
- For the whole body to be healthy, the individual cells must be healthy. These cells are dependent on an abundant supply of blood and lymph because these fluids supply nutrients and oxygen and carry away wastes and toxins.
- It causes changes in the blood. The oxygen capacity of the blood can increase 10–15 per cent after massage.

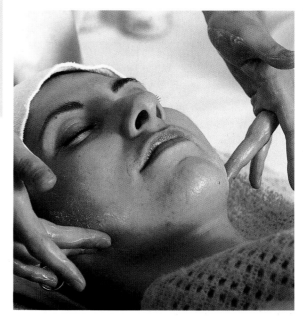

- Massage can help loosen contracted, shortened muscles and can stimulate weak, flaccid muscles. This muscle balancing can help posture and promote more efficient movement. Massage does not directly increase muscle strength, but it can speed recovery from the fatigue that occurs after exercise. Massage also provides a gentle stretching action to both the muscles and connective tissues that surround and support the muscles and many other parts of the body, which helps keep these tissues elastic.
- It increases the body's secretions and excretions. There is a proven increase in the production of gastric juices, saliva and urine. There is also increased excretion of nitrogen, inorganic phosphorus and sodium chloride (salt), suggesting that the metabolic rate (the utilization of absorbed material by the body's cells) increases.
- Massage balances the nervous system by soothing or stimulating it, depending on what you need at the time of the massage.
- Massage directly improves the function of the sebaceous (oil) and sweat glands, which keep the skin lubricated, clean and cooled. Tough, inflexible skin can become softer and more supple.
- By indirectly or directly stimulating the nerves that supply internal organs, blood vessels of the organs dilate and allow greater blood supply to reach them.

))))➤ *Aromatherapy*

## MAURY, MARGUERITE

In the 1950s, Austrian beauty therapist and biochemist Madame Marguerite Maury introduced the concept of using essential oils in massage and was responsible for setting up the first aromatherapy clinics in Britain, France and Switzerland.

## MEDITATION

The word meditation comes from the Latin *moderi*, meaning 'to heal'. Western medicine has been slow to catch on to the benefits of meditation but research has now shown that it can slow your heart rate, reduce negative emotions and produce a sense of calm. Meditation is a tool to make us aware of the peace within us, a place that the outside world cannot touch or influence.

))))➤ *Relaxation, Yoga*

## MELISSA
*Melissa officinalis*

Melissa, also known as heart's delight, has been used medicinally since the seventeenth century. The fresh lemony essential oil is distilled from the leaves and flowering tops. Dilute well as it may irritate the skin of some types of people.

### Properties and Uses

- Melissa helps to reduce high blood pressure and, because it also helps to calm palpitations and rapid breathing, it is a good remedy for shock
- The oil is often used for menstrual problems as it has a calming and regulating effect on the menstrual cycle, helps to ease period pain and improves missing or scanty periods
- Melissa can be used to reduce digestive spasms in colic, nausea and indigestion, relieve migraine and combat fever
- Low dilutions can be beneficial for eczema, and other skin problems; allergies affecting the skin and the respiratory system can benefit from its antihistamine properties
- Melissa calms the nervous system, relieves anxiety and has an uplifting effect on the emotions, dispelling sadness and loss, and counteracting hysteria
- It also has a general tonic effect on mind and body

))))➤ *Lemon Balm*

*FAR LEFT:* Origanum vulgare *(common marjoram).*
*NEAR LEFT: Massages increase the circulation of blood under the skin and around the vital organs; they also stimulate the lymphatic system to transport lymph around the body, thus improving toxic-waste elimination.*
*ABOVE RIGHT: Meditation can help you pace your breathing patterns, inducing a state of inner relaxation and clarity which is conducive to overall well-being.*

## MERC SOL
*Mercurius solubilis*

In Roman mythology, Mercury was the messenger of the gods. In recent centuries, the substance has been used for various medicinal purposes. Merc Sol is mainly used to treat conditions associated with foul-smelling secretions.

Conditions characterized by a smelly discharge are helped by this remedy, including chronic conjunctivitis, pus secretions from the ears, watery catarrh, nasal cold sores, glutinous saliva which stains the pillow during sleep, throat ulcers which make swallowing painful, phlegmy cough which is worse in the warmth and at night, drenching sweats, pus-filled skin eruptions, sores,

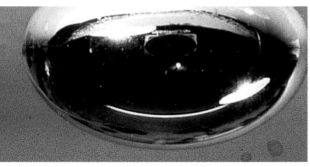

and in women, excessive vaginal discharge and green-looking stools flecked with blood. In the mouth and throat, gingivitis, thrush, bad breath, loose teeth in infected gums, swollen tonsils and ulcers can be helped.

The mercury type is fair-haired with smooth, clear skin. They tend to be outwardly detached, yet sensitive to criticism, with an inner sense of haste. Insecurity makes them cautious and suspicious of others. They dislike being contradicted and may react badly. When ill, they become slow, uncomprehending, forgetful and lack willpower. Children tend to appear very grown up, flirty and precocious, but inwardly are cautious and easily upset. They may also be shy and introverted with a tendency to stammer and prone to ear, nose and throat problems.

### Properties and Uses
- Relieves complaints accompanied by strong-smelling secretions, conditions affecting the mouth and throat and excessive sweating

- For the restless and anxious
- Alleviates fears about insanity and death, as well as harm to family
- Helps control explosive anger, even murderous feelings, if upset
- Alleviates burning secretions, eye complaints, skin conditions and aching joints
- Weak areas include the lining of the stomach and the respiratory system, skin, bones and joints, blood, mouth, throat and liver
- Symptoms improve in temperate weather and after rest, and worsen in changeable weather, when lying on the right side, if too hot in bed, when sweating and at night

## METHIONINE

Methionine is a sulphur-containing amino acid that is very important in numerous processes in the body. Research shows that it may help to prevent clogging of the arteries by eliminating fatty substances. The best sources of methionine are eggs, milk, liver and fish.

### Properties and Uses
- May help to eliminate fatty substances in the blood
- May help to regulate the nervous system
- In conjunction with choline and folic acid, it may prevent some tumours
- Necessary for the biosynthesis of taurine and cysteine

### Key Notes
- Supplements are not advised, although some doctors may suggest their use in specific circumstances.
- ⟫▶ *Amino Acids*

## MILK THISTLE
*Silybum marianum*

The mature seeds of the head of the milk thistle plant are used therapeutically. Milk thistle is primarily used to promote milk secretion, but it is also exceptionally good for the liver, making it work more efficiently by stabilizing liver-cell membranes and preventing damage from toxins.

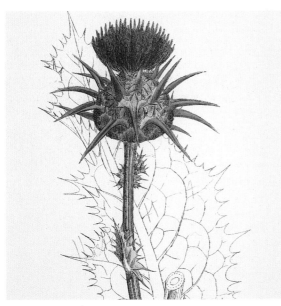

## Properties and Uses

- Hepatic, galactogogue, demulcent, cholagogue
- Milk thistle can be used to increase the secretion and flow of bile from the liver and gall bladder – its traditional use as a liver tonic has been supported by research showing that it contains constituents which protect liver cells from chemical damage; it is used in a whole range of liver and gall-bladder conditions, including hepatitis and cirrhosis
- It may also have value in the treatment of chronic uterine problems
- The herb is also used to promote milk secretion, and it is safe and good for nursing mothers

## Dosage

- Infusion: pour a cup of boiling water on to one teaspoonful of the ground seeds and infuse for 10–15 minutes. This should be drunk three times a day.
- Tincture: 1–2 ml three times a day.

))▶ *Detoxification*

*LEFT: Merc Sol is a homeopathic remedy which uses a small amount of mercury (pictured).*
*ABOVE RIGHT: Silybum marianum (milk thistle).*
*BELOW RIGHT: The Bach flower remedy Mimulus.*

## MIMULUS

*Mimulus guttatus*

This Bach flower remedy is prescribed for fear that can be identified, of known or worldly things. It should be taken for the everyday fears of pain, accident, poverty, being alone and misfortune. Fear dominates responses, either prodding into hasty action or freezing into inaction. These fears are easily identified and faced but underneath they are fed by insecurity and a negative attitude caused by past experience. Fear of flying, public speaking or snakes, for example, will all respond to this remedy.

### Key Notes

- Mimulus is for any fear that can be named. Anything from a trivial fear to serious phobia can be addressed, as long as it can be named.
- Typically, fear can lead to stammering, palpitations, indigestion, sleeplessness and troubled dreams. Mimulus liberates us from fear and helps us understand the rhythms and balances of everyday life.

))▶ *Bach Flower Remedies*

## MINERALS

Minerals are inorganic chemical elements, which are necessary for many biochemical and physiological processes that go on in our bodies. Inorganic substances that are required in amounts greater than 100 mg per day are called minerals; those required in amounts less than 100 mg per day are called trace elements. Minerals are not necessarily present in foods: the quality of the soil and the geological conditions of the area in which they were grown play an important part in determining the mineral content of food. Even a balanced diet may be lacking in essential minerals or trace elements because of the soil in which it was grown.

))▶ *Supplements, Trace Elements*

## MOLYBDENUM

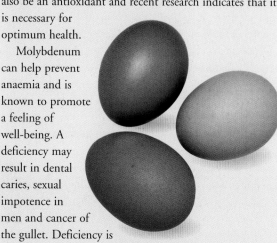

Molybdenum is an essential trace element, and a vital part of the enzyme which is responsible for the utilisation of iron in our bodies. Molybdenum may also be an antioxidant and recent research indicates that it is necessary for optimum health.

Molybdenum can help prevent anaemia and is known to promote a feeling of well-being. A deficiency may result in dental caries, sexual impotence in men and cancer of the gullet. Deficiency is usually the result of eating foods from molybdenum-deficient soils, or a diet that is high in refined and processed foods.

Molybdenum is toxic in doses higher than 10–15 mg, which causes gout (a build-up of uric acid around the joints).

The best sources are wheat, canned beans, wheatgerm, liver, pulses, whole grains, offal and eggs.

### Properties and Uses

- Aids in the metabolism of fats and carbohydrates
- Prevents sexual impotence
- Vital for the utilization of iron in the body
- Necessary for the excretion of uric acid from the body
- Protects against cancer
- Prevents anaemia
- Protects against dental caries

### Dosage

- The optimal intake is still undecided; adequate amounts are between 0.075–0.25 mg per day, but intake will differ between individuals. Experts suggest 50–100 mcg per day as a preventative measure.
))) ▶ *Minerals*

## MOUNTAIN DEVIL

*Lambertia formosa*

This essence helps one deal with feelings of hatred, anger, jealousy and the major blocks to expressing love. It is for people who tend to be suspicious of others; mountain devil helps to develop unconditional love and acceptance. It helps one express anger in a healthy way and so develop sound boundaries. This may open the way to forgiveness.

### Properties and Uses

- For hatred, anger, holding grudges, suspiciousness
- Brings unconditional love, happiness, healthy boundaries, forgiveness
))) ▶ *Australian Bush Flower Essences*

## MULLA MULLA

*Ptilotus atripicifolius*

Mulla mulla is for the personal recovery from shattering experience of burns from heat or fire. This essence reduces the negative effects of fire and the Sun's rays. It is for those with a fear of fire or flames (often from a past life). If this fear is unconscious it will often manifest in a lack of vitality.

### Properties and Uses

- For fear of flames and hot objects, distress associated with exposure to heat and Sun
- Reduces the effects of fire and Sun
- Encourages comfort with fire and heat

## MUSTARD

*Sinapis alba, Brassica nigra*

Mustard is an annual plant cultivated as a spice all over the world. It has been used for centuries as a pungent condiment and healing herb by the Chinese, the Greeks and the Ayur-vedics. Black and white mustards are used for culinary and medicinal purposes; the leaves, flowers,

*LEFT: Molybdenum is an essential trace element found in eggs.*
*BELOW LEFT: A mustard bath may have hidden restorative effects.*
*BELOW RIGHT: Commiphora myrrha (myrrh).*

seeds and oils of the black mustard are used, while only the seeds of the white mustard are useful. Black mustard powder is an important herbal remedy because it draws blood to the surface of the skin quickly, making it 'rubefascient' and warming.

Take care when using mustard seeds as they can burn the skin. Avoid contact with the mucous membrane and with sensitive skin.

## Properties and Uses

- Black mustard and white mustard are warming and can be used to draw infection or congestion away from its source (i.e. in the case of nasal congestion or an abscess)
- Rubefascient qualities make it useful for respiratory and circulatory disorders
- White mustard relieves pain, is a diuretic and an antibiotic
- Mustard flour is an antiseptic and deodorizer
- Mustard oil can be used for pain relief of arthritic conditions and chilblains
- An excellent expectorant and powerful emetic

))))➤ *Homeopathic Remedies*

## MUSTARD

*Synapse arvensis*

The Bach flower remedy mustard is used for dark clouds of gloom or deep, black depression that comes from nowhere. It is like being under a cloud which blocks out the warming rays and optimism of the Sun. There may be no known reason for the feeling, and it may lift just as suddenly as it arrived. While under the dark cloud it is hard to muster any feelings of happiness or hope. All clouds pass and mustard restores hope and the pleasure of living.

## Properties and Uses

- For depression of no known cause and melancholia
- For when thoughts turn inward and life lacks light and pleasure

- Although these attacks seem to come from nowhere there may be a deeply hidden reason; if it happens frequently, look for a cause
- Mustard lightens our mood and gives us faith and hope to keep on going

))))➤ *Bach Flower Remedies, Herbalism*

## MYRRH

*Commiphora myrrha*

Perhaps best known as one of the three gifts brought to the infant Jesus, myrrh was valued in ancient times as an ingredient in embalming preparations, incense and as a medicine. Do not use in high doses or at all during pregnancy.

## Properties and Uses

- Myrrh has an excellent soothing, antiseptic and healing effect on sore or inflamed gums, mouth ulcers, wounds, and cracked or chapped skin
- It can hasten the healing of weepy eczema and because of its anti-fungal properties it can be used as a vaginal wash for thrush or in a footbath for athlete's foot
- Myrrh is also an expectorant and a lung tonic, good for coughs, colds, bronchitis and flu
- It stimulates, tones and soothes the digestive system and is often used for diarrhoea, haemorrhoids and indigestion
- The oil acts a uterine tonic which can be helpful for menstrual irregularities
- Myrrh relieves agitation, calms fears and uncertainties and has a positive, balancing effect on the emotions

))))➤ *Herbalism*

## NAT MUR

*Natrum muriaticum*

Homeopathically, the Nat Mur remedy is made from rock salt, which is formed through the evaporation of salty water, leaving a crusty crystalline solid. The remedy is used to treat a number of conditions from emotional problems to ailments characterized by a discharge. It is also one of the 12 tissue salts.

Nat Mur works well on emotional problems such as distress, restlessness and depression, which tend to occur because of the suppression of other emotions, such as fear and grief. Conditions characterized by secretions or dis-charge, such as colds, catarrh, vaginismus, mouth ulcers, nasal boils, acne and cold sores, and other skin complaints such as hangnails, warts and a cracked lower lip are alleviated. In women, it helps with erratic periods, periods which have stopped due to stress, shock or grief, malaise, swollen ankles before and after a period, and for a dry or sore vagina. Headaches, caused by trauma or exercise; explosive headaches or blinding migraines also respond well.

The Nat Mur type is normally female, with a square or pear-shaped figure and greasy, pale skin. They tend to have dark or sandy hair, and watery, red-rimmed eyes. They are sensitive and often become quiet and introvert. They enjoy the company of others, but tend to be alone.

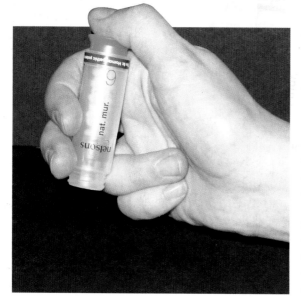

They either love or hate salty food, and prefer sour foods and beer. Children tend to be slow walkers and talkers, small for their age, responsible and diligent, but timid and easily upset although they dislike fuss. They are often prone to headaches and hangnails.

### Properties and Uses

- Relieves anxiety, depression, caused by suppression of emotions, conditions accompanied by secretions or discharge, skin complaints, irregular or absent periods, headaches
- For those who are impatient and easily upset when judged
- For those who are mildly depressed on waking
- For fear of enclosed spaces, crowds, business failure, insanity, death
- Helps worries about losing self-control and being hurt emotionally
- For dislike of the dark, being late, thunderstorms
- For a lower lip that has a centre crack
- For constipation
- For those who feel the cold but dislike heat
- Symptoms improve with fresh air, after sweating and avoiding food, and worsen in the cold, hot weather, sea air, in between 9 a.m. and 11 a.m., after over-exertion and if fussed over

▶▶ *Biochemic Tissue Salts*

## NATUROPATHY

Naturopathy is an umbrella term used in most Western countries to cover a range of therapies which come under the heading of natural medicine. Originally coined by the German pioneer Benedict Lust, naturopathy literally means 'natural treatment' and today its practitioners are generally those trained at specialist colleges in a range of skills that include acupuncture, herbalism, homeopathy, osteopathy, hydrotherapy, massage, nutrition and diet.

Naturopaths believe that four basic components make for good health:

- Clean air
- Clean water
- Clean food from good earth
- Exercise and healthy living

intestines and, according to naturopaths, contribute to toxicity, allergy and poor immunity. Some naturopaths even make use of a special treatment for washing the gut clean – called colonic irrigation.

Naturopaths usually follow three main principles when prescribing any treatment:

- The body has the power to heal itself so treatment should not be given to alleviate symptoms but to support the self-healing mechanism (the body's vital force).
- The symptoms of disease are not part of the disease itself but a sign that the body is striving to eliminate toxins and return to its natural state of balance, or homeostasis.
- As well as being as natural and gentle as possible, all treatments should take into account the mental, emotional and social aspects of a person as well as the physical.

Naturopathy is a philosophy for life rather than a set of inflexible principles. Naturopaths aim to prevent and treat the cause of disease by a system of detailed diagnosis and a wide range of treatments, many of which you must integrate into your lifestyle if you are to achieve lasting good health.

All naturopathic treatments work with some of these elements – and often all of them – to restore health and vitality. Naturopaths believe that infections seldom happen if the body is looked after in the way nature intended and that the body will cure itself of anything as long as it takes in only pure air and water, is kept clean, given the right food and undertakes healthy activity. But they also believe that getting ill is natural and that methods of cure should follow the same natural principles.

So, far from being suppressed, symptoms of illness should be encouraged to come out and the body helped and encouraged to fight back and find its proper balance – or homeostatis – again.

Naturopaths will routinely encourage brief fasting to get over simple infections such as flu and also address the health of the bowels, where important nutrients are absorbed by the bloodstream. Most naturopaths encourage special diets to clear the gut and eliminate the overgrowth of 'unfriendly' bacteria that can colonize the

Naturopathy can help with a wide range of acute and chronic problems, such as anaemia, allergies, arthritis, bronchitis, candida, circulation disorders, constipation, cystitis, eczema and other skin diseases, hangovers, irritable bowel syndrome, migraine, panic attacks, premenstrual syndrome, sinusitis, ulcers and varicose veins. In the case of life-threatening disease, it can improve resistance to infection so there is less risk of complications.

)))▶ **Fasting, Homeopathy, Nutrition, Osteopathy Homeopathy**

*LEFT: The homeopathic remedy* Natrum muriaticum.
*ABOVE: Exercise and healthy living is one of the four basic components that Naturopaths believe will ensure good health.*
*RIGHT: Naturopaths recommend that we should only intake clean water and clean food which has been grown in good soil.*

- Neroli helps to tone the skin and improve elasticity; added to cream or diluted in oil it is used to prevent stretchmarks, scarring, wrinkles and to soothe sensitive skin
- It is a gentle antidepressant and a nervous tonic, perhaps most helpful in treating anxiety, depression, nervous tension and stress-related problems
- As a sedative it can also combat associated insomnia

## NETTLE

*Urtica dioica*

The common stinging nettle – found in the British countryside and many gardens – is often considered a nuisance, but when infused or cooked in soup, it is a useful herbal remedy.

### Properties and Uses

- An iron tonic, mild diuretic, antihistamine, strengthening and styptic
- Useful for iron-deficiency anaemia; nourishing and building, good to take in pregnancy
- Lethargy, weakness, and feelings of heaviness in the body
- Good for nettle rash, allergies to strawberries and insect bites; use as tea and lotion
- Nervous eczema
- Relieves urinary gravel and water retention
- Helpful in arthritis
- Taken with cleavers as a spring tonic

### Key Notes and Dosage

- Leave to infuse for 15 minutes for best effect.
- The tops can be cooked as spinach or made into soup.

## NEGATIVE EMOTIONS

In flower essence therapy, and a variety of other natural therapies, it is believed that negative emotions depress the mind and immune system, repress activity and contribute to ill-health. According to Dr Edward Bach, all are rooted in one or more of the following:

- Fear
- Uncertainty
- Insufficient interest in present circumstances
- Loneliness
- Oversensitivity to influences and ideas
- Despondency or despair
- Overcare for the welfare of others

By addressing negative emotion, it is believed that peace and harmony can exist in the body, improving well-being and preventing and treating illness.

⫸ *Emotional Health, Homeopathy*

## NEROLI

*Citrus aurantium var. amara*

The blossom of the bitter orange tree is used to produce this oil.

### Properties and Uses

- Neroli tones the heart and circulatory system and its carminative and antispasmodic properties can relieve digestive problems such as indigestion, diarrhoea, flatulence and stomach cramps

## NOSODES

Nosodes are homeopathic remedies made from a disease product. Samuel Hahnemann's first nosode was made from scabies and was called psorinum. Later, homeopaths potentized other nosodes, including tuberculinum (from tubercular tissue), carcinosin (from cancer cells), syphilinum (from syphilis) and medorrhinum (from gonorrhea). Nosodes are indicated for constitutional remedies, and should only be prescribed by a homeopathic practitioner.

)))➤ *Homeopathy*

## NUTRITION

Our understanding of vitamins, minerals and other micronutrients, compounds and elements – and their role in our bodies – has improved dramatically over the decades. We now know that 'micronutrition' – or the vitamins, minerals and other health-giving components of our food, such as amino acids, fibre, enzymes and lipids – is crucial to life, and that by manipulating our nutritional intake, we can not only ensure good health and address ailments, but prevent illness and some of the degenerative effects of ageing. Exciting new discoveries related to the nutrient components of our food mean that more than half of us are now taking supplements in one form or another, convinced that diet itself – bearing in mind the stresses on our body and the polluted world in which we live – is inadequate to supply us with our nutritional needs.

In the late-nineteenth century naturopaths drew attention to the use of food and its nutritional elements as medicine, a concept which was not new, but which had not been acknowledged as a therapy in its own right until that time. Naturopaths used nutrition and fasting to cleanse the body, and to encourage its ability to heal itself. As knowledge about food, its make-up, and the effects it has on our body became greater with the development of biochemistry, the first nutritional specialists undertook to treat specific ailments and symptoms with the components of food.

By the middle of the twentieth century, scientists had put together a profile of proteins, carbohydrates and fats, as well as vitamins and minerals, which were essential to life and to health. More than 40 nutrients were uncovered, including 13 vitamins. It was discovered that minerals were needed for body functions, and a new understanding of the body and its biochemistry fed the growing interest in the subject. In the 1960s, doctors began to treat patients with special diets and supplements, prescribed according to individual symptoms, problems and needs. While conventional medical doctors still discussed nutrition in terms of basic food groups, nutritionists were prescribing vitamins in mega-doses. Other elements and compounds were soon identified as necessary to human life, and we are now able to purchase and take substances like amino acids, bee pollen, lipids (such as evening primrose oil and cod-liver oil), seaweeds, acidophilus (healthy bacteria) and dietary enzymes.

Nutrition has changed from being a mainly doctor-led dietary therapy, also called clinical nutrition, into a more profound theory of health based on treating the patient as a whole (holistic health), and looking for deficiencies which may be causing illness which are specific to each individual.

)))➤ *Diet, Herbalism, Minerals, Supplements, Vitamins*

*FAR LEFT: In flower essence therapy, negative emotions arising from anxiety, depression or fear can be overcome with time and treatment.*
*LEFT: Urtica dioica (nettle).*
*BELOW: Good nutrition is guaranteed when all four food groups are represented.*

## NUX VOMICA

 Made from the poisonous nut plant, which contains strychnine, this remedy is normally used for oversensitivity, irritability and digestive problems. It works well for those who bottle up their anger, who are never satisfied, are prone to arguments, dislike having to depend on others and prefer being left alone. It is also used for conditions such as nausea, vomiting, diarrhoea, indigestion, constipation and piles, which may be brought on by the overindulgence of certain foods or due to suppressing the emotions of mental overwork. Other problems it can alleviate include flu, retching coughs, colds with a blocked nose at night and runny nose during the day, chills, headaches which are worse due to mental exertion. In women, it helps with erratic, early or heavy periods, morning sickness, constant urination and labour pain.

The *nux vomica* type is usually male and hyper-sensitive. They have strained, lined faces and usually sallow skin. They are hypercritical, but cannot take criticism from others. They are competitive and enjoy a challenge, being verbally and mentally alert. They are, however, intolerant of others and easily angered. They are disgruntled when ill, and possibly dependent upon stimulants. Children tend to be hyperactive and easily irritated, dislike being contradicted, are prone to tantrums, diligent and competitive, but hate losing, moody on awakening and prone to stomach aches.

### Properties and Uses

- Relieves digestive upsets, oversensitivity and chills
- For fear of insects, failure, crowds and death
- For those who are quarrelsome, critical of others or fastidious
- Alleviates chills
- Reduces sensitivity to light, smell, noise
- For overindulgence of food, alcohol, coffee

- For aching, bursting, burning pains
- Symptoms improve when lying down and after sleep, in warmth and humidity, in the evening, after washing and with pressure, and worsen in cold, windy weather, in the morning, in open air or under the Sun, two hours after food and after mental exhaustion

## OAK

*Quercus robur*

This Bach flower remedy is useful for inappropriate focus and strength. Oak people are strong and brave fighters. They struggle through events and physical illnesses even when there is no hope, and blame themselves when there is no change. When their strength is inappropriate they can exhaust themselves by pushing blindly on in one narrow direction. Strength is a virtue, but it is pointless pushing against an immovable object. Oak helps us surrender, step back, look around and consider different answers.

### Properties and Uses

- Good for people who struggle on, never giving up
- The people who need oak may overwork, and drive themselves aggressively
- They can be obstinate and unless they rest or find another strategy, may exhaust themselves and break down
- Oak restores the true inner strength, which is flexible and adaptable

))))➡ ***Bach Flower Remedies***

## OATS

*Avena sativum*

Oats are a cereal plant, and are both extremely nutritious and useful therapeutically. Oats are one of the best sources of Inositol, which is important for maintaining blood cholesterol levels. Eaten daily, they provide a wealth of excellent effects. Oats do not contain gluten and are therefore appropriate for a gluten-free diet – particularly since they are so nourishing.

### Properties and Uses

- A tonic for general debility, used in the treatment of anorexia, and for convalescence and fatigue
- Lowers blood cholesterol levels
- Helps to control hormonal activity
- Cleansing – internally and externally; may protect against bowel cancer when taken internally
- Extremely rich in B vitamins and minerals
- Antidepressant, and can be used to treat depression, stress and nervous disorders
- Often used in the treatment of addictions
- Eat raw oats to ease constipation
- Oatmeal (unrefined) can be eaten on a regular basis to reduce the effects of stress and nervous disorders; cooked oats will relieve fatigue

- A compress of oatmeal, or an oatmeal bath soothes eczema and other skin conditions
- Boil a tablespoon of oats 275 ml or 10 fl oz of water for several minutes and drain; use as a nerve tonic and for its nourishing properties
- Eat oats daily to lower blood cholesterol and to experience tonic effects

))))➡ *Herbalism*

## OATS (WILD)

*Avena fatua*

A wild grass and the origin of cultivated oats (*Avena sativa*). The whole plant is used and picked while still green; this is called oat straw. Cultivated oats may be substituted. Groats, or oat grains, may also be substituted, although they are not quite as good as wild oats.

### Properties and Uses

- Nourishing and restorative to nerves and reproductive organs; antidepressant and strengthening
- A good remedy for 'keeping going', weakness and nervous exhaustion
- Eases restless sleep from over-excitement
- Use with valerian to ease withdrawal from tranquillisers
- Use with vervain for weakness following illness
- For PMS with scanty periods and cramps, exhaustion after childbirth and when breastfeeding
- For loss of libido in both sexes
- Use with horsetail to strengthen bones in children and in elderly people
- Baths and lotions are very soothing for eczema

### Dosage

- For oats in general buy the tincture. Use 20 drops every two hours when you need to keep going, or one teaspoon three times daily for weakened states.

*FAR LEFT: The homeopathic remedy* nux vomica.
*ABOVE LEFT:* Quercus robur *(oak).*
*LEFT: Cultivated oats (pictured) can be used instead of wild oats.*

## OINTMENTS AND CREAMS

 Ointments and creams made from pure, natural plant products offer one of the most versatile ways to use herbs, and even essential oils and flower essences. Ointments and creams stay on the surface of the skin longer than oils, which helps when there is a skin problem. They can provide a barrier between the skin and the outside environment, which protects and promotes healing. Simple creams and ointments can be made at home, using oils, beeswax and water, or flower waters. Thicker creams and ointments can be made from coconut oil or cocoa butter.

Elderflower & lavender Ointment

Marigold Cream

Comfrey Ointment

))➤ *Aromatherapy, Carrier Oils*

## OLIVE

*Olea europœa*

Olive, a Bach flower remedy, is used to treat extreme fatigue of mind, body or spirit. People in need of olive feel totally exhausted in every way. Life is hard and without pleasure. They feel that they have no more strength and at times hardly know how they manage to keep going. They burn the candle at both ends and become too tired to even think. They may depend on others for help. Olive helps people relax and switch off so that the simple things in life can be enjoyed. It can help ease overwhelming fatigue and the despair that often accompanies it.

### Properties and Uses

- Olive is for all exhaustion, physical and mental tiredness; exhaustion can be so profound that life loses its interest and spark
- Olive helps restore vitality by helping people to relax and take a more balanced attitude towards life, to allow quality time for unwinding, rest and spiritual renewal

))➤ *Bach Flower Remedies*

## OLIVE OIL

*Olea europea*

The leaves of the olive tree are used therapeutically as well as the oil from the fruit.

### Properties and Uses

- An excellent source of vitamin E; high in mono-unsaturated fats and has a high energy value; it does not contain any minerals
- Olive oil has a beneficial effect on the circulatory and nervous systems; it also benefits the digestive system
- May reduce the risk of circulatory diseases
- Beneficial to those suffering from hyperacidity as it reduces the level of gastric secretions
- The leaves of the olive are used to treat high blood pressure, stress and abrasions
- The oil can help in the treatment of constipation and peptic ulcers; it is also useful for dry skin and hair, particularly for the treatment of a dry, flaky scalp
- A useful carrier oil for aromatherapy essential oils

))➤ *Aromatherapy, Essential Oils, Nutrition*

## ONION

*Allium cepa*

The bulb of the onion is used in cooking and medicinally; like garlic, it warms the body and stimulates the circulation. Onions have long been considered the mainstay of every household remedy chest.

### Properties and Uses

- Onions are expectorant, antibacterial and diuretic
- Its stimulating effect aids in the secretion of digestive juices
- Onion juice has been used to treat infected wounds, amoebic dysentery, and at one time, juice applied to the ear was said to cure deafness!

*LEFT: Non-chemical, natural creams and ointments.*

*BELOW LEFT: Allium cepa (onion), the mainstay of any self-respecting household remedy chest.*

*BELOW RIGHT: An organic farmer proudly shows his produce.*

- May be used directly on the skin for natural relief from burns; simply place slices of raw onion on the burnt skin, or apply a homemade lotion of onion juice mixed with salt; this preparation is also effective for insect bites and stings
- For an antibiotic treatment, peel and eat (raw or cooked) one quarter of one sweet white onion, two to four times a day; the onion must be chewed, crushed, chopped or bruised to access its antibiotic effects
- Onions cause the body to 'weep', which releases toxins
- Onion increases circulation and can relax muscles
- Helps to reduce serum cholesterol after a fatty meal
- May provide some protection against cancer
- Mix onion juice with honey to relieve the symptoms of cold
- Onion poultices are used to treat bronchitis and can also help in the treatment of acne and boils
- Use a poultice of roasted onion for earache

)))**➤** *Homeopathy*

## ORGANIC

In 1995, the National Organic Standards Board (NOSB) in the US defined organic as follows: 'Organic is an ecological production management system that promotes and enhances biodiversity, biological cycles, and soil biological activity. It is based on minimal use of off-farm inputs and on management practices that restore, maintain and enhance ecological harmony.'

When you purchase organic foods and products, you are supporting a complete agriculture system that will affect the future of the world around us. If that sounds idealistic, it is not. Supporters of organic farming have emerged as a powerful voice against the introduction and use of farming methods that can damage health, wildlife, the environment and even the planet. It is more than just healthy eating and humane farming – it involves sustainable production and accountability. It is this all-encompassing approach that has drawn millions of advocates from around the world.

Organic produce is grown with no synthetic chemical pesticides, no synthetic chemical fertilisers and with great attention to the health of the soils, animals and eco-systems. Organic production has the following benefits:

- Reduces the amount of toxic and persistent chemicals in our food supply. This will have a dramatic effect on overall health.
- Uses practices that eliminate polluting chemicals and reduces nitrogen leaching, thus protecting and conserving our water resources.
- Protects the health of future generations by creating long-term solutions to agricultural problems. The choices we make today will have a dramatic impact in the future.
- Encourages the growth and protection of rural life.
- Creates a safer, healthier food supply.
- Improves the quality of the soil.
- Creates healthier habitats for humans and wildlife. Organic agriculture places the balance of the ecosystem at the top of the priority list.
- Preserves a true economy. Organic food may seem to cost more, but conventional farming costs society much more in terms of environmental and health costs. Choose organic whenever possible.

)))**➤** *Diet, Herbalism*

## OSTEOPATHY

Osteopathy, like chiropractic, is a manipulative therapy based on the belief that the skeleton and organ systems are dependent upon one another, and therefore body functions will only work effectively if body structure is properly aligned. Misalignment of the spine and skeleton can cause organs to dysfunction and impairs the circulation of blood and lymph.

Most osteopaths will work on posture, joints and muscles, not just to correct structural problems, but because structural integrity also affects internal organs and tissue. Structural disorders can also be affected by unhealthy emotional problems, especially in the case of recurring conditions. Osteopaths work on the soft tissue of the body using a specific type of manipulation.

Osteopaths believe that we function as a complete working system – our body structure, organs, systems, mind and emotions are all interrelated and mutually interdependent. Consequently, problems that affect the structural body upset the balance of the body generally. Similarly, internal problems can reveal themselves in the body's structure as it adapts to accommodate pain, discomfort or disease. By manipulating the body structure, osteopaths aim to restore health and balance in the whole person, not just at the site of pain.

Much of osteopathic practice focuses on easing muscular tension, which does more than simply alleviate pain and stiffness. The osteopathic belief that a relaxed muscle is a well-functioning muscle is based on the physio-

*BELOW LEFT: Osteopathy is a type of manipulative therapy which operates around the central belief that skeletal structure and organ position work in connection with each other and so the two must be perfectly aligned.*
*RIGHT: Petroselinum crispum (parsley).*
*BELOW RIGHT: Pogostemon cablin (patchouli).*

logical fact that muscles use up an enormous amount of the body's energy when they contract. Stress, either mental or physical, can cause muscles to contract, wasting energy and making the muscles less elastic so that they are more prone to damage. Tense muscles can also impede the circulation of blood and lymph which flow through them. By relaxing tight muscles these important fluids can flow freely, allowing blood to carry nutrients and oxygen to where they are needed and enabling waste-carrying lymph to drain them away. The ribs and diaphragm are also surrounded by muscles. Work in this area can improve existing respiratory conditions such as asthma and chronic bronchitis.

Only when the body is able to work efficiently is it able to attain optimum health and well-being, enabling it to fight off illness and disease, and using its own resources to heal itself.

⫸ *Manipulative Therapies, Natural Therapies, Naturopathy*

## PARSLEY

*Petroselinum crispum*

Native to the eastern Mediterranean, this popular herb is cultivated worldwide. The leaves, seeds and roots are used for medicinal purposes.

### Properties and Uses

- Used as a diuretic, expectorant, emmenagogue, carminative, antispasmodic and hypotensive remedy
- The essential oil is obtained from the leaves and the seeds, and is used in aromatherapy
- Parsley is a tonic in its effect on the blood vessels and is sometimes used externally in the treatment of haemorrhoids
- Applied as a compress to bruises, parsley helps to shrink the broken blood vessels below the skin
- The principle action of parsley is as a diuretic, and is used in the treatment of urinary tract problems, in particular kidney and bladder stones

- It is a cell regenerator, good for ageing skins and promoting wound healing
- Acts as a diuretic
- Often recommended for cellulite and as a general tonic

**Caution**
- Keep all essential oils out of children's reach

## PAW PAW
*Carica papaya*

Paw Paw is used for the assimilation and integration of new ideas and information, especially where there is a tendency to feel overwhelmed by the quality and quantity of that information. A feature of this plant is its very narrow stem which, at the top, branches into a mass of foliage to bear large and ponderous fruits. This essence should be used when one is unable to solve a problem. It will activate the 'higher self', where we have the answer to all our problems. It will ease the burden of problems as it activates the intuitive processes to provide solutions.

**Properties and Uses**
- For people who feel overwhelmed, and are unable to resolve problems or are burdened by decisions
- Helps improve access to the 'higher self' for problem-solving and the assimilation of new ideas
- Brings calmness and clarity

)))➤ *Australian Bush Flower Essences*

**Caution**
- Do not use during pregnancy in medicinal dosage

## PATCHOULI
*Pogostemon cablin*

Patchouli is the aromatic oil extracted from a south-east Asian shrub of the mint family. It has many uses, and is especially pleasant when used as part of a blend.

**Properties and Uses**
- An important antidepressant, nervous tonic and reputed to be an aphrodisiac, patchouli is valued in treating depression, anxiety, nervous exhaustion, lack of interest in sex and stress-related problems
- It is astringent, antiviral, antiseptic and anti-inflammatory, good for cracked skin and open pores; it is also effective for acne, eczema and dermatitis
- Its fungicidal and deodorant actions make it one of the best choices for treating dandruff and fungal infections on the skin

## PEACH KERNEL OILS

A popular carrier oil, peach kernel is rich and nourishing, and is thus good for dry and ageing skins. It is a good source of vitamin E, and helps to encourage healing.

))))▶ *Carrier Oils, Massage*

## PEPPERMINT

*Mentha piperita*

One of the most popular herb teas in the world, the herb peppermint is easily grown in the garden.

### Properties and Uses

• Digestive, carminative, antispasmodic, mild stimulant, emmenagogue
• Cooling on the skin
• For indigestion, colic, wind, nausea, vomiting, depressed appetite, period pains and gall-bladder pain; a couple of drops of the essential oil in hot water, or sucking a strong peppermint sweet is also effective
• Use with elderflower and yarrow for colds, sinus problems and blocked nose; inhale the steam as you drink
• A strong tea, used as a lotion, is good for hot, itchy skin problems

### Dosage

• Take freely. A small amount of peppermint may be added to most herb teas for flavour.

))))▶ *Aromatherapy*

## PEPPERMINT

*Mentha piperita*

Peppermint is best known as a remedy for digestive problems. The essential oil is both a tonic and a stimulant, with a particular affinity for nervous disorders, nervous vomiting, flatulence and colitis.

### Properties and Uses

• Refreshing and stimulating, peppermint tones and settles the digestive system – it relieves indigestion, flatulence, spasms, diarrhoea, nausea, stomach cramps and travel sickness; it also helps tone the stomach, liver, intestines, and the nervous system
• It is a valuable expectorant in the treatment of bronchitis, colds and flu, and it can reduce fevers by inducing sweating and cooling the body
• Peppermint is a painkiller, beneficial for toothache, headaches and some migraines
• It relieves itching, is a useful antiseptic for acne and congested skin, and is an emergency remedy for shock
• Muscle and mental fatigue are relieved by peppermint

### Caution

• Do not use during pregnancy. Never use peppermint oil undiluted, as it can provoke a reaction. Avoid using if you are taking homeopathic remedies, as it acts as an antidote.

))))▶ *Herbalism*

## PERSONAL REMEDIES

Every flower essence has specific properties so you will need to discover which is the most effective for you. Often a blend is the most effective, and your choice of remedies will depend upon your overwhelming emotional characteristics at the time. This forms the basis of your personal remedy. You will need a 30 ml glass amber dropper bottle, 30 ml of spring water (or 10 ml brandy) and 20 ml of spring water.

*LEFT: Mentha piperita (peppermint).*
*ABOVE RIGHT: Citrus aurantium var. amara (petitgrain).*
*RIGHT: Every combination of flower remedies can be personalised or tailored to meet the individual needs of specific patients. These personal remedies can be taken singly or in combination with each other.*

Decide which remedies are most applicable. Usually between one and six is enough. If you think you need several then simplify to four, covering immediate issues and check again in a few weeks.

Put four drops of each remedy into a clean 30 ml amber glass dropper bottle. This is the standard amount, but read the label as occasionally seven drops are used. If the remedies are to be used within a week, fill the bottle with clean spring water. If the remedies are to taken for a prolonged period add 10 ml of brandy and then fill with spring water.

The standard dose is to take four drops, under the tongue, four times a day. At times of crisis two drops can be put into a glass of water (or, in an emergency, any drink) and sipped as needed. If, for any reason, it is impossible to take anything by mouth, put the drops on your skin or in your bath water.

## PETITGRAIN

*Citrus aurantium var. amara*

Petitgrain is often regarded as a cheaper alternative to neroli. It is distilled from the leaves and twigs of the bitter orange tree, whereas neroli comes from the blossom.

### Properties and Uses

- Petitgrain can refresh or relax, depending on the oils with which it is blended
- Strengthens and tones the nervous system, and as such it can calm many stress-related problems such as nervous exhaustion and insomnia
- Feelings of apathy, irritability, mild depression, anxiety, loneliness and pessimism, can all get a lift from petitgrain's antidepressant properties
- This oil also has a tonic effect during convalescence or when you are feeling run down; it has a notable antispasmodic effect and helps to tone the digestive system, relieving flatulence and indigestion
- Petitgrain is a deodorant, sometimes used to control excessive perspiration; it is also used to control the overproduction of sebum in the skin and has gentle antiseptic properties, making it ideal for many greasy skin and scalp conditions, especially acne and greasy hair

))))➤ *Neroli*

## PHENYLALANINE

L-Phenylalanine is an essential amino acid, necessary for a number of biochemical processes, including the synthesis of neurotransmitters in the brain. It is said to promote sexual arousal and to release hormones that help to control appetite.

The best sources of phenylalanine are proteins, cheese, almonds, peanuts, sesame seeds and soya.

### Properties and Uses

- May help to alleviate depression
- May help to control addictive behaviour
- Encourages mental alertness
- Promotes sexual arousal
- Reduces hunger and cravings for food

### Dosage

- L-Phenylalanine is usually available in 500 mg doses. Take on an empty stomach for best effect and do not take with protein.

### Caution

- If you suffer from skin cancer, do not take L-Phenylalanine. People with high blood pressure should only take supplementary L-Phenylalanine with their doctor's supervision. It is not suitable for use with monoamine oxidase inhibitors (MAOI) antidepressants. Pregnant women should not take this amino acid.

))))➤ *Amino Acids*

## PHOSPHORUS

Phosphorus is a mineral which is essential to the structure and function of the body. It is present in the body as phosphates, and in this form aids the process of bone mineralization and helps to create the structure of the bone.

Phosphorus is also essential for communication between cells, and energy production. Phosphorus appears in many foods and deficiency is rare. Because of its role in strengthening our bones, we should eat twice as much calcium as phosphorus.

The best sources of phosphorus are yeast, dried milk and milk products, wheatgerm, hard cheeses, canned fish, nuts, cereals and eggs.

### Properties and Uses

- Forms bones and teeth
- Produces energy
- Burns sugar for energy
- Acts as a co-factor for many enzymes and activates B-complex vitamins

- Increases endurance
- Fights fatigue
- Forms ribonucleic acid (RNA) and deoxyribonucleic acid (DNA)

### Key Notes
- Phosphorous deficiency usually accompanies deficiency in potassium, magnesium and zinc, so ensure a good multivitamin and mineral supplement has all four.
- Supplementation should only be undertaken with supervision.

### Caution
- Phosphorous can be toxic at dosages or intake above 1 g per day, in some cases causing diarrhoea and the calcification of organs and soft tissues, making the body unable to absorb iron, calcium, magnesium and zinc.

)))▶ *Minerals*

## PHOSPHORUS

Our bodies need phosphorus for the healthy functioning of our teeth, bones, bodily fluids and deoxyribonucleic acid (DNA). In conventional medicine it has been used to treat conditions as diverse as measles and malaria. Homeopathically, it is mainly given to those suffering from anxiety and digestive disorders.

Phosphorus is used to treat symptoms such as exhaustion, insomnia, nerves which are caused by underlying stress, anxiety and fears, for instance, due to exam pressure, overwork or fears of dying. Other problems that can be helped include digestive problems such as nausea and vomiting due to coughing, stress or food poisoning; cravings for certain foods and pressure in the stomach; symptoms of poor circulation such as cold or over-heated fingers and toes; excessive bleeding, such as bleeding gums, nose bleeds and heavy periods; respiratory problems such as acute bronchitis or asthma; difficulty in breathing; tight chest; pneumonia; dry, tickly coughs and red-tinged phlegm.

The phosphorus type is normally tall and lean, with fine hair and pale skin that blushes easily. They tend to be intelligent, outgoing and are sometimes artistic, as well as being open and affectionate. They can be enthusiastic, but not for sustained periods. They are imaginative and love attention. Children tend to be tall for their age, smooth-featured, but blush easily; they like company but becomes restless and nervous; they are often perceptive, artistic and affectionate, but dislike homework, the dark and thunderstorms.

### Properties and Uses
- Relieves anxieties, fears, digestive complaints, circulatory and bleeding conditions, respiratory problems
- Enhances mental awareness
- For those who are nervous under pressure
- Good for people who tend to bottle things up
- Relieves indifference to family and friends when ill
- For fear of illness and death
- Weak areas include digestive organs, circulation, nervous system, the left side of the body, liver
- Treats bleeding, such as nosebleeds
- For respiratory problems
- For headaches
- Symptoms improve in fresh air, after sleeping, when touched and when lying on the right side, and worsen in the morning and evenings, after mental or physical exertion, after hot food or drinks, when lying on the left side and in thunderstorms

*ABOVE LEFT: Phenylalanine is an essential amino acid found in most protein-rich foods such as walnuts and bananas.*
*LEFT: Phosphorus keeps our bones and teeth healthy but it is also known to relieve headaches.*
*BELOW: Dairy products such as hard cheese are the best source of phosphorous.*

## PHYTOCHEMICALS

Phytochemicals are literally plant chemicals or antioxidants that occur naturally in most fruit and vegetables. These have a major impact on our body systems, helping to promote health and prevent disease. They are not nutrients as such, in that they are not essential, but they are biologically active compounds that play a vital role in the biochemistry of our bodies. Phytochemicals cannot be stored in the body, so must be eaten regularly, hence the importance of a diet rich in fresh fruit and vegetables. There are over 100 phyto-chemicals now identified. Here are just some of their main properties:

- Capsaicin, found in hot peppers, helps to protect DNA from damage
- Allium, found in garlic, onions, leeks, chives and shallots, helps to protect against cancer and has a beneficial effect on the immune system
- Bioflavonoids act as potent antioxidants, binding to toxic metals and ensuring their elimination from the body
- Isothiocyanates and indoles, found in cruciferous vegetables, including cabbage, broccoli, cress, radishes and turnips, have been linked to a lower risk of cancer, particularly of the colon

## PILLS/TABLETS

Many supplements come in tablet form and these are the most practical for many people because they can be easily stored and will keep for a long time. Check the label to see what is added to your tablets in the form of binders or fillers, which are added to preserve or bulk out the active ingredient.

'Chelated' is a term which will appear on mineral supplements, and it means combined with amino acids to make assimilation more efficient. Most nutritionists recommend chelated minerals because they are three to five times more effective.

Time-release formulas are created with a process that allows them to be released into the body over an eight to 10-hour period. These are particularly useful for water-soluble vitamins, any excess of which is excreted within two or three hours of taking the supplement. Studies show that time-release formulas are most effective, and provide stable blood levels during the day and night.

*LEFT: Phytochemicals can be found at submolecular level in green vegetables, such as cabbage.*
*ABOVE: Making homeopathic pills at an alternative medicine pharmacy.*
*RIGHT: Pinus peuce (Macedonian pine).*

## Properties and Uses

- Inhalations of pine are wonderful for colds, catarrhal conditions including hayfever, and sore throats
- The oil, which is expectorant, antiseptic and anti-viral, helps to clear chest infections, sinuses and ease breathing
- Pine stimulates the circulation and helps to relieve rheumatic and muscular aches, pains and stiffness
- Pine is also deodorizing and insecticidal; it is good for excessive perspiration and to clear lice and scabies
- Its refreshing aroma dispels apathy, relieves mental fatigue, nervous exhaustion and stress-related problems

## Caution

- Use only small amounts in the bath or in massage. Do not use if you have an allergic skin condition. Always check the source of your oil as oils are distilled from several species of pine, some of which are unsuitable for use in aromatherapy.

))))➡ *Flower Essences*

Herbal remedies take this form less frequently since it is more difficult to mix more than one herb and to control the quantities. Some of the more common remedies will be available from professional herbalists or health-food shops, or you can press your own with a domestic press.

))))➡ *Nutrition, Supplements*

## PINE

*Pinus sylvestris*

The Arabs, Greeks and Romans all made use of the medicinal properties of the pine tree, while Native Americans are believed to have used pine to prevent scurvy and infestation with lice and fleas.

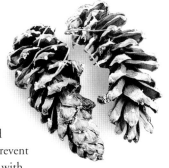

## PINE

*Pinus sylvestris*

Pine is a very specific remedy for those who blame themselves and are suffering from feelings of self-reproach. Even when successful, they are never content with the results and always feel that they could have done better. Pine people feel the need to control all aspects of their lives and have a personal script of high ideals. They burden themselves with duty and a personal responsibility for the world.

## Key Notes

- For people burdened with self-reproach and guilt – frequently groundless. They may carry the blame for others' actions.
- For people who have self-punishing or self-destructive behaviour.
- For people with masochistic tendencies.
- Pine helps us understand that responsibility is the ability to respond. If we respond honestly and freely then there can be no blame, and we can move on.

))))➡ *Bach Flower Remedies*

## POLARITY THERAPY

Polarity therapy is the science of balancing opposite energies within the body to promote mental, physical and emotional health. It is a combination of Eastern and Western approaches to health. The name 'polarity' was chosen to convey the image of the body as a living magnet where electromagnetic energy flows between its positive and negative poles.

According to polarity therapy, disease can go by many names, but ultimately the only cause of disease is blocked energy. Energy can become blocked by internal emotional stresses or by external factors such as poor diet and lack of energy. Once unblocked, free-flowing energy can again restore mind and body to health.

The therapy is based on the belief that the body is governed by the opposite poles of positive and negative, similar to the Chinese philosophy of the opposites of yin and yang. Energy is seen as electromagnetic, so in order for it to flow around the body it must have poles to flow between, just as the Earth's electromagnetic waves flow between the North and South Poles. The flow of energy is governed by five energy centres in the body, called *chakras. Chakras* are like energy substations that are constantly working to replenish stores of energy and generate it through the whole person.

Each *chakra* governs the energy needed for the health of that body part, but is also responsible for emotional patterns, so that the flow of energy affects the mind, body and emotions.

The role of polarity therapy is not simply to unblock the energy, but to help you resolve the problems that created the blockages in the first place. To do this the polarity therapist uses four techniques:

- Bodywork – using touch on specific parts of the body to balance, remove blocks and improve vitality
- Awareness skills – teaching that shock and overwhelming situations can be held in the body's energy, causing blockage; therapists help you work through issues to prevent energy from being affected
- Diets – prescribed according to your specific type and characteristics; detoxification, to unblock and stimulate energy, is often advised, as is maintaining an acid/alkaline balance
- Exercise – stretching postures are a series of yoga-type postures for each *chakra* that are designed to release stagnant energy

## POTASSIUM

Potassium is one of the most important minerals in our body, working with sodium and chloride to form electrolytes, essential body salts which make up our body fluids. Potassium is crucial for body functioning, playing a role in nerve conduction, heartbeat, energy production, synthesis of nucleic acids, and proteins and muscle contraction.

Sweating can cause a loss of potassium, as does chronic diarrhoea and diuretics. People taking certain drugs, including corticosteroids, high-dose penicillin and laxatives, may have potassium deficiencies, and symptoms of deficiency can include vomiting, abdominal distension, muscular weakness, loss of appetite, low blood pressure and intense thirst.

The best sources of potassium are fresh fruit, particulary bananas, and vegetables.

## Properties and Uses
- Activates enzymes which control energy production
- Prevents and treats high blood pressure
- May protect against stroke
- Improves athletic performance
- May help treat and prevent cancer
- Maintains water balance within cells
- Stabilizes internal structure of cells
- Acts with sodium to conduct nerve impulses

## Dosage
- Eat more fresh fruit and vegetables to increase potassium intake. Diuretic users and those in a hot climate may need up to 1.5 g in supplementary potassium daily.
- Take with zinc and magnesium for best effect.

## Caution
- In excess (doses above 17 g), potassium may cause muscular weakness and mental apathy, eventually stopping the heart.

)))➤ *Minerals*

## POTENCY

Homeopathy uses preparations containing infinitesimal amounts of the original substance, such as *belladonna*, salt or even snake venom. For example: to make the 6 potency (properly called the 6 centesimal potency) of lycopodium, one part of the wolf's claw plant is added to 99 parts of milk sugar or alcohol and succussed, and this process is repeated 6 times. A 30 potency has gone through the same process 30 times. Although a 30 potency has been diluted more than the 6 potency, the succussion has made it more powerful and it is usually taken for more serious problems than a 6 potency. (The number on the label tells you just how many dilutions the remedy has been through.)

*FAR LEFT: Polarity therapy, like yoga (pictured) endeavours to balance opposite energies existing within the body to generate better health.*
*NEAR LEFT: Potassium levels are generally high in all types of fruit, but especially in bananas.*
*ABOVE RIGHT: The late nineteenth-century herb and plant press at the Homeopathic Central Pharmacy of Dr Wilmar Schwabe in Leipzig, Austria.*

Remedies can also be diluted according to the decimal scale i.e. one part to nine. In this case, there will be an 'x' next to the number, e.g. 6x.

Homeopaths prescribe potencies based on a wide range of factors, including how long you have had the condition, what the person's energy and the energy of the condition are like, how well the remedy fits the symptom picture, and whether they believe the overriding factors are emotional, mental or physical.

- 6C dilutions are best for physical conditions, and you can confidently self-prescribe these for acute conditions
- 30C dilutions are prescribed for physical conditions that have a good emotional symptom picture; again, these are safe to use for self-prescription
- 200C is prescribed when there are strong physical and emotional factors present
- 1M and above is prescribed when the condition has a strong emotional base

## Caution
- Do not play around with the higher potencies, particularly those that have a dramatic effect on mental or emotional health.

## POWDERS

Many herbs are ground into a powder for external and internal use. This is a versatile form in which to take herbs, as it allows you to control the dosage, and also to make external applications, such as blending with a mild talcum for treating athlete's foot, using as a deodorant, creating a paste for teeth, wounds, gums or lesions, and adding to other herbal concoctions. Herbs in this form can be added to food or drinks, or put into capsules for easier consumption and convenience. You can make your own powder by crushing dried plant parts with a mortar and pestle, or chop them finely in a food processor or coffee-grinder.

Many supplements also come in powder form, which will usually provide you with extra potency, with no binders or additives, which is useful for people with allergies or those who find it difficult to swallow a tablet. Powders are particularly useful for children – sprinkle a little powder in their breakfast juice, or stir it into some yoghurt.

))))➤ *Nutrition*

## PRACTITIONER

Natural practitioners, such as aromatherapists, herbalists, and homeopaths address each case on an individual basis. On the basis of a full physical and emotional assessment, you will be given treatment that works to balance your body's vital force, or energy. Natural medicine is holistic, which means that it takes into consideration your mind, body and spirit, not just the physical symptoms of disease that present themselves when you are ill.

When you visit a natural health practitioner you will be expected to give details of everything about you and your health in order for your therapist to make an informed decision about treatment. Your symptoms will not be treated, rather, their root cause will be investigated and dealt with. You can occasionally expect your symptoms to become worse before they get better, which is a sign that your body is res-ponding to treatment and beginning to help itself. The basis of all natural therapies

is that they stimulate your body to heal itself.

The success of alternative therapies can be enormously dependent on a good practitioner–patient relationship, and your choice of a therapist is as important as the choice of therapy. Take your time, check the therapist's qualifications, ask for recommendations from friends, your doctor or another therapist, and do not commit yourself until you are sure you will have a rapport. Because you will be imparting a great deal of information about yourself to the therapist, who must be able to take it on board and diagnose and treat on that basis, you must feel comfortable with any practitioner, and feel able to be honest about yourself and your complaint.

Always choose a practitioner who is qualified and registered with the appropriate governing body. You can ask to see evidence of this. Try to get a referral or a rec-ommendation from a friend, your doctor, another therapist, or from a governing body. Then you can be sure that you are placing yourself in the hands of someone who is capable of doing the job correctly.

## PSYCHOTHERAPY

The mind and emotions are regarded as an integral and vitally important part of total health. All complementary therapies promote the idea of the body as

*ABOVE: LEFT Gingibar officinale (root ginger) ground into powder form.*
*ABOVE: A Chinese herbalist practitioner.*
*RIGHT: Pulsatilla homeopathic tablets.*

a whole, and that treating it holistically will result in overall health and well-being. Psychological influences, such as stress, worry, anxiety and depression can have an enormous impact on health, and have been implicated in a number of conditions. Psychotherapies aim to address the parts of the body that some Western medicine has yet to reach successfully.

There are a number of types of psychotherapies (properly known as psychological therapies), including behavioural, analytical, humanistic, integrative and even counselling.

Many therapies adopt a form of psychotherapy in their consultation and in further sessions, as a part of treatment. For example, naturopaths approach mental health from the perspective of removing destructive emotions. They are not equipped to deal with serious mental illness such as schizophrenia, but can pinpoint and eliminate the origins of psychosomatic illnesses, mostly through counselling and the use of relaxation techniques.

)))▶ *Counselling, Naturopathy*

## PULSATILLA
*Pulsatilla nigricans*

This homeopathic remedy is made from the pasque flower, or windflower. Pulsatilla can help relieve a number of digestive problems, such as rich food causing lack of sleep; a tight stomach on waking in the morning; bad reactions to rich or fatty food, particularly pork, heaviness under breastbone after eating; cravings for sweet foods and a rumbling stomach. In women, lack of periods or late periods, particularly if due to shock or illness, thick, stinging discharge and menopausal problems, all of which tend to be accompanied by crying and depression, can be helped. Moodiness, depression and fears of being alone can also be treated. Ailments characterised by excessive discharge or secretions, such as conjunctivitis, catarrh with yellow phlegm, sinusitis and a runny nose, can also be alleviated.

### Properties and Uses
- Relieves digestive disorders, gynaecological conditions, emotional traumas
- For people who avoid confrontations
- To treat depression
- For the self-conscious
- For those who cry easily
- For fear of being alone, the dark, insanity and death
- Treats ailments characterized by discharge
- For gynaecological conditions
- For digestive problems
- For a bad taste in the mouth, dry mouth
- Relieves aching joints
- Symptoms improve in fresh air, with gentle movement and with sympathy, and worsen in the heat, after eating rich foods, after lengthy standing, when lying on the left side and in the evening
- The pulsatilla type is normally female, and fair, with blue eyes. They tend to blush easily, be on the plump side, and are kind, popular and good-natured. While they lack assertiveness and tend to do anything to avoid confrontation, they are easily influenced by others and often led by their emotions. They are compassionate and concerned about distress in others. Children tend to be either small and fair with delicate features, easy-going, affectionate yet shy, blushing easily; or darker-haired, small, listless, needing reassurance and attention, but slow in returning it. Both types are scared of the dark, dislike weather changes, particularly the cold, which can trigger ailments, and are prone to colds.

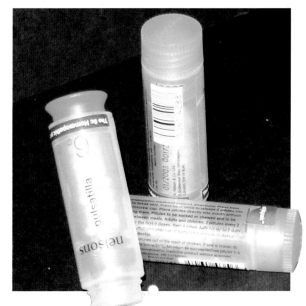

## RADIONICS

Radionics is based on the belief that the vital energy, or life force, of humans can become blocked, stagnant and thrown into a state of disharmony by infection, stress, pollution, injury, disease, psychological states, malnutrition and poor hygiene. Practitioners believe that radionics open up the channels of energy so that it flows freely, allowing the body to heal, and reversing the cause of the illness. They claim that every person's energy patterns or rhythms are as unique to them as their fingerprints, and every part of their body, down to cellular level, reflects these vibrations. When illness or disease causes these rhythms to become unbalanced or interrupted, the energy pattern is altered. This altered pattern can be read from any part of the body and treated by sending messages (in a kind of numerical form, with the use of a machine) to the body in order that it may heal itself through a restored flow of energy.

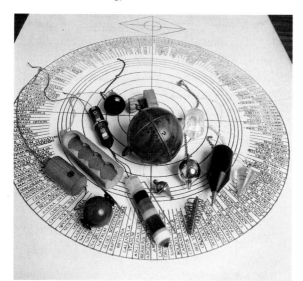

A 'witness', which may be a lock of hair, a drop of blood or a fingernail clipping from the patient, is given to the therapist, who places it in a 'black box' containing various magnets and resistors which will pick up its energy rhythms. Dials on the box are operated until the practitioner senses a resistance, which means that the machine has captured the same energy patterns or rhythm as the witness. From there, treatment involves sending coded messages back to the patient, through the box,

correcting imbalances discovered through the initial analysis. Effectively, the healing energies are transmitted to the patient through the practitioner and the black box. The most remarkable part of the therapy is that there is no need for the patient to be anywhere near the machine for healing to take place. The effects have been felt by patients several thousand miles away. Some radionic practitioners also suggest colour, music, herbs, homeopathy and osteopathy to correct imbalances.

)))▶ *Energy, Homeopathy, Osteopathy*

## RASPBERRY

*Rubus idaeus*

The leaves of the common raspberry plant are used in herbal medicine, and they have a long tradition of use during pregnancy.

### Properties and Uses

- Astringent, tonic, parturient
- Raspberry leaves strengthen and tone the tissue of the womb, assisting contractions and checking any haemorrhage during labour
- As an astringent it may be used in a wide range of cases, including diarrhoea, leucorrhoea and other loose conditions

*LEFT: Instruments used in radionics.*
*ABOVE: Rubus idaeus (raspberry)*
*RIGHT: Aeschulus carnea (red chestnut).*

- Valuable in the easing of mouth problems such as mouth ulcers, bleeding gums and inflammations; as a gargle it will help sore throats; raspberry is also very rich in iron and calcium

### Key Notes and Dosage
- Infusion: pour a cup of boiling water on to two teaspoonfuls of the dried herb and let infuse for 10–15 minutes. This may be drunk freely.
- Tincture: take 2–4 ml of the tincture three times a day.
- Do not take during the first three months of pregnancy, unless under medical supervision.

### RDA
Three sets of figures are used to assess the adequacy of diets for the population. In the United States, a Food and Nutrition Board has been established for the purpose of determining vitamin and mineral requirements. This board is composed of distinguished scientists and nutritionists and is under the auspices of the National Academy of Sciences. Since 1940 the Board has periodically prepared a brochure listing the Recommended Dietary Allowances (RDA) of vitamins and other nutrients, based on existing knowledge.

These allowances are intended as a guide for all persons involved in planning food supplies and in the interpretation of food consumption levels. The RDA figures, however, are estimates based on the present state of knowledge of the needs of most human beings; particular requirements will be less or more, depending on numerous individual factors such as genetics, environmental influences, and presence or absence of disease processes.

In Europe and the UK, the Reference Nutrient Intake (RNI) is used, which represents the amount of a nutrient that is deemed by the government to be sufficient to meet the needs of almost all healthy people – even those with higher than average needs. In the UK, this figure is roughly the same as the old RDA (Recommended Daily Amount), which was formerly the only set of figures used.

The Estimated Average Requirement (EAR) is the amount of a nutrient that is considered to be sufficient to meet the needs of an average, healthy person.

The Lower Reference Nutrient Intake (LRNI), represents the amount of a nutrient that is almost certain to be inadequate. For example, the average intake of the trace element selenium in the UK falls well below this figure.

))))➤ *Minerals, Supplements, Vitamins*

### RED CHESTNUT
*Æsculus carnea*

Red chestnut, a Bach flower remedy, is for those who suffer fear and anxiety for others. They may have forsaken worrying about themselves, but project their fear on to their loved ones. They often anticipate that some unfortunate accident or illness (the worst scenario) will befall friends and relations and ceaselessly worry. This inappropriate fear limits the social interactions of both the sufferer and their loved ones.

Red chestnut helps us realize that the anxiety is a projection of personal fear. It brings the calm necessary to be sensitive to the real problems and concerns of our loved ones and to give empathetic support.

### Properties and Uses
- For fear that something awful may happen to loved ones
- For the over-fussing, possessive and those who are intrusive into others' lives
- Calms unnecessary fear, over-worry, even hypochondria on another person's behalf
- Red chestnut encourages calm and rationality – a response based on sensitivity to others and not projected fear

))))➤ *Bach Flower Remedies*

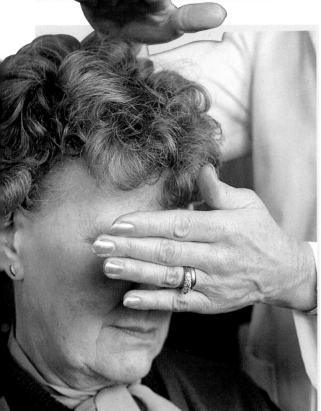

## REISHI MUSHROOMS

*Ganoderma lucidum*

Reishi mushrooms have been popular for centuries in the Far East, where they are believed to promote longevity. These mushrooms, like shiitake mushrooms, are used to treat a variety of disorders and to promote vitality.

### Properties and Uses
- Used to prevent high blood pressure and heart disease
- Control and lower cholesterol
- Build up resistance to, and treat, fatigue and viral infections
- Anti-tumour properties are valuable in treating cancer

### Key Notes and Dosage
- Available in fresh or dried form, as well as in capsule, pill and extract form. Follow instructions on the label. Soak dried mushrooms for 30 minutes in warm water before using.

⫸ *Herbalism, Immunity*

## REIKI

Reiki means 'universal life energy' in Japanese, and it is a form of healing based on tapping into the unseen flow of energy that permeates all living things. It is believed that reiki originally evolved as a branch of Tibetan Buddhism, and that knowledge of its power and use was transmitted from master to disciple.

Treatment by a reiki master is intended to promote physical, emotional and spiritual well-being. Clients lie or sit fully clothed while the practitioner's hands are placed on specific parts of the body, starting with the head. Some reiki practitioners do not touch the physical body, but transmit healing into the aura around the body.

Reiki is aimed at encouraging the healing energies in the body, and involves transmitting the healer's own energy to the sufferer. Most emotional, physical and spiritual conditions will respond to treatment, including many that are considered to be untreatable by the conventional medical profession.

⫸ *Healing*

## REFLEXOLOGY

Reflexology involves stimulating, massaging and applying pressure to points on the hands and feet which correspond to various systems and organs throughout the body in order to stimulate the body's own healing system. These points are called reflex points, and each point corresponds to a different body part or function.

Reflexologists believe that applying pressure to these reflex points can improve the health of the body and mind. Depending on the points chosen, reflexology can be used to ease tension, reduce inflammation, relieve congestion, improve circulation and eliminate toxins from the body. Like many other complementary therapists, reflexologists do not claim to cure anything, rather they

*ABOVE LEFT: Reiki is an ancient Japanese practice which triggers off healing by tapping into the invisible energy flow which connects all living things.*
*ABOVE: Like shiitake mushrooms (pictured), reishi mushrooms are believed to promote good health and longevity.*
*RIGHT: Foot reflexology being performed on a patient.*

aim to stimulate the body to heal itself. They do this by working on the physical body to stimulate the healing at the physical, mental and emotional levels.

Pressure applied to nerve endings can influence all the body systems, including the circulation and lymphatic systems. Improvements in circulation and the lymphatic system result in improved body functioning because nutrients and oxygen are transported more efficiently around the body and toxins are eliminated with greater ease. Energy pathways are opened up so that the body is able to work more effectively, and harmony or 'homeostasis' is restored.

Reflexologists believe that the body is divided into 10 vertical zones or channels, five on the left and five on the right. Each zone runs from the head right down to the reflex areas on the hands and feet, and from the front through to the back of the body. All the body parts within any one zone are linked by nerve pathways and are mirrored in the corresponding reflex zone on the hands and feet. By applying pressure to a reflex point or area, the therapist can stimulate or rebalance the energy in the related zone.

Each zone is a channel for energy (called *chi* in Eastern disciplines), and stimulating or working any zone in the foot by applying pressure with the thumbs and fingers affects the entire zone throughout the body. For example,

working a zone on the foot along which the kidneys lie will release vital energy that may be blocked somewhere else in that zone, such as in the eyes. Working the kidney reflex area on the foot will therefore revitalise and balance the entire zone and improve functioning of the organ.

Reflexology is an excellent whole-body system, and can be used both to prevent illness and to encourage the body to heal. It is particularly useful for stress and related disorders, emotional disorders, digestive problems, circulatory disorders, menstrual problems, insomnia, fatigue, and most chronic and acute illnesses.

)))**▶ *Natural Therapies***

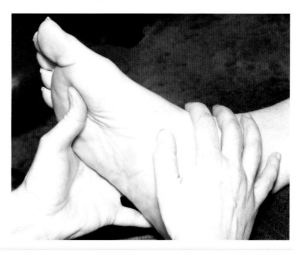

## RELAXATION AND BREATHING

Research has shown that mental activity has a direct effect on the body; that a relaxed mind can produce significant physical benefits, and if your body is relaxed, your mind will be too.

It has been found that relaxation can reduce the heart rate, lower blood pressure, and regulate breathing and metabolic rate. It also reduces adrenaline levels and allows the immune system to function more efficiently. Stress is a normal and necessary part of life, which provides motivation, stimulation and the drive to meet challenges with enthusiasm. The key to controlling it is relaxation.

True relaxation is a healing process that focuses on relaxing the mind and body. You will learn how to control and resolve the effects of stress rather than suppressing them with short-term measures, such as alcohol or overeating. Relaxation is a skill. Practised correctly, it can both prevent and treat disease, and improve your sense of well-being. Once you have learned how to do it, relaxation is a state that you can bring about wherever you are and whatever you are doing.

Therapists use and teach a number of different types of physical and mental relaxation techniques and in some cases induce very deep relaxation.

### Physical Relaxation

- Active muscular relaxation: in this exercise, you tense your muscles and then release them to feel the physical and mental release that accompanies each movement. You will be taught how to work around your body, possibly starting with an arm or leg and focusing on every detail, including fingers and toes. A therapist can guide you around your body, asking you to hold various muscles for about 10 seconds. At the end of the session, which usually lasts for 20–30 minutes, he or she will tell you that the session is ending and when you open your eyes and stretch you will feel relaxed and refreshed.

- Passive muscular relaxation is similar to tense-release, but instead of tensing a muscle group you focus your attention on it, acknowledge the tension already held there and then release it. You may be asked to imagine a slow wave of relaxation washing through the muscles, lengthening and expanding them, loosening any points of tension.

Relaxation is safe for anyone, and is particularly useful for small children. It can be used to treat most stress-related complaints, including insomnia, nausea, vomiting, loss of appetite, pain, anxiety, panic attacks, asthma, constipation, blood pressure, heart disease, arthritis and stress management. It is most commonly used for pain control, anxiety and insomnia. Relaxation has also been successful in treating some types of cancers, and conditions like ME and hyper-activity in children.

⟫▶ *Meditation, Natural Therapies, Yoga*

## RESCUE REMEDY

Rescue Remedy, a Bach flower remedy, can be bought as a remedy and as a cream. It is made from equal amounts of the five following essences:

- Cherry plum – for feelings of desperation
- Rock rose – to ease terror, fear or panic
- Impatiens – to soothe irritability and tension

- Clematis – to counteract the tendency to drift away from the present
- Star of Bethlehem – to address the mental and physical symptoms of shock

Rescue Remedy rebalances the body after any emotional or physical upsets. When a person feels in need of rescue or is unsettled; this may be after a shock, an accident, an argument, a trying event like a divorce or separation, or any circumstance which has demanded supreme nervous effort. Rescue Remedy also hastens healing after accidents, operations and dental surgery.

Use Rescue Remedy cream after sunburn, cuts, bruises or damage from accidents. Rescue Remedy can be added to any skin washes, douches or compresses if some element of rescue is needed. This method is also useful if nothing is allowed by mouth.

))))▶ *Bach Flower Remedies*

## RHUBARB

*Rheum palmatum* and *officinale*

Chinese rhubarb is also known as 'turkey rhubarb'. Garden rhubarb is a hybrid.

### Properties and Uses
- Laxative, astringent, bitter tonic, cooling
- Alleviates constipation, acute liver and gall-bladder diseases, feelings of congestion and fullness in the stomach
- For stomach acidity, gastroenteritis and diarrhoea from food poisoning
- Treats gout
- Traditionally used in cancer
- Use as a poultice for abscesses

### Dosage
- Half a teaspoon to a cup of water for decoction or 30–40 drops of the tincture, three times daily.

))))▶ *Nutrition*

*CENTRE LEFT: Yoga positions are always accompanied by relaxation and breathing exercises.*
*LEFT: Bach Rescue Remedy.*
*ABOVE RIGHT: Rhus toxicodendron (rhus tox).*

## RHUS TOX

*Rhus toxicodendron*

Poison ivy, or a variety of it, poison oak, is the basis of this homeopathic remedy. Uses include skin complaints characterized by red, itchy, puffy skin which feels like it is burning and which tends to form a scaly surface, such as eczema, herpes, nappy rash, and raised patches of skin where there is a clear demarcation line between the affected and unaffected part. Muscle and joint pain, such as that associated with rheumatism, osteoarthritis, cramps, restless legs, stiffness in the lower back, numbness in arms and legs and strains can also be alleviated.

The rhus tox type is lively, extrovert and a hard worker. They also tend to be restless, and will cry for little reason. They seem always to be thirsty.

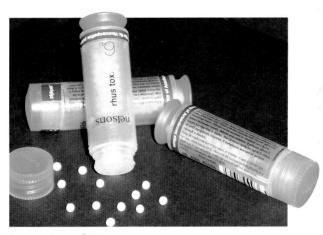

### Properties and Uses
- Relieves joint, muscle pain and stiffness, red, itchy skin eruptions
- For fear of being poisoned
- For those who are anxious at night
- For people who are depressed and may contemplate suicide
- For headaches after being cold or damp
- Alleviates backache
- For blistering skin problems
- Symptoms improve in the warmth, with movement or changing position, after stretching, and worsen during cold, wet weather, with rest, when lying on the back or right side and at night.

## RNI

*See RDA*

➤ *Minerals, RDA, Supplements, Vitamins*

## ROCK ROSE

*Helianthemum nummularium*

The Bach flower remedy rock rose is one of the main remedies in the Rescue Remedy. It can be taken in all cases of extreme fear, terror, panic, urgency or danger. It can also be taken when there is danger to the mind, threatened thoughts of suicide or insanity, nervous breakdown, fear of death or hopeless depression.

The person who needs rock rose feels intense fear and panic. At root the fear is an unrecognized terror at the prospect of loss of life or personal identity. Rock rose gives courage to face life and death, and accept change with courage.

### Properties and Uses

- For feelings of helplessness and hopelessness
- For terror, blind panic and nightmares
- For fear and its effects: palpitations, heart jitters or panic attacks
- Rock rose should be given for any perceived threat to the person, self-image or personal integrity

➤ *Bach Flower Remedies*

## ROCK WATER

This is water taken from a natural well or spring, preferably one with a traditional reputation to heal. There are many half-forgotten springs and wells. The water should be open and free flowing. Choose one which is open to the air and sunshine, and is as natural as possible. Do not use water from a well dedicated to a saint or within a church or shrine.

Rock water is suitable for people who are very strict with themselves and unforgiving. They practise self-discipline and deny themselves anything which might distract them from their goal. They have high ideals and are often hard on themselves. Rock water gives the flexibility of water.

### Key Notes

- The people who need rock water may be rigid, narrow-minded and very strict with themselves, to the point of self-denial
- They tend to be perfectionists with exaggerated ideals
- They may also be rigid in body, suffering from stiffness or arthritis
- Rock water encourages flexibility in reaching goals; goals which are truly in harmony with the natural order of the world

➤ *Bach Flower Remedies*

## ROLFING

Rolfing is named after its founder, Dr Ida Rolf (1896–1979), an American biochemist. Rolfing is intended to integrate manipulative forms of treatment with bioenergetics (the study of energy in living things).

When our bodies are well-aligned, gravity can flow through us, allowing ease of movement. A poor alignment is pulled down by gravity and struggles to keep balance, compensating and making changes until the entire structure is weakened. Rolfing realigns body structure and restores balance.

It relies mainly on deep massage of the muscles and connective tissues, to return the body to a state of balance. When the body is balanced, the mind, nervous system and all the organs and tissues to which it relates can function more efficiently. The body's innate healing system can therefore work at optimum level.

Movement and psychology have become part of training, so both emotional and physical problems can be dealt with. Rolfing is best used for ailments affecting the musculoskeletal system (caused by mechanical stress), poor posture and breathing difficulties.

))))➤ *Manipulative Therapies, Natural Therapies*

## ROSE

*Rosa centifolia, Rosa damascena*

 The rose has many therapeutic properties but its oil is very expensive to produce. The oil is distilled from the blossoms of the rose, usually from two types of roses, although there are many variations. The oils vary slightly in colour and fragrance, but have similar properties and uses. Rose oil can be used in tiny quantities and still be extremely effective.

### Properties and Uses

- A renowned aphrodisiac, sedative and a tonic with antidepressant properties. It has an affinity with the female reproductive system, helping to regulate the menstrual cycle and alleviate PMS or postnatal depression

*LEFT: Rock water.*
*ABOVE: The pink* Zephirine drouhin *rose.*

- Broken veins, ageing or wrinkled skin also benefit from treatment with the essential oil
- Useful in treating headaches, earache, conjunctivitis, coughs and hayfever
- In some cases it can help to encourage the production of healthy sperm, and is used for the treatment of male infertility
- Often used in the treatment of stress-related conditions such as insomnia and nervous tension
- Regulates appetite, prevents and relieves digestive spasms, constipation and nausea
- Soothes cracked, chapped, sensitive, dry, inflamed or allergy-prone skin, stops bleeding and encourages wound healing
- Rose oil is a powerful antiseptic against viruses and bacteria. Rose oil acts as a tonic for the heart, circulation, liver, stomach and uterus, and helps to detoxify the blood and organs.

### Caution

- Do not use during the first three months of pregnancy and not at all if there is a history of miscarriage.

))))➤ *Herbalism*

## ROSE

*Rosa damascena*

Rose oil is normally used therapeutically, but red roses may also be used as a herb.

### Properties and Uses

- A valuable tonic for the heart and lungs
- As a tea, the petals are astringent and have a tonic effect on the gut and liver
- It has a diuretic action and is said to increase appetite
- Has a soothing effect on the skin
- Rose petals are a good addition to any herbal remedy when there are emotional aspects, particularly a feeling of 'holding back'

### Key Notes

- Use in a tea, in gentle creams for the skin, and in the bath.

))))➤ *Aromatherapy*

## ROSEMARY

*Rosmarinus officinalis*

The word *Rosmarinus* means 'dew of the sea', and it relates to three species of evergreen flowering shrubs. Rosemary is one of the best-known and most used of the aromatic herbs.

### Properties and Uses

- Rosemary oil tones the skin, liver and gall bladder; it is used to treat acne, eczema, dandruff, lice and hair loss
- Helps to clear catarrh, coughs and colds and headaches
- Antiseptic and antibacterial, anti-fungal and a diuretic, generally cleansing and useful for fluid retention; it has properties that help to relieve painful periods and clear vaginal discharge, flatulence, indigestion and constipation
- Works as a tonic for the nervous system and is an antidepressant; it relieves stress-related disorders, mental exhaustion and promotes mental clarity
- A powerful circulation stimulant, excellent for low blood pressure, muscle fatigue, poor circulation, aches, pains and strains; it is both refreshing and rejuvenating, and acts as a perfect pick-me-up
- Rosemary prevents and reduces digestive spasms, relieves wind and regulates digestion
- The oil is perhaps best known for its effectiveness as a hair treatment; it is a tonic and conditioner of dark hair especially, helping to retain the colour; a little oil can be added to shampoos or rinses, and can help to reduce dandruff and prevent alopecia

### Caution

- Do not use during pregnancy. Rosemary is not suitable for people with epilepsy or high blood pressure.

)))➤ *Herbalism*

*ABOVE RIGHT: Rosmarinus officinalis (rosemary).*
*RIGHT: Royal jelly (produced by the queen bee inside her colony) has long been valued by naturalists for its rejuvenating properties.*
*FAR RIGHT: Ruta graveolens (ruta grav) ointment eases the discomfort experienced after strains and sprains.*

## ROSEMARY

*Rosmarinus officinalis*

Rosemary has many traditional uses and stories. Most uses are based on elements of truth. Ophelia gave Hamlet a sprig for remembrance. It is planted in cemeteries for the same reason and it does help improve the memory by improving the circulation. During the Plague in Europe posies of herbs, including rosemary, were carried to ward off the disease. The queen of England still carries a small posy during the ceremony on Maundy Tuesday.

### Properties and Uses

- Lifts the spirits and improves circulation, carminative, gentle bitter tonic
- Alleviates depression
- For headaches associated with gastric upsets; use with chamomile for stress headaches
- For poor circulation if taken regularly; a useful addition to any herbal medicine for conditions associated with cold and poor circulation
- Treats poor digestion, gall-bladder inflammation, gall stones and liverishness feelings
- Use as a gargle for sore throats; it is a useful substitute for sage during pregnancy
- Use with horsetail for hair loss due to stress and worry
- Use the infused oil for massage for cold limbs and aches and pains
- Rosemary encourages the circulation of the blood; good circulation to the head strengthens the brain and improves the quality and strength of hair; two cups of rosemary tea a day will prevent hair-loss through poor circulation and restimulate growth after chemotherapy

### Key Notes and Dosage

- Standard doses used freely.
- Rosemary tea can be used as a conditioning hair rinse for dandruff but also for gloriously glossy hair (especially for dark hair) use rosemary vinegar.

)))➤ *Aromatherapy*

## ROYAL JELLY

Royal jelly has been used for centuries for its health-giving and rejuvenating properties, and it is rich in vitamins, amino acids and minerals. It is also the prime source of fatty acid, which helps to increase alertness and act as a natural tranquillizer (when necessary). Royal jelly is secreted in the salivary glands of the worker bees to feed and stimulate the growth and development of the queen bee.

### Properties and Uses

- Antibacterial
- May prevent the development of leukaemia
- Has a yeast-inhibiting function, preventing conditions such as thrush and athlete's foot
- Contains the male sex hormone testosterone, which may increase libido
- Used in the treatment of sub-fertility
- Controls blood cholesterol levels
- Boosts the immune system
- Used in the treatment of skin problems, including eczema, psoriasis and acne

## RUTA GRAV

*Ruta graveolens*

Based on the herb *rue*, which was traditionally used in the sixteenth and seventeenth centuries to prevent the spread of typhus, this homeopathic remedy is useful for bruised bones and tendon injuries, aching bones, deep-aching pain, rheumatism, sciatica, which is worse when lying down and for the restlessness which goes with having to be still or lying down. It is also good for eyestrain, when the eyes feel hot and sore from overuse or reading small print, and accompanying headaches. Other conditions treated include infection after tooth extraction, weak chest with breathing difficulties, prolapsed rectum, constipation with stools that are alternately large and difficult to pass or loose, containing blood and mucus.

### Properties and Uses

- Relieves bruises, strained tissue and ligaments, restlessness and eyestrain
- For people who contradict and criticize others
- For depression when ill
- For restlessness
- For those who are anxious or troubled
- For those who are dissatisfied with themselves and others
- Treats painful, aching limbs
- Treats bruises
- Alleviates headaches due to eyestrain
- Symptoms improve with movement, and worsen in the cold and damp, when resting or lying down

LEFT: *Herbs provide a safer and more natural way of healing and improving one's health than traditional medicine.*
BELOW: *A* Salvia officinalis *(sage) bush.*
BELOW RIGHT: *Salt (sodium chloride), apart from being used as a food condiment and preservative, also has many therapeutic advantages.*

## SAGE

*Salvia officinalis*

The actions of red sage and sage are very similar, and can be used to treat any inflamed and septic mouth conditions.

### Properties and Uses

- Astringent, stimulant, antiseptic, carminative, antispasmodic, nervine and generally strengthening
- Alleviates depression and nervous exhaustion, post-viral fatigue, general debility
- Treats anxiety and confusion in elderly people or accompanying exhaustion and weakened states
- Soothes indigestion, wind, loss of appetite and mucus on the stomach
- For excessive sweating and night sweats; taken cold
- Good for weak lungs with persistent and recurrent coughs and allergies
- For menopausal hot flushes, period pains and premenstrual painful breasts (as a tea and compress)

## SAFETY

Most natural remedies are safe to use at home, and because many of the elements of treatment are close by, their use can save many a trip to the doctor. If you are concerned about any health matter, it is best to see your doctor or alternative practitioner before attempting to treat yourself at home. Home treatment is appropriate for most illnesses that are not life-threatening. Natural remedies can normally be undertaken alongside orthodox medical care – although you must tell your doctor or health practitioner about any remedies you are using yourself.

As with all medicines, natural remedies must be treated with respect and taken with due regard to any potential adverse effects. All foods may produce side-effects or adverse reactions. Side-effects may be desirable or undesirable, but are not usually life-threatening.

If you are taking prescriptive drugs for an illness see your general practitioner before self-medicating with any natural medicine. Pregnant and lactating women, people with chronic gastrointestinal complaints and the elderly should also seek the advice of a reputable, qualified practitioner, as should parents who are thinking of treating their children with natural medicines.

Natural therapies are equally safe for the majority of people to use, but every case should be assessed individually. See individual entries for safety notes.

- Cold sage tea taken every few hours will usually dry up breast milk
- As a gargle and mouth-wash for sore throats, laryngitis, tonsillitis, mouth ulcers and inflamed and tender gums
- As an antiseptic wash for dirty and slow to heal wounds

**Dosage**
- Traditionally, one cup a day maintains health in old age. For extra-strength gargle add five drops of tincture of myrrh (from chemists or herb shops) to a cup of sage tea. Sage tincture can be taken, instead of the cold tea, for stopping night sweats. Four teaspoons daily, in a little water. Do not give in pregnancy.

))))➤ *Aromatherapy*

## SAGE
*Salvia officinalis*

The properties of sage (see above) make this oil useful on its own, or as a part of blend. It is effective in warming massages and acts as a general tonic.

**Properties and Uses**
- For nervous and physical debility
- Where there are rheumatic pains
- After a cold, use in the bath to warm
- Has a softening effect on overworked muscles

**Caution**
- Do not use in pregnancy, in feverish conditions, or in cases of high blood pressure.

))))➤ *Clary Sage, Herbalism*

## SALT
*Sodium chloride*

Salt has been used traditionally as a preservative and as a seasoning for food. It also has therapeutic uses, some of which are based on folk medicine. The body needs salt to maintain water in the body and help distribute carbon dioxide through the blood.

**Properties and Uses**
- Salt has cleansing and antiseptic properties, and acts as a digestive and a laxative
- Salt is sometimes recommended as an emetic

- Salt is used in the form of saline solution or salt tablets to treat salt depletion resulting from excess production of sweat in very high temperatures, from excessive vomiting and diarrhoea and as a result of shock and haemorrhage; saline solution is usually administered intravenously
- A small bag of salt, previously warmed, pressed against the ear may help to relieve earache
- Dissolving a pinch of salt in the mouth before going to bed is sometimes recommended for the prevention of night cramps
- A warm salt gargle can ease inflammation of the throat
- To exfoliate the skin, put a little salt on a face flannel and rub gently over the face and body

**Key Notes**
- Too much salt in the diet may lead to fluid retention and hypertension. People with high blood pressure should restrict their intake of sodium chloride.

))))➤ *Nutrition, Sodium*

## SANDALWOOD

*Santalum album*

 Sandalwood oil is one of the main remedies used in Ayurvedic medicine (ancient Indian medicine), and it is used to treat a wide variety of diseases. Its woody, sweet fragrance is often used in perfume and soap, particularly in Europe. The best sandalwood oil comes from India, where it is distilled from the mature tree.

### Properties and Uses

- Sandalwood is an antiseptic, particularly effective for all urinary disorders, especially cystitis, probably because of its antibacterial and antiseptic properties
- Clears catarrh and is effective for respiratory conditions such as bronchitis, dry coughs and sore throats
- The oil helps to soothe the stomach, reduce digestive spasms, relieve fluid retention and reduce inflammation
- Sandalwood encourages wound healing, and skin problems such as dry, chapped skin, acne, psoriasis, eczema and shaving rash can all benefit from its soothing, rehydrating and antiseptic action
- It is an antidepressant oil that calms the nervous system
- The oil is also considered to be somewhat aphrodisiac

### Caution

- Do not use undiluted on the skin

*ABOVE: Santalum album (sandalwood) aromatherapy oil.*
*RIGHT: Tomatoes are a good source of the trace mineral selenium.*
*FAR RIGHT: Sepia homeopathic pills.*

## SCLERANTHUS

*Scleranthus annuus*

 Scleranthus, a Bach flower remedy, is for those who are unable to decide and suffer much from hesitation, procrastination and uncertainty. It is also useful for confusion. People who need Scleranthus tend to be quiet and are not inclined to discuss their opinions with others. Scleranthus gives the stability to listen to the inner self and to integrate the emotional and intellectual ex-tremes into a balanced and sustained action.

### Key Notes

- This remedy is for people who are unable to decide between two things or courses of action. They will be characterized by uncertainty, indecision, vacillation and procrastination.
- There may be mood swings, and many of them will suffer from motion sickness.
- Scleranthus brings harmony, stability and balance. It creates a balanced position from which to change uncertainly into certainty, and provides the stability to act decisively.

⟫▶ *Bach Flower Remedies*

## SELENIUM

Selenium is an essential trace element which has recently been recognized as one of the most important nutrients in our diet. It is an antioxidant, and is vitally important to the human metabolism. Selenium has been proved to provide protection against a number of cancers, and other diseases.

The best sources of selenium are wheatgerm, bran, tuna fish, onions, tomatoes, broccoli and wholemeal bread.

### Properties and Uses
- Maintains healthy eyes and eyesight
- Stimulates the immune system
- Improves liver function
- Protects against heart and circulatory diseases
- Can detoxify alcohol, many drugs, smoke and some fats
- Useful in the treatment of arthritis
- Helps treat dandruff

### Notes
- Selenium supplementation should be taken with 30 to 400 IU of vitamin E to ensure that selenium works most efficiently.
- Selenium can be toxic in very small doses; symptoms of excess include blackened fingernails and a garlic-like odour on the breath and skin. Take no more than 500 mcg daily, unless supervised by a registered practitioner.

))))▶ *Antioxidants, Minerals*

## SEPIA

*Sepia officinalis*

Medicinally, cuttlefish ink has historically been used to treat conditions such as kidney stones, hair loss and gonorrhoea. Today, the homeopathic remedy sepia is most commonly used by women and is used to treat complaints such as menstrual problems and hormonal imbalances.

Useful for women who feel dragged down both physically and emotionally. Useful for complaints relating to the vagina, ovaries and uterus, such as heavy or painful periods, PMS, menopausal hot flushes, thrush, conditions associated with pregnancy, and the feeling of a sagging abdomen, accompanied by the need to cross the legs. Pain during sex, aversion to sex or exhaustion afterwards can also be treated. Also, any situation where the woman is feeling emotionally and physically tired and lacking in energy. It is also useful for headaches with nausea, hair loss, dizziness, offensive sweating, indigestion, skin discoloration and circulatory problems.

The sepia type tends to be female, tall, dark and with sallow skin. They are dignified and attractive, love dancing, but tend to be detached emotionally, often playing the martyr role. They have strong opinions, hating to be contradicted, and are often resentful of responsibilities. Children tend to be sallow, sweaty-skinned, tire easily; are sensitive to weather; moody and negative, dislike being left alone and parties; and have a tendency to constipation.

### Properties and Uses
- Relieves menstrual problems, conditions associated with hormonal imbalance, complaints accompanied by exhaustion
- For fear of poverty, being alone, insanity
- For those who are irritable with family and friends, but good in company
- For people who bottle up anger
- For those who find it hard to conceal thoughts
- For those who are prone to sudden weeping
- For those who are easily chilled
- Relieves a dragging sensation in the abdomen
- Treats burning or throbbing pains
- Symptoms improve after food, exertion, especially dancing, sleep and in the warmth, and are worse on the left side, after physical and mental exertion, in the early morning and evening, in thundery weather and if near tobacco

massage. To work with the body's energy the pressure must reach through the superficial layers of the body to its centre. Sometimes this feels deeply relaxing and sometimes this can be quite sharp.

Shiatsu is given on a Japanese mattress which means the giver and the receiver are at floor level. The receiver remains clothed which helps the practitioner contact the body's energy rather than the skin.

Shiatsu:
- Relaxes
- Restores and balances energy
- Eases tension and stiffness
- Improves breathing
- Improves circulation
- Heals the body and mind
- Enhances well-being

Shiatsu at the hands of a qualified therapist is perfectly safe for everyone and particularly beneficial for pregnant women. Some therapists also specialise in the treatment of small children and the elderly. Shiatsu is not suitable, however, for people with cancer of the blood or lymphatic systems.

Shiatsu involves the giver leaning on the receiver and moving along the meridians. Shiatsu differs from an oil massage as there are moments of stillness in the movement for the giver to contact the energy.

))))➤ *Natural Therapies*

## SHIITAKE MUSHROOMS

*Leninus edodes*

Like reishi mushroom, shiitake mushrooms were traditionally believed by Chinese Taoists to confer immortality.

### Properties and Uses
- Contain 18 amino acids
- Rich in B vitamins
- When sun-dried, they contain high amounts of vitamin D
- Their effectiveness at treating cancer has been reported in several studies
- Contain immune-boosting polysaccharides

## SHIATSU

Shiatsu is a Japanese form of body work. It was developed from different disciplines of Oriental medicine, including acupuncture, herbalism, diet and exercise. Shiatsu, like many forms of massage, works to relax and invigorate the body. Shiatsu also makes use of the energy of the body and originated as a holistic therapy for the treatment of mind, body and spirit. When used correctly it remains a holistic therapy, taking into consideration the mind, body and spirit. It is as useful for emotional pain as it is for physical problems.

The word shiatsu can be broken down into *shi*, which means 'finger' and *atsu*, which means 'pressure'. In reality shiatsu may be thumb, finger, elbow or even knee pressure. The quality of the pressure is the main feature that differentiates shiatsu from other forms of

## Key Notes

- Available in fresh or dried form, as well as in capsule, pill and extract form. Follow instructions on the label. Soak dried mushrooms for 30 minutes in warm water before using.

))))➤ *Herbalism, Immunity, Reishi Mushrooms*

## SILICA

Also called silicea, this homeopathic remedy is prepared from silicon dioxide. It is also one of the 12 tissue salts identified by Dr Wilhelm Schüssler. It is good for complaints that have occurred as a result of low immunity due to undernourishment, such as colds, ear infections and catarrh. Also for skin and bone conditions, such as acne, weak nails, slow growth or fontanelles which are slow to close in babies, slow-healing fractures, expelling splinters, glass shards or thorns from body tissue, problems associated with the nervous system, such as colic and migraines. Other problems alleviated include catarrh with thick, yellow discharge, enlarged lymph nodes, offensive sweat, headaches which start at the back of the head and move over the forehead, glue ear and restless sleep.

The silica type tends to be slim and small-boned with lank hair. They have a neat appearance but are prone to cracked lips, brittle and uneven nails. Often fragile-looking, they are tenacious and strong-willed, although often lack confidence and are tired. Children tend to be

*LEFT: Unlike other forms of massage, where there is direct contact with the skin, recipients of shiatsu massage remain fully clothed to help the practitioner contact the body's energy, rather than the skin.*

*ABOVE: Taoists originally believed that Shiitake mushrooms (pictured), like their counterparts, Reishi mushrooms, conveyed immortality.*

*RIGHT: Silica relieves conditions caused by low immunity, such as colds and catarrh.*

neat, small but with large sweaty heads, feel the cold easily, are shy but strong willed, conscientious but lack confidence.

## Properties and Uses

- Relieves conditions caused by low immunity due to malnourishment, bone and skin conditions, expulsion of foreign bodies
- For fear of failure, exertion, sharp objects
- For those who are timid and lack self-confidence
- Alleviates worries about future events
- For fear of commitment because of being hurt
- Treats sweaty feet
- For chills
- Hastens healing
- Treats discharges
- For cracked lips, brittle nails
- Symptoms improve in heat and when wrapped up, and worsen in draughts cold and damp, when lying on the left side, after washing, by suppressing sweat, in the morning

))))➤ *Biochemic Tissue Salts*

## SKULLCAP

*Scutellaria laterifolia* or *Scutellaria galericulata*

 This is one of the main sedative herbs, but it also has a tonic effect on the entire nervous system.

### Properties and Uses

- Strengthens and calms the nervous system, antispasmodic
- Relieves anxiety, tension headaches, PMS, examination nerves and post-examination depression
- Use with valerian or chamomile and linden flowers for insomnia, disturbed sleep and for tranquillizer withdrawal
- Use with vervain for workaholics; the mixture is relaxing without sedating
- Supportive treatment in epilepsy and for people on major tranquillizers; reduces anxiety without interfering with their medication.

### Key Notes

- There are many relaxing tablets in the shops containing skullcap and other herbs; follow the dosage on the box.

## SLIPPERY ELM

*Ulmus fulva*

The bark of this small American tree is used therapuetically, mainly for its mucilaginous qualities.

### Properties and Uses

- Soothing, mucilaginous
- Forms a lining over the wall of the stomach, soothing ulcers that are irritated by stomach acid, as in the case of colitis and other inflammatory conditions
- For any sort of inflammation or irritation in the digestive tract: nausea, indigestion, wind, food allergies, stomach ulcers, acidity, heartburn, hiatus hernia, colitis, diverticulitis and diarrhoea
- Mix with sufficient water to make a paste for drawing splinters

### Dosage

- A level teaspoon of powder stirred into a drink, three times daily before meals. Tablets flavoured with carminative herbs are especially useful. Take one or two with a glass of water or milk before meals. For travel sickness and nausea during pregnancy suck one tablet slowly.

## SOUND THERAPY

Sound therapy is an ancient method of healing. The theory is that as everything in the Universe is in a constant state of vibration, including the human body, even the smallest change in frequency can affect the internal organs. Modern sound therapists consider that there is a natural resonance or 'note' for each part of the body, and for each individual. They direct specific sound waves to specific areas to affect the frequency at which that part is vibrating. In this way, health is restored and balanced.

Sound therapy may use machines that transmit healing vibrations, but more usually it involves direct application of the voice, music or a combination of sounds. Specifically directed sounds can be used in the treatment of a variety of disorders, and have been very effective in the past with disabled children and adults.

))))➤ *Cymantics*

*LEFT:* Ulmus fulva *(slippery elm).*
*ABOVE RIGHT: Your spirit can keep you feeling young even in old age.*
*FAR RIGHT: Spirulina tablets.*

## SPIRIT

Many of us have an instinctive understanding of spirit, a sense of our own life force and being. We may be sensitive to the energy of others and aware of the impact of our own energy. As parents, we can witness the impact of negative energy on our children – a baby becomes anxious and cries when his mother is distressed; a child throws a temper tantrum when his father is rushed and under pressure.

Spirit is a kind of life energy. Some people call it a soul or 'the spirit', but you do not have to be religious to understand the concept that there is a unique and conscious entity that inhabits and animates the human form. Spirit is seen in terms of love and light and peace. It involves a fundamental personal belief and power, which affects the way you live your life on a daily basis. Spirit is what makes you an individual, and it is something that we all share.

Spirit is an essential element in holistic therapies, and as important as physical and emotional health. So not only will therapists take into consideration the health of your spirit when diagnozing and treating, but they will aim to balance your health on all levels so that you become more in touch with spirit.

## SPIRULINA

Spirulina are *cyanobacteria*, or blue-green algae. They are rich in gamma linolenic acid (GLA) and a wide variety of nutrients, including beta-carotene. Spirulina is used as a staple food by the Aztecs of Mexico and is now marketed as a high-protein food supplement.

The best sources of spirulina are fresh or freeze-dried spirulina.

### Properties and Uses

- Rich in nutrients and high in protein (particularly useful for vegetarians)
- May help to suppress appetite
- Used to maintain skin health and to treat skin disorders
- May contribute to the health of the intestines
- General tonic properties
- May help to rejuvenate
- Many have anti-cancer properties

## SPONGIA

*Spongia tosta*

Sponge was first noted for its medicinal purposes more than 600 years ago, when it was used as a treatment for goitre, the swelling of the thyroid gland, which is brought on by a deficiency in iodine. The homeopathic remedy spongia works particularly well for children's croup, characterized by sneezing and a hoarse, dry barking cough, with the patient waking in alarm with the feeling of suffocation, later followed by thick mucus which is difficult to bring up. Associated symptoms of coughs, such as hoarseness, dryness of the larynx from a cold, headaches which are worse when lying down, but improve when sitting up, bronchitis, dry mucous membranes and feeling heavy and exhausted are also helped. Laryngitis, where the throat is raw and dry and feels like it is burning, responds well. It is also good if chest conditions or tuberculosis run in the family.

The spongia type tends to be lean, light-haired and blue-eyed, with a 'dried up' appearance.

### Properties and Uses

- Relieves croup, coughs and laryngitis
- Relieves anxiety
- For fear of suffocation and death
- For those who wake from sleep in fear
- Alleviates chest or heart region congestion
- For palpitations
- For laryngitis
- Symptoms improve with warm food and drinks and when sitting up, and worsen when talking, swallowing, eating sweet food or cold drinks, moving, touching the affected area, lying with the head lower than the feet and around midnight

## STAR OF BETHLEHEM

Star of Bethlehem is used in Rescue Remedy to ameliorate the effects of shock; the shock of bad news, of loss, of an accident – even of being born. People 'jump' with shock; waves ripple outwards through the body affecting every cell and tissue. Time is needed for everything to settle, to be comfortable in the body, but sometimes the trauma may be so extreme, or the shock unrealized or repressed that the effects are still resonating years later. Star of Bethlehem neutralizes the effects so that the body can find peace and comfort.

## Properties and Uses

- For shock and all the physical and emotional effects of shock
- Long repressed shock or trauma may lead to psychosomatic symptoms
- Combats grey pallor, poor appetite and poor sleep
- The effects of shock must be fully acknowledged and not trivialized
- Star of Bethlehem neutralizes the effects of shock, releasing residue blockages so that the body and mind can find equilibrium and comfort

))))➤ **Bach Flower Remedies, Rescue Remedy**

## STEAM INHALATIONS

Inhalations have been traditionally used to ease problems with the respiratory tract, including colds, sore throats and coughs. The best way to create a steam inhalation is to add three to four drops of essential oil to a bowl of boiling water. Bend over the bowl, cover your head with a towel and breathe deeply for a few minutes.

Vaporizers can be electric or a ceramic ring that is heated by a light bulb, but most are ceramic pots warmed by a small candle. Add water and six to eight drops of oil to the vaporizer. Alternatively, add the oil to a bowl of water and place by a radiator. The heat of the steam opens up airways and pores, and allows the essential oil to be absorbed more quickly and effectively. Herbs and infused herbal oils can also be added to steam inhalation, with great effect.

Children need close supervision during an inhalation, to ensure that they are not scalded. Do not use steam inhalations in the case of asthma, hayfever or other allergies without a 30-second 'trial' period. If all is well, increase time to one minute but do not exceed.

))))➤ **Herbalism**

## ST JOHN'S WORT

*Hypericum perforatum*

St John's wort has become one of the most popular antidepressant herbs, and recent studies show that it is as effective, if not more so, than the drug Prozac. It does, however, have a wide variety of other therapeutic uses.

## Properties and Uses

- Strengthens and speeds healing in the nervous system, analgesic, anti-viral, anti-inflammatory
- Treats neuralgia, sciatica, pain with tingling in hands or feet and back pain
- For pain from deep wounds – internally and externally
- For mild to moderate depression
- Alleviates depression and nervousness of menopause
- Use as a tincture as lotion for shingles, cold sores and herpes
- Use as a cream for sore skin, inflamed rashes and cuts
- Use infused oil as base oil for aromatherapy back massage and with lavender essential oil for neuralgia

## Key Notes

- It may be a week before depression begins to lift. The best preparations for external use are the infused oil and creams based on the infused oil; see box for instructions. For nerve damage you may need to persist for some months. Hypercal cream, available from homeopathic chemists, is made from St John's wort and marigold. It is a good first aid cream. Do not take with prescription drugs, unless on the advice of a registered herbalist.

))))➤ **Hypericum**

*ABOVE: Star of Bethlehem.*

*LEFT: To soothe a sore throat, cold or cough, add three or four drops of essential oil to a bowl of boiling water, cover your head with a towel and breathe in deeply.*

*RIGHT: Hypericum perforatum (St John's wort).*

in more oxygen to fuel the muscles, blood sugar increases to supply added energy, digestion slows, and perspiration increases. In the second stage of stress, the body begins to repair the damage caused by the first stage. If the stressful situation is resolved, the stress symptoms vanish. If the stressful situation continues, however, a third stage, exhaustion, sets in, and the body's energy wears out. This stage may continue until vital organs are affected, and then disease or even death can result.

Stress is a major factor in diseases whose physical symptoms are induced or aggravated by mental or emotional problems. Stress-related disorders compose 50 to 80 per cent of all illnesses, though stress may not be the only cause.

## STRESS

Stress comes in many forms, and it can be fairly safely described as anything that places undue pressure on the mind, body or spirit. Stress can come from obvious sources: divorce, bereavement, financial problems, overscheduling, inadequate relaxation and moving house. It can also stem from anything that causes the body to work harder, including a poor diet, inadequate sleep or exercise, constant noise, pollution, chemicals in food and the environment and even injury.

### Symptoms of stress include:
- Increased breathing and heart rate
- Nausea
- Tense muscles
- Inability to relax
- Irritability (including temper tantrums)
- Insomnia
- Allergies
- Skin problems
- Headaches
- Fatigue

All stress factors have an effect on our body, causing it to make a series of rapid physiological changes, called adaptive responses, to deal with threatening or demanding situations. In the first stage of stress, hormones are poured into the bloodstream. The pulse quickens, the lungs take

*LEFT: Sustained stress takes a toll on our health and our body's ability to cope.*
*BELOW: If you want to be this happy and recover from a deep hurt or sadness,*
*Sturt desert pea can work miracles.*
*BELOW RIGHT: Sulphur brimstone is extracted from sulphur crystals (pictured).*

## STURT DESERT PEA

*Clianthus formosus*

Sturt desert pea is the floral emblem of South Australia. It is for deep hurts and sorrows. Aboriginal legends connect this flower with grief and sadness. This is one of the most powerful of all the essences and, like so many of the bush essences, it can help the person bring about amazing changes in their life.

### Properties and Uses

- For emotional pain, deep hurt and sadness
- Brings about letting-go
- Triggers healthy grieving
- Releases deep held grief and sadness

)))) ***Australian Bush Flower Essences***

## STURT DESERT ROSE

*Gossypium sturtianum*

This essence is for guilt. It is also for following your own inner convictions and morality, helping you to follow through with what you know you have to do. It can restore self-esteem that has been damaged by past actions you may have felt guilty about.

### Properties and Uses

- For guilt, low self-esteem and being easily led
- Brings courage, conviction and makes us true to ourselves
- For integrity

)))) ***Australian Bush Flower Remedies***

## SULPHUR

*Sulphur brimstone*

This homeopathic remedy is extracted from the mineral and the remedy is given to treat digestive and skin disorders. It is useful for hot, red, itchy skin associated with problems such as eczema and nappy rash, digestive complaints such as vomiting and diarrhoea which occur in the morning, indigestion which is made worse by drinking milk and hunger pangs, which can be alleviated with sulphur. It can also treat offensive odours, such as foul-smelling sweat or discharge, premenstrual symptoms such as irritability and headaches and menopausal symptoms, such as flushing and dizzy spells. It is also useful when another remedy has not worked as hoped

or if the picture remedy is not clear. Other problems, such as lack of energy, restless sleep, depression, fever, burning pains and eruptions, congestions and back pain can also be helped.

The sulphur type is either round and red-faced or lanky with bad posture, dry, flaky skin and dull hair. They tend to be selfish, self-centred and egocentric, but can be giving and good-natured. They are full of ideas, but cannot carry them out, lacking willpower. They fuss over minor details, are quickly angered, but just as quickly calm down. They are often sensitive to smell. Children tend to be either well-built, with thick hair and a rosy complexion or thin and pale with dry skin. Both types eat well, look dishevelled, are happy when stimulated, take care of their possessions and are difficult to get to bed.

### Properties and Uses
- Relieves inflamed, itchy skin conditions, digestive complaints, offensive odours, women's conditions, conditions other remedies do not seem to be helping
- For the selfish and egotistical
- For the argumentative and aggressive
- For fear of ghosts, height and failure
- For those who are prone to lethargic depression
- For people who are full of bright ideas which fade away
- Treats burning, itching sensations
- For inflammation of affected part
- For offensive odours
- Alleviates thirst
- Weak areas include left side of the body, circulation, digestive organs and skin
- Symptoms improve when lying on the right side, in warm, dry, fresh air, after physical activity, and worsen in stuffy atmospheres, in the morning, particularly around 11 a.m. and at night, in the damp and cold and after washing

*RIGHT: Sunshine wattle, an Australian bush essence, can bring on optimism and completely change someone's outlook.*
*FAR RIGHT: Vitamin supplements are now a commonplace feature of our nutritional habits.*

## SUNSHINE WATTLE
*Acacia terminalis*

Sunshine wattle is for people who have had a difficult time in the past and who are stuck there. They bring their negative experiences of the past into the present. Life is seen as being grim and full of struggles. When they look at life they only see bleakness, hard times and disappointment continuing into the future. In a more positive mode these people will see the beauty, joy and excitement in the present and optimistically anticipate the future.

### Properties and Uses
- For being stuck in the past and expecting a grim future; for struggles.
- Brings optimism
- Brings acceptance of the beauty and joy in the present
- Opens a bright future

)))➤ *Australian Bush Flower Essences*

## SUPPLEMENTS

Supplements are elements of nutrition that are given supplementally. There is a wide range of vitamins, minerals and other substances available in supplement form, and these are discussed throughout this book. There are also a number of other food supplements that do not fall strictly within the definitions of vitamins, minerals, lipids and amino acids. These include various elements that either have healing properties or are now known to be crucial to health.

Supplements are not a replacement for food, and they cannot be ingested without food. Supplements are no substitute for a poor diet, but they will enhance a good one. People suffering from chronic conditions or who smoke or drink regularly may need to take supplements to ensure optimum health.

It is important to remember that micronutrients work in conjunction with one another, and taking large doses of any one supplement can upset the balance within the body. A good vitamin and mineral supplement will ensure that you are getting the correct amounts of each, according to the relationships between them. Extra supplements should only be taken on the advice of a registered nutritionist or medical practitioner. Where supplements are taken to discourage the course of illness – for example, vitamin C for colds or flu – it is safe to take larger doses than usual. Read the packet for further information.

When should supplements be taken?
- The best time for taking most supplements is after meals, on a full stomach, although some vitamins and minerals work best on an empty stomach. Read the label on any supplement you plan to take to find out the best time to take it.
- Time-release formulas need to be taken with food, for their nutrients are slowly released over a period of hours. If there is not enough food to slow their passage through the body, they can pass the sites where they are normally absorbed before they have had a chance to release their nutrients.
- Take supplements evenly throughout the day for best effect.

)))▶ *Minerals, Vitamins*

## SWEET CHESTNUT

*Castanea sativa*

Sweet Chestnut is for those moments when the anguish is so great that it becomes unbearable. It is ideal for people who feel that they have reached the end of their tether and are being stretched beyond endurance. Sweet chestnut helps to bring out hidden reserves, opening boundaries and expanding limits. It gives strength the chance to grow.

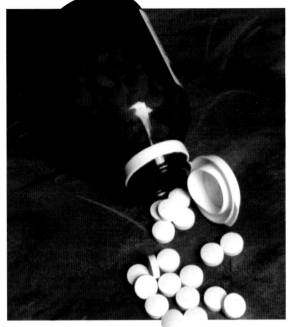

**Key Notes**
- When it feels as if the mind or body will give way, that something will snap and all that is left is annihilation, sweet chestnut is the right remedy. Bach called this feeling the 'dark night of the soul'.
- Associated symptoms include anxiety, sleep disturbances, hopelessness and despair. This distress is often hidden so that collapse seems lonely and inevitable.
- Sweet chestnut restores hope, widening outlook to enable transformation.

)))▶ *Bach Flower Remedies*

## SYMPHYTUM

Symphytum is used in herbal as well as homeopathic form. Symphytum has always been used for healing wounds.

### Properties and Uses
- For broken bones
- For injured cartilage
- For backache
- For injury to the eyes
- Can be applied externally where there is swelling; use after a broken bone has been set to hasten the knitting process of the bone

## TABACUM

Tabacum is made from the tobacco plant. Its main use is to cure travel sickness, although it is also good for vertigo and morning sickness.

### Properties and Uses
- Effective for seasickness
- Treats nausea, vomiting and vertigo
- For palpitations
- For pallor and sweating
- Relieves itchy skin
- For impaired mental faculties

## T'AI CHI

T'ai chi or t'ai chi ch'uan means 'supreme ultimate power' and is often referred to as 'mediation in motion'. A Chinese martial art, t'ai chi was founded by a Taoist monk more than 5,000 years ago. Chairman Mao incorporated it into general Chinese health practice in 1949 in order to relieve stress and associated disorders. Derived from Confucian, Buddhist and Taoist teachings, this art or therapy is a complete physical and mental discipline, which promotes health and well-being.

T'ai chi is a series of flowing actions based on the movements of nature. The Chinese theory of chi, or energy, is incorporated into this discipline, and this therapy is designed to gently stir or stimulate the flow of chi to unblock any points of stagnation or poor circulation, and allow the flow to reach any weakened parts of the body. Illness and disease are believed to be the result of an imbalance of chi in the body.

Traditionally t'ai chi has 128 postures, all of which must be taught and worked through at a specific, slow pace. These postures run together in a flowing movement, which can have a powerful effect on physical and psychological health.

## TAURINE

Taurine is a non-essential amino acid that is produced by the body. Its main role is to regulate the nerves and muscle, and help to co-ordinate neuro-transmission. Studies performed on animals show that a diet low in taurine can cause degeneration of the retina and impaired vision.

An excessive intake of taurine can cause depression and other symptoms. Doses of up to 3 g are used to treat high blood pressure, epilepsy and other conditions relating to the eyes; 50 to 100 mg is usually prescribed, taken two to three times a week.

Good sources of taurine are meat, fish and eggs, but none of the plant foods.

### Properties and Uses
- Mild antioxidant
- Works with zinc to protect against cataracts
- Regulates nerves and muscles, and electrical activity

⫸ *Amino Acids*

## TEA TREE
*Melaleuca alternifolia*

This small tree or shrub is a traditional remedy among the Aboriginal people of Australia, but it was not until after World War I that serious study of the oil began. From the 1920s until World War II it became increasingly famous, and was supplied to the Royal Australian Navy and to the Army to prevent infection and to encourage healing of the wounded.

The oil experienced a renaissance in the 1970s and once again returned to the medical forefront, having been proven to combat all types of infection. People with sensitive skin should introduce the oil with caution.

## Properties and Uses

- Primarily an anti-infection oil, tea tree has anti-fungal, antibacterial and antiviral properties; it is frequently used for skin problems such as spots, acne, warts, verrucae, athlete's foot, rashes, insect bites, burns and blisters
- Used to clean cuts and infected wounds and helps skin to heal by encouraging the formation of scar tissue
- Tea tree is effective against dandruff, cold sores, and urinary or genital infections such as cystitis and thrush
- An expectorant that also alleviates inflammation and is a valuable immune stimulant; tea tree is known to boost the immune system, and is used in the treat-ment of colds, flu, respiratory infections, catarrhal problems and infectious illnesses; it is also used to reduce a fever
- It is now a popular choice for delousing children's hair, providing effective treatment without the side-effects of drugs

*LEFT: Tobacco obtained from the* nicotiana tabacum *plant can be used to combat morning sickness.*
*ABOVE:* Melaleuca alternifolia *(tea tree) cream is a superb antiseptic.*
*RIGHT: The herb thyme is a popular addition to recipes.*

## THYME
*Thymus vulgaris*

This herb is popular in cooking. There are many different garden varieties with distinctive foliage: white thyme, yellow thyme, variegated thyme. Although not as strong as common wild *thymus vulgaris*, they can be used in all recipes if nothing else is available.

### Properties and Uses
- Antiseptic, antibacterial, anti-fungal, expectorant, digestive tonic
- For whooping cough and any cough with infected or tough phlegm; helpful, if taken regularly, in asthma
- Relieves indigestion, wind and intestinal infections
- Use with marshmallow for cystitis
- Intestinal worms in children
- Use as a weak tea to prevent nightmares
- Thyme vinegar is antifungal for athlete's foot; dilute with an equal amount of water for washes and douches for thrush

### Dosage
- Take freely. Large doses might be needed for coughs. For an infant's coughs two or three teaspoons of syrup up to four times daily. Make a chest rub from the infused oil.
- For children's worms, use quarter to half a cup of strong tea before breakfast, for two weeks.

⤷ *Aromatherapy*

## THYME

*Thymus vulgaris*

One of the most useful medicinal herbs in natural healthcare, thyme was also one of the first plants to be used for its healing properties. The oil, distilled from the leaves and tiny purple flowering tops, has a fresh green scent.

### Properties and Uses

- Thyme is antiseptic and antibiotic, disinfectant and strongly germicidal; it is valuable for all infections especially gastric and bladder infections as it also has digestive and diuretic properties
- The oil's anti-rheumatic and antitoxic properties are beneficial in treating arthritis, gout and cellulite; rubefascient and stimulant actions also help with muscle and joint pain and poor circulation
- Stimulates the immune system to effectively fight off colds, flu and catarrh and ease coughing
- Diluted oil is good for cleaning wounds, burns, bruises and clearing lice
- Used as a mouthwash it helps to soothe and heal abscesses and gum infections
- Thyme has an uplifting fragrance, which can relieve depression, headaches and stress

### Caution

- Dilute well as thyme may cause irritation and sensitization in some people. Do not use if you have high blood pressure. Best avoided during pregnancy. Do not use if you are taking homeopathic remedies.

⟫ *Herbalism*

## TINCTURES

Tinctures are one of the most powerful and concentrated forms of herbal medicine. Powdered, fresh or dried herbs are placed in an airtight container with alcohol and left for a period of time. Alcohol extracts the valuable or essential parts of the plant and preserves them for the longest possible time. You can make your own tincture at home. Dosages are usually 5–20 drops, which can be taken directly or added to water.

## TISANES

*See Infusions*

## TRACE ELEMENTS

Minerals are inorganic chemical elements, which are necessary for many biochemical and physiological processes that go on in our bodies. Inorganic substances that are required in amounts greater than 100 mg per day are called minerals; those required in amounts less than 100 mg per day are called trace elements. Minerals are not necessarily present in foods – the quality of the soil and the geological conditions of the area in which they were grown play an important part in determining the mineral content of food. Even a balanced diet may be lacking in essential minerals or trace elements because of the soil in which it was grown.

Trace elements, or minerals required in quantities under 100 mg per day include:

- Chromium
- Zinc
- Selenium
- Silicon
- Boron
- Copper
- Manganese
- Molybdenum
- Sulphur
- Vanadium

))))➤ *Minerals*

## TRADITIONAL CHINESE MEDICINE

Traditional Chinese Medicine (TCM) is a holistic system of medicine that embraces a wide range of therapies, including herbalism, acupuncture, acupressure, diet, massage, exercise (including *Qi Gong*) and lifestyle factors. It can be enormously helpful for children suffering from chronic and acute health conditions, and for preventative healthcare. Many parents swear by the Chinese approach, which believes that health is not just the absence of symptoms, but the presence of a vital and dynamic state of well-being. Many conditions can be cured completely with appropriate treatment suggested by a registered TCM practitioner, including asthma, skin diseases, menstrual problems, neurological disorders, allergies, arthritis, depression, digestive disturbances (including colic) and migraine (including abdominal migraine, common in children), colds, coughs, flu, sore throats, period pains (common in young girls), nausea and vomiting, nasal blockages, insomnia, constipation, aches and pains (including growing pains) and earaches.

))))➤ *Acupressure, Acupuncture,*
*Chinese Herbalism*

*FAR LEFT: Thymus vulgaris (thyme).*
*NEAR LEFT: Tinctures are made from a solution of herbs left to ferment in alcohol in an airtight container.*
*LEFT: Copper (pictured, copper ore), one of the trace minerals required by the human body for optimal health.*
*BELOW: Traditional Chinese Medicine (TCM) is a holistic discipline which embraces natural therapies including herbalism (pictured), acupuncture and massage.*

## TRAVEL ESSENCE

This combination is made from the essences of banksia robur, bush iris, bottlebrush, bush fuchsia, crowea, fringed violet, macrocarpa, mulla mulla, paw paw, she oak and sundew. The use of this essence is beneficial for distress associated with all forms of travel, although it particularly addresses the problems encountered with air travel. It enables a person to arrive at their destination feeling balanced and ready to go.

### Properties and Uses

- Helps when we feel depleted, drained and disorientated
- Centres
- Refreshes
- Maintains sense of personal space

))))➤ *Australian Bush Flower Essences*

## TRYPTOPHAN

This essential amino acid is used by the brain, along with several vitamins and minerals, to produce serotonin, a neuro-transmitter. Serotonin, which regulates and induces sleep, is also said to reduce sensitivity to pain. It was one of the first amino acids to be produced for sale as a supplement, and it is useful as a natural sleeping aid.

The best sources of tryptophan are cottage cheese, milk, meat, fish, turkey, bananas and proteins.

### Properties and Uses
- May help to encourage sleep and to prevent jet lag
- Reduces sensitivity to pain
- Reduces cravings for alcohol
- Natural antidepressant and may help to reduce anxiety and panic attacks

### Dosage
- Used to prevent panic attacks and depression, it should be taken between meals with juice or water (no proteins). To help induce sleep, take 500 mg along with vitamin B6, niacinamide and magnesium an hour or so before bedtime.

### Caution
- There is some evidence that tryptophan may cause liver problems in high doses, and although studies vary, it is now believed that it can be toxic in very high doses. Take only with the advice of your doctor.

⟫➤ *Amino Acids*

## TURMERIC
*Curcuma longa*

Turmeric holds a place of honour in Ayurvedic medicine. It is a symbol of prosperity, and was believed to be a cleanser for all the systems in the body. Turmeric was prescribed as a digestive aid, a treatment for fever, infections, dysentery, arthritis and jaundice.

### Properties and Uses
- Antiseptic, warming and astringent
- Turmeric acts as a stimulant, an alterative and carminative with vulnerary and antibacterial properties
- Reduces fat, purifies blood and aids circulation
- Benefits digestion and can help rid the body of intestinal parasites

### Key Notes
- A turmeric infusion will benefit all these conditions, and reduce arthritis pain. Warm one cup of milk. Remove from heat before boiling. Stir in one teaspoon of turmeric powder. Drink up to three cups a day.

### Caution
- Do not use in cases of hepatitis or pregnancy. Turmeric is said to reduce fertility, and would not be recommended for someone trying to conceive.

⟫➤ *Herbalism*

## URTICA

*Urtica urens*

The stinging nettle is the basis for this homeopathic remedy. Used both as an internal remedy and external cream, urtica is useful for skin conditions, particularly if the skin is stinging or has the sensation of burning. It is good for rashes, where the skin is blotchy and blistered, such as urticaria (hives) and bee stings, or when there is an allergic reaction, for instance, after eating strawberries. Other conditions alleviated include rheumatism, neuralgia, neuritis, gout, excess uric acid, and in women, vulval itching and painful breasts when there is a block to milk flow.

### Properties and Uses

• Relieves stinging, burning skin conditions, rheumatic pain and neuralgia
• For cystitis
• For gout
• Symptoms improve after massaging the affected area and when lying down, and worsen in cold, damp air, if touched and with water

))))➤ *Herbalism*

## URTICA URENS

*See Nettles*

))))➤ *Homeopathy*

## VACCINATION

Immunization prepares our bodies to fight against diseases with which we may come into contact in the future. Immunization against polio, for example, stimulates the immune system to produce antibodies against the polio virus. These antibodies recognize the disease if and when it enters the body at a later date and are ready to fight it. Some types of immunization, such as those that work against polio, measles, mumps and rubella and against diphtheria, pertussis and tetanus (DTP), are aimed at the general population, primarily at young children. Others are intended for specific people, such as those exposed to dangerous infections during local outbreaks. In many countries, including the US (but not the UK), immunization against certain infections is a requirement for entry to school.

*ABOVE LEFT: Curcuma longa (turmeric) powder.*
*FAR LEFT: Bananas are just one food source containing the essential amino acid tryptophan.*
*LEFT: Urtica urens, (stinging nettle).*

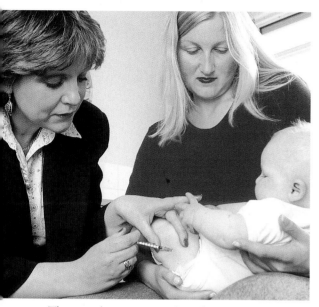

There are, however, a number of studies that show how vaccination disrupts normal immune function. When we contract an illness naturally, our bodies begin to build up defences long before symptoms become evident. An illness has to get past the skin, sneezing reflexes, respiratory secretions (mucus), tears, fever, intestinal flora and other elements of immunity before it can gain access to major organs and tissues of the body. As it passes these sites, immunity is built up against the invader. The disease itself is the peak of the 'antibody response'. In other words, symptoms are an indication that our bodies are fighting off the disease.

A child who gets measles, for example, will have 100 per cent immunity to the disease, and the infection will have prepared him or her to respond even more promptly and effectively to other infections acquired in the future.

When the vaccine viruses are injected or squirted directly into the child's body, they bypass the normal immune system response. In other words, it is a fairly serious shock to the body to find itself with a virus at hand, and none of its immune responses prepared. By introducing viruses directly into the bloodstream, far from preventing diseases, it actually pushes the disease into a chronic form and deeper into the body, where it then attacks vital organs. It has been suggested

that by suppressing measles and other infectious diseases in this manner may lead to cancer and other chronic and auto-immune diseases.

Despite government assurances to the contrary, there are protesters who are concerned by the link between bowel disorders, encephalitis, epilepsy, MS, diabetes and autism and immunization.

Many natural health practitioners are against the idea of vaccination for all of these reasons. There are homeopathic alternatives available that can be taken instead of vaccinating, but of course this is a very personal choice that must be thought about carefully.
))))▶ *Homeopathy, Immunity, Nosodes*

## VALERIAN

*Valeriana officinalis*

This strong-smelling herb is used to relieve conditions that have been induced by anxiety and nervous tension.

### Properties and Uses
- Sedative, nerve restorative, calms the heart, antispasmodic, carminative
- Good for anxiety, confusion, migraines, insomnia and depression with anxiety
- Useful when flying
- Helps palpitations and withdrawal from tranquillizers
- Helpful in treating high blood pressure due to stress
- Use with chamomile for colic and nervous indigestion

### Dosage
- The cold decoction is best: soak one teaspoon in a cup of cold water overnight, dose half to one cup. Tincture: 20–60 drops three times daily. More may be needed to help tranquillizer withdrawal. Relaxing tablets containing valerian are widely available; follow dose on box.

## VALNET, DR JEAN

French army surgeon Dr Jean Valnet successfully used essential oils to treat soldiers wounded in battle and patients in a psychiatric hospital. In 1964 Valnet published *Aromathérapie,* still considered by many to be the authority on aromatherapy and the use of essential oils. This is the classic textbook of serious aromatherapy practice. Valnet is President of the Societe Francaise de Phytotherapie et d'Aromatherapie, which is world-renowned for the study of aromatherapy. Valnet is widely believed to have given aromatherapy a credible standing in the world of science and medicine.

))))➤ *Aromatherapy*

## VAPORIZER

*See Steam Inhalations.*
))))➤ *Herbalism*

## VERVAIN

*Verbena officinalis*

This herb is good for anxiety and is often given for anxious states during pregnancy because of its high iron content.

### Properties and Uses

- Use as a tonic, fever herb, nerve restorative, anti-spasmodic, carminative, diuretic, promotes milk flow, emmenagogue
- For exhaustion and post viral fatigue; exhaustion from overwork; a useful general tonic
- For nervous depression
- Treats fevers and flu, especially with headaches and nervous symptoms.
- For insomnia and excessive dreaming; feelings of paranoia
- For indigestion, worms and parasites; digestive discomfort following treatment for parasites
- Treats liverishness with nausea, heavy headaches and depression, irritable bowel syndrome with mucus in the stools
- Helpful in asthma – relieves chest tension
- Sip the tea throughout labour to encourage regular contractions; continue after the birth to encourage milk flow; treats postnatal depression

*LEFT: Vaccinating our children has become a standard procedure; however, there are homeopathic alternatives available if you disagree with vaccination.*
*ABOVE: A vaporiser with a night light.*
*RIGHT: Verbena officinalis (vervain).*

- For period pains and to restore periods stopped by stress
- Treats post-operative tiredness and depression
- As a compress for inflamed eyes

### Dosage

- Standard-strength teas taken every two hours in fevers or three cups a day for chronic complaints. For worms and parasites make double-strength tea and drink before breakfast for some weeks or until better.
- Vervain tea is an ideal restorative for people strained by over-work, especially mental work. This is also one of the indications for the use of the flower remedy.

))))➤ *Flower Essences*

# VERVAIN

*Verbena officinalis*

Vervain is used to treat stress. The people who need it have fixed ideas and principles. They are strong-willed and rarely change their views; they think they are right and obstinately maintain a stance, or fight on when others would have conceded. They are great doers and wish to convert all those around them. They strive with mental energy and will-power, but the effort of battling against the will of others is extremely stressful, even exhausting. Vervain brings calm and tolerance.

## Properties and Uses

- Vervain is for self-driven activity, often with over commitment; it can be used for overwork and stress-related illnesses
- Common accompanying symptoms include anxiety, indigestion, insomnia and sleep disorders
- Vervain brings calm and a space for reflection. It relieves stress and helps to bring the personal will into harmony with the world

))))➤ *Herbalism*

# VIBRATIONAL MEDICINE

Vibrational medicine involves using substances or treatments that work on the natural energy field of the body. Homeopathy and flower essences are good examples of this type of treatment. Because the remedies are so diluted, they often contain only a vibration of the original substance, and it is this vibration that works on the body's natural energy field. It is rather like radio signal rather than an overt substance, but it is that subtle signal that effects a cure.

))))➤ *Flower Essences, Homeopathy*

# VINE

*Vitis vinifera*

Vine is for capable, confident and successful people; for those who 'would be king'. They believe they know best and that others would be happier if they followed. They can bully and dominate, disabling others and gaining authority at the expense of other people's confidence. Even in illness, from the sick bed, they can be ruthless and dominating, ordering their carers around. Vine encourages equality and the respect each of us as humans are due.

## Properties and Uses

- For dominating and bullying types who can be cruel and callous through thoughtlessness
- Good for stress-related illnesses
- Vine allows us to stand back and let others express themselves; to respect the absolute authority of each person over their own inner life and to acknowledge their personal choices

))))➤ *Bach Flower Remedies*

*LEFT: Vervain, an original Bach flower remedy works well to relieve stress and to bring calmness into our world.*
*BELOW LEFT: Vitis vinifera (vine).*
*RIGHT: Vinegar is obtained from a fermentation of alcohol and can be used to preserve herbs for medicinal purposes.*

## VINEGAR

*Acetic acid*

Vinegar (from the French *vinaigre*, 'sour wine') is an acidic liquid obtained from the fermentation of alcohol and used either as a condiment or a preservative. Vinegar usually has an acid content of between four and eight per cent; in flavour it may be sharp, rich or mellow. Vinegar is often used to preserve herbs, and is used on its own for medicinal purposes. Apple cider vinegar is the most useful medicinally.

### Properties and Uses

- Helps to make more efficient use of calcium in the body, and can help to encourage strong bones, hair and nails
- Vinegar is antiseptic, astringent and excellent for urinary tract infections
- Antispasmodic
- Antibacterial
- Improves functioning and adjustment of the body so that there is efficient use of the food you eat (i.e. it balances metabolic activity)
- Anti-fungal, used in the treatment of thrush
- Apple cider vinegar is a good tonic and relieves sore throats
- Sip first thing in the morning, and just prior to meals to reduce appetite and encourage efficient digestion of food
- Simmer cider vinegar in a pan, cover with a towel and inhale to reduce the spasms of bronchitis and to help reduce any excess catarrh
- Drink a glass of warm apple cider vinegar with honey half an hour before bed to encourage restful sleep; excellent for insomniacs
- Vinegar can be drunk (warm, with a little honey) to treat digestive disorders and urinary infections
- Apply vinegar to wasp stings to reduce swelling and ease discomfort

- Coughs, colds and infections will respond to a cup of warm water with two tablespoons of vinegar and some honey; arthritis and asthma may also be treated with the same drink, adding slightly more vinegar
- Apply cider vinegar on the skin to treat athlete's foot, ringworm and eczema
- Drink vinegar daily to treat thrush, and apply to the exterior of the vagina (mixed with a little warm water) to ease itching
- Add vinegar to bath water to soothe skin problems, to help draw out toxins from the skin and ease thrush

## VINEGARS

Herbal tinctures can also be made using vinegar, which contains acetic acid and acts as a solvent and preservative in a way similar to alcohol. Choose apple cider vinegar, which has its own therapeutic qualities. Steep macerated spices or aromatic herbs in vinegar. Cover tightly and keep the container in a warm place for two weeks, shaking twice a day. Strain, and pour the tincture into a dark bottle. This can be used for health purposes and in cooking.

NORMANDY CIDER VINEGAR
MADE IN FRANCE
*Ideal in Salad Dressings and Marinades*

## VISUALIZATION

This technique can be easily learned and used to great effect. Visualization is the conscious use of the imagination to create images that you can use to heal or change aspects of your life. It can help to deepen the relaxation process and overcome many of the mental and emotional problems that can lead to ill health. It is often goal-directed, which means you set yourself a mental goal such as 'I feel calm and in control' or 'I am slim', and your mind learns to accept it. Relaxation therapists encourage you to use the skill to picture yourself overcoming a problem or an illness and to replace negative and destructive emotions with positive, life-enhancing alternatives.

Visualization uses the power of the mind to enhance the benefits of physical relaxation. The brain is divided into two hemispheres: the left which is concerned with logic and reason and the right which relates to creativity, imagination and emotions. Most of the time we use the left side to work, study and cope with daily life. The right side is used much less, but any images which we create in it are believed to be directly linked to physical responses in the body. So

remembering an embarrassing situation can bring on all the symptoms of the stress experienced in the situation. Given that children have such intense and strong memories of anything they consider to be traumatic. It is extremely useful to learn the balancing art of positive visualization. Soothing or positive images can provoke a corresponding sense of calm or well-being in the body.

Visualization encourages right-brain activity and uses the images it provides to override destructive effects wrought by the left side. It is based on the belief that imagination is stronger than intellect. If we give our minds a positive image they will accept it, providing the image is strong and believable.

))))➤ *Meditation, Relaxation*

## VITAL FORCE

Chinese medical practitioners believe that a vital force, called *chi*, flows through our body in channels, or meridians. When this vital force, or energy, becomes blocked or stagnant, disease and disharmony result. Similarly, homeopaths and most other therapists believe that there is a vital energy that drives and animates our bodies and mind.

Different therapies and disciplines have a variety of names for this force: spirit or energy, for example. But the concept remains the same. It is the body's controlling energy. It vitalizes the physical body, and it is the link between the body, soul and mind. Some complementary medical disciplines believe that energy flows through our bodies, and that illness or 'dis-ease' is caused by blockages and imbalance. Others believe that it is simply a governing force that can be weakened by environmental factors (diet, trauma, stress, pollution, sleep patterns, for example), so that it can no longer keep the whole body (that is, mind, body and spirit) balanced. The vital force is not a material substance, such as water or air, but it is

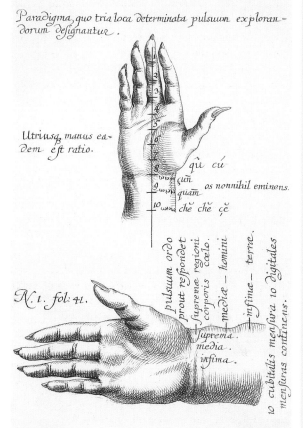

*Paradigma, quo tria loca determinata pulsuum explorandorum designantur.*

*Utriusq̃ manus eadem est ratio.*

qȗi cȗ
ḡun
quam̃ os nonnihil eminens.
chễ chễ çễ

*pulsuum ordo prout respondet suprema regioni corporis coelo.*
*media – homini.*
*infima – terræ.*

*Suprema.*
*media.*
*infima.*

*10 cubitalis mensura 10 digitales mensuras continens.*

*N. 1. fol: 41.*

equally indispensable for life. Its presence distinguishes living things from inanimate matter. When illness occurs, it appears first as a disturbance in this natural energy long before it manifests itself as physical symptoms.

The concept of the vital force also helps to explain the differences between us – why some of us are more susceptible to environmental factors than others.

▶ **Energy, Spirit, Traditional Chinese Medicine**

*LEFT: Visualization as a conscious use of the imagination to aid relaxation and healing is often practiced during meditation.*
*ABOVE: The Chinese believe that chi, or vital force, flows through our body in channels, or meridians. This belief underpins the Chinese theory of pulses (pictured) showing where blood-flow can be accessed and used for healing purposes.*
*RIGHT: Milk contains large amounts of fat-soluble vitamin A.*

## VITAMIN A

Vitamin A is a fat-soluble vitamin which comes in two forms: retinol, which is found in animal products like liver, eggs, butter and cod-liver oil, and beta-carotene, which our body converts into vitamin A when it is required. Beta-carotene is found in any brightly coloured fruit and vegetables.

Vitamin A was for many years called a miracle vitamin because of its positive effect on the immune system and growth. It is necessary for healthy skin and eyes, and allows us to see in the dark. Beta-carotene is an antioxidant, and it has anti-carcinogenic properties.

The best sources for vitamin A are cod-liver oil, liver, kidney, eggs and dairy produce. Beta-carotene can be found in carrots, tomatoes, watercress, broccoli, spinach, cantaloupe and apricots.

### Properties and Uses
- Anti-carcinogenic
- Prevents and treats skin disorders and ageing of skin
- Improves vision and prevents night blindness
- Improves our bodies' ability to heal
- Promotes growth of strong bones, hair, teeth, skin and gums
- May help in the treatment of hyperthyroidism

### Dosage
- The RDA is believed to be inadequate, and people with special needs (e.g. following illness, suffering from infections or diabetes), should have a higher level
- As vitamin A, up to 6000 mcg if you are not pregnant
- As beta-carotene, 15 mg can be taken as a preventative measure against illness

### Caution
- Vitamin A as retinol is toxic and should not be taken at all by pregnant women. Beta-carotene is not toxic and is considered to be safe for adults and children alike.

▶ **Antioxidants, Beta-carotene, Vitamins**

## VITAMIN B9 (FOLIC ACID)

Folic acid is a water-soluble vitamin which forms part of the B-complex family. It is also known as vitamin Bc or vitamin B9. Low levels of folic acid may lead to anaemia. Folic acid is essential for the division of body cells, and needed for the utilization of sugar and amino acids.

Recent findings indicate that folic acid can prevent some types of cancer and birth defects, and it is helpful in the treatment of heart disease. Most folic-acid deficiency is the result of a poor diet because it is abundant in leafy green vegetables, yeasts and liver. Taken from just before conception, and particularly in the first trimester of pregnancy, folic acid can prevent spina bifida.

The best source of folic acid are green leafy vegetables, wheatgerm, nuts, eggs, bananas, oranges and organ meats e.g. liver.

### Properties and Uses
- Improves lactation
- May protect against cancer
- Improves skin
- A natural analgesic
- Increases appetite in debilitated patients
- Needed for metabolism of RNA and DNA
- Helps form blood
- Builds up resistance to infection in newborns and infants
- Essential for genetic code transmission
- Prevents spina bifida

### Key Notes and Dosage
- There are many people at risk of deficiency, including heavy drinkers, pregnant women; elderly and those on low-fat diets. Supplementation at 400–800 mcg is recommended for those at risk.
- It is best taken with a good multivitamin and mineral supplement.
- Folic acid is toxic in large doses and can cause severe neurological problems. High doses may cause insomnia and interfere with the absorption of zinc in the body.

⟫➤ *Vitamins*

## VITAMIN C (ASCORBIC ACID)

Vitamin C is water-soluble, which means that it is not stored by the body; we need to ensure that we get adequate amounts in our daily diets. More people take vitamin C than any other supplement and yet studies show that a large percentage of the population is still deficient.

Vitamin C is also known as ascorbic acid, and it is one of the most versatile of the vitamins needed to sustain life. It is one of the antioxidant vitamins and is believed to boost immunity and to fight cancer and infection.

The best sources of vitamin C are rosehips, blackcurrants, broccoli, citrus fruits, and also in all fresh fruit and vegetables.

### Properties and Uses
- Reduces cholesterol and helps prevent heart disease
- Hastens healing of wounds
- Maintains healthy bones, teeth and sex organs
- Acts as a natural antihistamine
- May help to overcome male infertility
- Fights cancer
- Boosts immunity and reduces the duration of colds and other viruses
- Helps maintain good vision
- Antioxidant

### Key Notes and Dosages
- At least 60 mg is necessary for health, but more is required by smokers (25 g is depleted with every

*ABOVE: Water-soluble Vitamin C, found in fresh fruit and vegetables, helps counteract the effects of high cholesterol levels.*
*ABOVE RIGHT: Cod-liver oil capsules.*
*RIGHT: Vegetable oils have high concentrations of vitamin E.*

cigarette), and people who are under stress, taking antibiotics, suffering from an infection, drink heavily or after an accident or injury.

- Daily dosages of up to 1500 mg per day appear to be safe, but take in three doses, preferably with meals and in a time-release formula.
- Vitamin C may cause kidney stones and gout in some people, others may suffer from diarrhoea and cramps at high dosages, although the vitamin is considered to be non-toxic at even very high levels.

))))➤ *Antioxidants, Immunity, Vitamins*

## VITAMIN D

Vitamin D is a fat-soluble vitamin which is found in foods of animal origin, and is known as the sunshine vitamin. Vitamin D can be produced in the skin from the energy of the Sun, and it is not found in rich supply in any food.

Vitamin D is important for calcium and phosphorus absorption, and helps to regulate calcium metabolism. Recent research suggests that it could have a role in protecting against some cancers and infectious diseases. Deficiency is caused by inadequate exposure to sunlight, and low consumption of foods that contain vitamin D.

The best sources of Vitamin D are animal produce, such as milk and eggs, oily fish, butter and cheese; cod-liver oil is also a good source.

### Properties and Uses
- Protects against osteoporosis
- May help in the treatment of psoriasis
- Boosts the immune system
- May help in protection against and treatment of cancer
- Necessary for strong teeth and bones

### Key Notes and Dosage
- Supplementation between 5–10 mcg is suggested for those at risk of deficiency.
- Vitamin D is the most toxic of all the vitamins, causing nausea, vomiting, headache and depression, among other symptoms. Do not take in excess of 10 mcg daily.

))))➤ *Vitamins*

## VITAMIN E

Vitamin E is fat-soluble and one of the key antioxidant vitamins. Its key function is as an anti-coagulant, but its role in boosting the immune system and protecting against cardiovascular disease are becoming increasingly clear.

Apart from its crucial antioxidant value, vitamin E is important for the production of energy and the maintenance of health at every level.

Unlike most fat-soluble vitamins, vitamin E is stored in the body for only a short period of time and up to 75 per cent of the daily dose is excreted in the faeces.

The best sources of Vitamin E are wheatgerm (fresh), soya beans, vegetable oils, broccoli, leafy green vegetables, wholegrains, peanuts and eggs.

### Properties and Uses
- Antioxidant; helps to slow the process of ageing
- Protects against neurological disorders
- Boosts immunity
- Protects against cardiovascular disease
- Alleviates fatigue
- Accelerates healing – particularly of burns
- Reduces symptoms of PMS
- Treats skin problems and baldness
- Aids in the prevention of miscarriage
- Acts as a natural diuretic
- Prevents thick scar formation

### Key Notes and Dosage
- Available in many forms (dry is best for people with skin problems or oil intolerance).
- Daily dosage may be from 250–80 mg daily, but you may be advised to take higher doses in some cases.
- Vitamin E is non-toxic, even in high doses, but it is not suggested that you take in excess of 350 mg unless you are supervised by a registered practitioner

))))➤ *Antioxidants, Vitamins*

## VITAMIN K

The K vitamins are fat-soluble, and are necessary for normal blood clotting. They are often used to treat the toxic effects of anticoagulant drops, such as warfarin, and in people who have a poor ability to absorb fats.

Vitamin K occurs naturally in foods as vitamin K1, and is produced by intestinal bacteria as vitamin K2. Synthetic vitamin K is known as K3. Vitamin K1 injections are routinely given to newborn babies to prevent haemorrhage, but since a recent scare linked the vitamin with childhood leukaemia, it is now more often given as oral drops.

The best sources of Vitamin K are vegetables, such as cauliflower, spinach and peas, and wholegrain cereals.

### Properties and Uses
• Controls blood clotting

### Key Notes and Dosage
• Most people produce sufficient quantities of the vitamin in the intestine, but it is estimated that we need between 500 and 1000 mcg from our diet.
• There are no reports of toxicity, but because of the possibility that injected vitamin K may be related to childhood leukaemia, oral drops are suggested for newborns.

))))➤ *Vitamins*

## VITAMINS

Vitamins are compounds needed by the body in small quantities to enable our bodies to grow, develop and function. They work with enzymes in the body, and other compounds, to help produce energy, build tissues, remove waste, and ensure that each system works effectively and efficiently. Ideally vitamins are present in roughly the same quantity in various foods.

))))➤ *Diet, Natural Health, Phyto-chemicals*

## WALNUT

*Juglans regia*

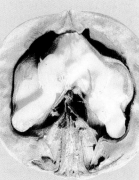

Walnut is for people who need to find constancy and protection from outside forces. People who are indecisive or clingy need to move on and break links and old patterns with people and things, but are reluctant to do so. Walnut frees the person from interference and gives protection so that it is possible to break inappropriate ties and pursue personal freedom. Walnut is useful for people on the brink of some major decision or change e.g. children leaving home, the menopause, marriage or having babies.

### Key Notes
• Walnut is for change. It is useful during any of the milestones of life, such as puberty, marriage, leaving home, a change of job or even a change of school.
• A walnut person may be indecisive and clingy; they can see the advantages of moving but find it impossible to do so.
• It is also useful for those who become temporarily distracted or dominated by the enthusiasm, salesmanship or strong opinions of others.

))))➤ *Bach Flower Remedies*

## WARATAH

*Telopea speciosissima*

For the person who is going through the 'black night of the soul' and is in utter despair, waratah gives them the strength and courage to cope with their crisis and will bring their survival skills to the fore. This remedy will also enhance and amplify those skills. It is for emergencies and great challenges. This powerful remedy often only needs to be used for four or five days. The waratah essence was made with great assistance and guidance in profound metaphysical circumstances, from what was known to be the last flowering waratah shrub of the season.

### Properties and Uses

- For hopelessness and an inability to respond to a crisis
- Brings, courage, tenacity, adaptability and strong faith
- Enhances survival skills

))))➤ *Australian Bush Flower Essences*

## WATER

About 65 per cent of our bodies are made up of water, so it is not surprising that water is the most essential element of our diets. Without food we can last for several weeks. Without water, we would be dead within a few days.

### What Does It Do?

- Water is essential to the digestive process. If we do not drink enough between meals, the saliva flow slows down and digestion is less efficient.

- Almost two litres of water is excreted from our bodies every day through our skin, urine, lungs and gut, and many toxins are removed from our bodies this way. If we are losing this much water, we need to replace it. The more water we drink, the greater the number of toxins eliminated.

- Without water our cells cannot build new tissue efficiently, toxic products build up in our bloodstream, blood volume decreases so that we have less oxygen and nutrients transported to our cells, all of which can leave us weak, tired and at risk of illness.

))))➤ *Diet, Hydrotherapy*

*FAR LEFT: Vitamin K is contained in vegetables like cauliflower.*
*NEAR LEFT: Cross-section of a walnut.*
*ABOVE: Water is an essential component of our planet and our bodies.*
*RIGHT: Waratah works to reinforce our survival skills.*

## WATER VIOLET

*Hottonia palustris*

Water violet is for self-reliant people, with an aloof, live-and-let-live attitude. They are quiet and spend much time alone, keeping others at a distance. When ill they keep to themselves and do not wish to be of any trouble to those around them. They find it hard to share. In their isolation they may feel special, or chosen, a sensation which can distort their sense of belonging and self-worth.

Water violet gives the confidence to share strengths and weaknesses, the ups and downs, all of life's rich tapestry.

### Key Notes

- The person needing water violet is reserved and self-contained. The self-reliance can be seen as aloofness and pride, leading to loneliness.
- For solitary yet proud people.
- Associated symptoms may include stiffness, arthritis, or hardening of the arteries.
- Water violet acknowledges the inner self as a starting point from which to expand, communicate with the world and share from the heart.

)))》 *Bach Flower Remedies*

## WEDDING BUSH

*Ricinocarpus pinifolius*

Wedding Bush is for people who have difficulty committing themselves to relationships, whether they be personal, social or business. This essence can be taken when people begin a union or partnership. It is usually used for people who flit from one relationship to another, or when the initial attraction fails.

### Properties and Uses

- For difficulty with commitment
- Brings commitment to relationships and dedication to life purpose

## WHITE CHESTNUT

*Æsculus hippocstanum*

This Bach flower remedy is for when the mind is full of unwanted thoughts, ideas or persistent and worrying mental arguments, overactive and exhausting mental chatter, going round and round in a never-ending circle. It is for people who cannot switch off.

### Properties and Uses

- For people who cannot switch off and suffer from constant mental chatter, persistent thoughts and worries
- Treats insomnia, tiredness, irritability, headaches and an inability to concentrate
- For sleeplessness due to worry
- White chestnut switches off unwanted thoughts so that it is possible to find peace and mental clarity
- If thoughts persist, the chatter is a subconscious distraction and other remedies might be needed to address the root cause

)))》 *Bach Flower Remedies*

## WILD OAT

*Bromus ramosus*

This Bach flower remedy is for capable people who have ambition to do something meaningful in their lives but have not yet found their true calling. They may have several choices or directions they could follow and may be working hard on a given path, but basically they are dissatisfied and frustrated. Somewhere they know that they have not found their true calling in life and are emotionally or spiritually unsatisfied.

Wild oat helps to tune the heart and find true meaning and purpose. It helps make choices, sometimes difficult, which unite all aspirations and bring harmony to inner and outer calling; it balances the needs of spirituality and making a living.

### Properties and Uses

- For uncertainty and frustration with current activities, a desire to find a purpose despite aimless drifting from one job or relationship to another
- For dissatisfaction and headaches
- Wild oat helps us listen for our calling, find our true vocation and gives the strength of character to act on this

))》 *Bach Flower Remedies*

## WILD ROSE

*Rosa canina*

Dr Bach recommended wild rose for fatalists who have become resigned to all that happens. They glide through life passively, taking it as it is,

*TOP LEFT:* Hottonia palustris *(water violet).*
*LEFT:* Bromus ramous *(wild oat).*
*RIGHT:* Rosa canina *(wild rose).*

without motivation or expectation. They are apathetic about change and ask, 'What is the use?' They have given away their power and interest in life. Wild rose stimulates interest in life and an appreciation of its colour and joy. The remedy encourages action and a purposeful pleasure in being and doing.

### Properties and Uses

- For people who are fatalistic; resigned to events and apathetic about change
- Treats exhaustion, deficiency illnesses and general weakness, lingering trivial ailments and lack of vitality
- Wild rose helps us to interact with all aspects of life and make an impact by creating our own unique and dynamic reality

))》 *Bach Flower Remedies*

## WILD YAM

*Dioscorea villosa*

The rhizome of a Mexican wild yam. Wild yam is the starting point for synthesization of hormones for the contraceptive pill and for 'natural progesterone' which is used in a prescription cream for the menopause.

### Properties and Uses

- Anti-inflammatory, anti-spasmodic
- For stomach cramps, nausea, vomiting, hiccups, recurrent colicky pains, pain of diverticulitis and gall bladder pains; use with a little ginger for a quicker action

- Relieves period pain and pain on ovulation
- For menopausal symptoms and vaginal dryness
- Use for rheumatoid arthritis

### Key Notes

- Works especially well on persistent and recurrent problems.

## WILLOW

*Salix alba var. vitellina*

Willow is for people who find injustices hard to accept and are embittered. They take problems personally and life becomes a personal trial to endure, without hope or happiness. They blame the world when things go wrong. Willow helps them see that with this self-pitying outlook they are creating their own oppression by negative thoughts.

### Key Notes

- The people who need willow may be sulky and selfish, even embittered, with self-pity and ungrateful for help.
- Physically there may be stiffness and arthritis, as well as psychosomatic illness and tearfulness.
- Willow helps us see that we create our own reality by focusing on different elements of our lives. It encourages a more positive and mature attitude. Willow may also be taken for a brief temporary embitterment, such as that which follows a job loss or the end of a marriage.

)))⯈ *Bach Flower Remedies*

## WITCH HAZEL

*Hamamelis virginiana*

Witch hazel is a common tree, grown in America. Its leaves or roots are used for medicinal purposes. This herb can be found in most households in the form of distilled witch hazel. It is the most applicable and easy to use astringent for common usage. As with all astringents, this herb may be used wherever there has been bleeding, both internally and externally.

### Properties and Uses

- Astringent, anti-inflammatory
- Useful in the easing of haemorrhoids; it has a deserved reputation in the treatment of bruises and inflamed swellings, also with varicose veins
- Witch hazel will control diarrhoea and aid in the easing of dysentery

)))⯈ *Herbalism*

## YARROW

*Achillea millefolium*

Yarrow is a sacred plant to many cultures. In China, yarrow stalks were used to cast the *I Ching*, to read the future for the emperor. Ayurvedics use the herb as a 'heal-all' because it has so many uses – allowing you to keep your head in the heavens and your feet on the ground. Yarrow balances emotional upsets, and is a frequent addition to treatments during menopause.

### Properties and Uses

- Diaphoretic, anti-inflammatory, antiseptic, anti-spasmodic, styptic, gentle bitter tonic
- For early stages of fevers, especially with hot, dry skin
- Treats catarrh, sinusitis, hayfever and dust allergies
- Useful in high blood pressure, with hawthorn and linden
- Use with a little ginger for cold feet
- Use internally and externally for varicose veins and spontaneous bruising, for thrombosis and to prevent blood clots
- Supportive for people undergoing radiotherapy and intestinal infections
- Treats diarrhoea, colicky pains, liverishness, weak digestion
- For irregular menstrual bleeding, period pains and vaginal discharges; improves pelvic circulation

*LEFT: Hamamelis virginiana (witch hazel).*
*ABOVE: Achillea millefolium (yarrow).*

- Use with sage and marigold for pelvic infections and pelvic congestion with period pains and pain before periods
- Use as a tea or tincture to disinfect wounds and stop bleeding
- Use as a cream or compress for bleeding piles
- Apply the infused oil to inflammations associated with varicose veins
- Bathe to relieve aches and pains

### Key Notes and Dosage

- For a bath simmer a handful of fresh leaves in 500 ml, or one pint, of water for 15 minutes. Strain and add to your bath water.
- The fresh leaf can be chewed and applied to cuts to stop bleeding. Chew the root to relieve toothache.

## YELLOW DOCK

*Rumex crispus*

This nutritious herb helps with poor liver functioning and helps to increase bile flow. It also acts as a laxative and can be used externally for ringworm or scabies.

### Properties and Uses

- An astringent, laxative, bitter tonic, alterative
- Alleviates chronic constipation
- For liver congestion with poor fat digestion and feelings of heaviness after eating
- For stomach acidity and irritable bowel syndrome with constipation
- Use for food poisoning and intestinal infections, to clear the source of irritation from the digestive system
- Use with burdock for chronic, hot and itchy skin diseases

### Dosage

- Make the decoction using 12 g for 500 ml of water (half an ounce to one pint of water). For constipation one cup of decoction or two teaspoons of tincture daily. More might be needed for short periods. Use half this dose for chronic conditions, for children and for constipation in pregnancy.

## YLANG YLANG

*Cananga odorata*
*var. genuina*

Ylang ylang is distilled from trees known as perfume trees, which originated in the Philippines and have now spread through-out Asia. The oil is distilled from the freshly picked flowers. The oil is very liquid, clear and has a heady fragrance with high notes of hyacinth and narcissus.

### Properties and Uses

• An adaptogenic oil, which means that it can help to rebalance – working as either a stimulant or a relaxant
• Sedative, antidepressant and a tonic for the nervous system; depression, anxiety, tension, irritability, and stress-related insomnia can all benefit from its sooth-ing properties
• Helps to rebalance sebum production in oily skin, acne and both dry and greasy scalps; it can also be used to calm irritated skin as well as bites and stings
• Ylang ylang has also been attributed with aphrodisiac properties and can be used to treat sexual problems
• Acts as a circulatory tonic and works to rebalance body functions generally; it can help to reduce blood pressure and slow breathing and heart rate in cases of shock or panic; experts recommend that people suffering from palpitations or low blood pressure should carry a small bottle of the oil to inhale when necessary

### Caution

• Can cause nausea or headaches in high concentrations. May irritate some hypersensitive people
ᗕ▶ *Essential Oils*

## YOGA

Yoga encourages flexibility, relaxation skills and breathing. Used therapeutically, yoga can help with the following: muscle joint mobility, flexibility, breathing disorders, musculo-skeletal pain, nervous system and endocrine disorders, digestive problems, fatigue, insomnia and stress-related conditions.

The word yoga means 'unity' or 'oneness' and is derived from the Sanskrit word *yug* which means 'to join'. In spiritual terms it refers to the union of the individual consciousness with the universal consciousness. On a practical level yoga is a means of balancing and harmonizing the body, mind and emotions, and is a tool that allows us to withdraw from the chaos of the world and find a quiet space within. It utilizes the innate life force within the body and teaches how to tap into, harness and direct it skilfully. To achieve this, yoga uses movement, breath, posture, relaxation and meditation in order to establish a healthy, vibrant and balanced approach to living.

Yoga exercises are comprised of *asanas*, or postures, that involve stretching, bending, turning and relaxation. Each posture has a specific therapeutic effect. There are

six main groups of yoga postures: standing, inverted, twist, back bend, forward bend and side bend.

**Key Notes**
- Standing – improves efficiency of the muscular, circulatory, respiratory, digestive, reproductive, endocrine and nervous systems.
- Inverted – balances endocrine system and metabolism. Enhances thinking power and revitalizes internal organs.
- Twisting – aids digestion, helps relieve back pain, improves intercostal breathing.
- Back bend – invigorating, encourages deep breathing.
- Forward bend – improves blood circulation, aids digestion and calms emotions.
- Side bend – stimulates main organs such as liver, kidney, stomach and spleen.

### YOGHURT

As a food, yoghurt is a rich source of protein and all of the vitamins and minerals found in milk. Live yoghurt, which contains active bacteria, is most often used therapeutically and should be eaten to increase the healthy bacteria in the body, which help our body to fight infection.

**Properties and Uses**
- Live yoghurt may help to reduce blood cholesterol levels
- Live yoghurt should be eaten to increase beneficial bacteria following a course of antibiotics; eat daily for two to three weeks for best effect

*ABOVE LEFT: Ylang ylang.*
*LEFT: Yoga teaches that a unity of body and spiritual consciousness promotes longevity and that correct breathing techniques increase the body's natural stamina.*
*ABOVE: A daily intake of yoghurt can help prevent heart-related diseases, reduce blood cholesterol levels and help fight infection.*

- Apply live bacteria to areas affected by thrush; can be used internally as a douche
- Daily intake of yoghurt may prevent heart disease

))))➤ *Acidophilus, Nutrition*

### ZINC

Zinc is one of the most important trace elements in our diet and it is required for more than 200 enzymic activities within the body. It is the principal protector of the immune system and is crucial in the regulation of our genetic information. Zinc is also essential for the structure and function of all cell membranes.

Zinc is an antioxidant and can help to detoxify the body. A zinc deficiency can cause growth failure, infertility, impotence and in some cases, an impaired sense of taste. Eczema is commonly linked to zinc deficiency: new research points to the fact that post-natal illness may be a direct result of insufficient zinc in the diet. A weakened immune system and a poor ability to heal may indicate deficiency.

The best sources of zinc are offal, meat, mushrooms, oysters, eggs, wholegrain products and brewer's yeast.

**Properties and Uses**
- Boosts the immune system
- Prevents cancer
- Prevents and treats colds
- Maintains senses of taste, smell and vision
- May help to prevent degenerative effects of ageing
- Prevents hair loss
- Treats acne and other skin problems
- Useful in the treatment of rheumatoid arthritis
- Prevents blindness associated with ageing
- Increases male potency and sex drive
- Used in the treatment of infertility

**Dosage**
- Take 15–30 mg daily, and increase copper and selenium intake if taking more zinc
- Very high doses (above 150 mg per day) of zinc may cause some nausea, vomiting and diarrhoea.

))))➤ *Antioxidants, Immunity, Minerals*

# GLOSSARY

**ABCESSES**
Localized pus-forming bacterial infection on the surface of the skin. Treatment requires removal of the tissue through the skin with a needle or open surgical drainage requiring local anaesthesia.

**ACUTE ILLNESS**
Short-lasting illness with a sudden, rapid onset, such as flu or tonsillitis. Recovery almost always takes place without medical intervention.

**ALKALINE**
A chemical compound which belongs to a class of substances that are soluble in alcohol and water, and are able to combine with oils and fats to form soap. They neutralize acids by forming salts.

**ALLERGY**
State of oversensitivity produced by exposure to particular substances which trigger off an exaggerated response in the immune system.

**ANAEMIA**
Condition associated with low red blood cell count (and hence iron) in the bloodstream which causes weakness, giddiness and produces a pale complexion.

**ANAESTHETIC**
Any drug or agent used to produce the partial loss of feeling or sensation of pain. Usually used to perform surgery and other painful procedures.

**ANTIMICROBIAL**
Any substance that prevents microorganisms from multiplying and producing widespread infection.

**APHRODISIAC**
Sexual stimulant, usually credited with increasing vitality and stimulating the growth and function of vital organs.

**ASTRINGENT**
Binding and contracting effect on the mucous membrane, to give it a protective coating against irritants or infective organisms. Good natural examples include lemon, sage and thyme.

**ATHEROSCLEROSIS**
Progressive narrowing and hardening of arteries over time, usually associated with ageing, but can also be caused by high cholesterol levels and obesity.

**BITTER**
Quality of food which stimulates appetite. One of the six Ayurvedic tastes, found in barks, tannins and resins.

**CALCIFICATION**
Degenerative process by which organic tissue becomes hardened by deposits of calcium salts.

**CARDIOVASCULAR**
Belonging to or associated with the heart and the blood vessels (veins, arteries, arterioles, venules, capillaries).

**CARMINATIVE**
Any substance that relaxes digestive tensions and spasms. Good natural examples include cloves, coriander, fennel, parsley, peppermint and thyme.

**CAROTENOID**
Photosynthetic pigment occurring in plants and bacteria with a high affinity to fats. They are found in chloroplasts and aid the process of photosynthesis.

**CHAKRAS**
Circles thought to be found along the midline of the body, in line with the spinal column. In Eastern medicine, they are considered channel pathways through which *qi* or *chi* flows.

**CHEMOTHERAPY**
Treatment of disease by means of chemicals that have a specific toxic effect upon the disease and selectively destroy cancerous tissue (a malignant tumour or growth).

**CHRONIC ILLNESS**
Long-lasting disorder which, unlike an acute illness, has a gradual onset and leads to a weakened state of health. Medical intervention is normally required.

## COLIC
Spasms of the intestines that cause a baby to scream. It can be made worse by a mother's mood and diet, especially if she is breast-feeding.

## CONJUNCTIVITIS
Inflammation of the clear inner coating of the eyelid and swelling of the surface of the eye, usually associated with a discharge.

## DIAPHORETIC
Any substance that promotes perspiration. Good natural examples include brandy, cayenne peppers, ginger root and horseradish.

## DEMENTIA
Organic mental disorder characterized by a general loss of intellectual abilities involving impairment of memory, judgement and abstract thinking, as well as changes in personality. The most common causes include Alzheimer's disease and Parkinson's disease.

## DEMULCENT
Any substance that soothes irritated tissues. Good natural examples include barley, cucumber and honey.

## DIURETIC
Any substance that relieves retained fluids by stimulating urine production and drainage. Good natural examples include cucumber, fennel, juniper berries, lemon and parsley.

## DOSHAS
Basic constitutional types in Indian medicine–vata, pitta and kapha–collectively known as the 'tri-doshas'. When they are normal, they are known as the three dhaatus. Doshic imbalances govern the internal biochemical charges that will eventually lead to a higher or lower metabolism.

## EMETIC
Any substance that promotes an involuntary contraction of the digestive tract to produce vomiting. Good natural examples include nutmeg and salt.

## EPILEPSY
Condition caused by momentary disturbances in brain function which manifest as episodic events of violent shaking and difficulty in processing sensory information.

## EXPECTORANT
Any substance that helps to free and remove mucus from the respiratory system. Good natural examples include cloves, garlic, ginger, honey, marjoram, onion and thyme.

## FASTING
Abstaining from all or some kinds of food, usually accompanied by some form of meditation or religious purpose.

## FREE RADICALS
Highly reactive molecules in the environment produced by both healthy and disease-causing processes. They are known to cause tissue damage through factors like radiation, chemicals and ageing.

## GYNAECOLOGICAL
Belonging to or associated with a branch of medicine dealing with the diagnosis and treatment of disorders affecting the female reproductive organs.

## HOLISTIC
Any method of treatment which deals with the whole person through body, mind and spirit, rather than just through presenting symptoms.

## HUMOURS
Four body fluids (blood, phlegm, choler and melancholy) which are believed to determine emotional and physical disposition.

## HYPOTENSIVE
Characterized by or causing diminished tension or pressure as in abnormally low blood pressure.

## INSOMNIA
Inability to sleep or abnormal wakefulness. Symptoms of insomnia include an oversensitivity to light, smell, noise and touch. It can be helped by taking regular amounts of exercise and abstaining from eating late in the evening.

## IRRITANT
Substance that causes inflammation following immediate, sustained or repeated contact with the skin.

## LARYNGITIS
Inflammation of the voice box characterized by hoarseness and dryness of the throat or mucous membrane, difficulty in coughing and swallowing.

**LYMPH**
Colourless fluid, which contains mainly white blood cells, collected from the tissues of the body and transported through the lymphatic system.

**MENOPAUSE**
Cessation of mentrual flow in females, usually occurring at the age of 50, after which prescriptions of hormones are given.

**MONOAMINE OXIDASE INHIBITORS (MAOIS)**
Controversial chemical antidepressants used in the treatment of depression.

**MUSCULAR DYSTROPHY**
Group of diseases characterized by progressive deterioration and loss of muscle fibres without nervous system involvement.

**NATUROPATHY**
Method of healing which makes exclusive use of natural remedies (light, heat, cold, water, vegetables and fruits). No drugs are prescribed and no surgery is used.

**OSTEOARTHRITIS**
Non-inflammatory joint disease occurring chiefly in older individuals, accompanied by pain and stiffness of the bones, particularly after prolonged activity.

**OSTEOPOROSIS**
Reduction in the amount of bone mass, leading to the occurrence of fractures due to brittle bones.

**OXALIC ACID**
Substance present in plants and animals which binds with calcium, causing the precipitation of calcium-containing compounds and preventing calcium uptake in the gut.

**PANCHAKARMA**
Indian term meaning internal cleansing, which consists of five forms of therapy, including vomiting, purging, two types of enema and nasal inhalation. It is said to prevent disease and rebalance vitality.

**PHLEGM**
Disharmony of the body fluids producing either external (visible) phlegm, or internal (invisible) phlegm.

**PHOTOSYNTHESIS**
Biochemical process by which green plants, algae and some bacteria absorb light (energy) from the sun and use it to build carbohydrate compounds. This reaction occurs inside chloroplasts, cells unique to plants, which contain a pigment called chlorophyll.

**POULTICE**
Moist and heated dressing applied to inflamed skin and covered with a towel to trap heat and draw out toxins.

**PRANA**
Vital energy that runs through our bodies. Also known as our life force in Indian medicine.

**PREMENSTRUAL SYNDROME (PMS)**
Combination of emotional, physical and psychological mood disturbances occurring after ovulation and normally ending with the onset of mentrual flow.

**PURGATIVE**
Substance or agent which brings on the elimination of waste from the intestines by stimulating bowel movement.

**QI (CHI)**
According to Qigong theory, the essential energy of the universe which is fundamental to all elements of life. It runs through the whole body in channels or meridians and it is the alleged vital force that underlies the proper functioning of body, mind and spirit.

**RADIOTHERAPY**
Treatment of disease by ionising radiation which brings on the dislodgement of electrons from an atom and literally 'burns off' damaged tissue.

**RESTORATIVE**
Any substance which strengthens and promotes well-being after an illness which has caused debilitation of the patient.

**RHEUMATIC**
Relating to any discomfort or disease associated with the painful swelling of joints and muscles. If acute, these pains can bring on very high fevers.

## SALTY
One of the six Ayurvedic tastes. Salty taste is found in rock salt, seaweed, sea salt and vegetables.

## SANSKRIT
Ancient Indo-European language sacred to Hinduism. Ayurvedic medicine and its teachings are derived from sacred texts written in Sanskrit known as the Vedas.

## SCHIZOPHRENIA
Serious mental disorder manifesting most major psychotic symptoms, as well as thought disturbances, such as hallucinations or delusions.

## SCIATICA
Syndrome characterized by pain radiating from the back into the buttock, or pain present anywhere along the length of the sciatic nerve in the hipbone.

## SEDATIVE
Any substance that calms the nerves. Good natural examples include chamomile and lettuce.

## SEPTICAEMIA
Disease associated with the presence of disease-carrying microorganisms or their toxins in the bloodstream.

## SOUR
One of the six Ayurvedic tastes found in fats, amino acids, fermented products, fruits and vegetables.

## STIMULANT
Any substance that increases activity in specific organs or systems, warms the body and increases energy production.

## TANNINS
Plant-derived compounds characterized by their ability to precipitate proteins in solution. Some are toxic, others are harmless, such as those found in tea or coffee.

## TINCTURE
Medicinal extract of herbs made by soaking in alcohol and water. One of the initial stages in making a homeopathic remedy, is preparing a 'mother' tincture.

## TINNITUS
Symptomatic noise in the ears such as ringing, buzzing, clicking. Sometimes these sounds are heard by others other than the patient.

## TONIC
Any substance that balances, nourishes and promotes well-being by stimulating circulation and enhancing effective organ function.

## TONSILLITIS
Uncomfortable swelling of the tonsils, the lympathic tissue located at the back of the throat, which form part of the body's immune system.

## TOXIN
Poison produced inside the body. A build up of these harmful substances can produce poor breathing patterns, circulation and waste elimination.

## VASODILATOR
Agent that dilates blood vessels and increases blood flow, often producing flushes and resulting in a rise in temperature.

## VULNERARY
Assisting in the healing of wounds by protecting against infection and stimulating cell growth.

## YANG
In Chinese philosophy, the active male principle of the universe, which is associated with creativity, heaven, heat and light.

## YIN
In Chinese philosophy, the passive female principle of the universe which is associated with earth, dark and cold.

# FIRST AID

## BOILS

**Homeopathy** Belladonna 30 can be used at the onset when there is much throbbing, redness and heat, and the boil is much worse from pressure. Hepar Sulph is known as the homeopath's 'lance'. Use when the boil is ripening and the pus needs to be expelled. The boil will be much worse from touch and will feel very painful. Silica 6 or 30 can be given when the boil is slow to heal, oozing a thin pus.

**Medical Herbalism** A poultice can be made from marshmallow leaf or cabbage leaf to draw out the pus. Bathe in a solution of Echinacea tincture to control the infection.

## BRUISING

Apply a cold compress or bag of ice to the injured area immediately after damage has occured. If bruising is severe or seems to spread, this may indicate internal bleeding and medical advice must be sought immediately.

**Acupuncture** Apply a moxa stick to the bruised area. This has the effect of stimulating the circulation of *Qi* (*chi*) energy and blood to the area, which relieves pain and helps the bruise to disperse.

**Homeopathy** Take Arnica 30 immediately after the injury and repeat at two-hourly intervals until the pain has subsided. This will reduce suffering and swelling, and may well prevent bruising if given soon enough. Do give Arnica even if some time has lapsed after the bruising. If the bruised area becomes swollen and black and blue use Ledum 30. Take one dose every four hours, for three doses. Arnica ointment can be applied to the bruise if the skin is not broken.

**Medical Herbalism** Apply a compress soaked in cold water with a few drops of essential oil of lavender, or a chilled infusion of comfrey. Remove the compress when it is dry. When the swelling has subsided, apply comfrey ointment to the bruise.

## BURNS (minor)

Place the affected part under cold (not icy) water for several minutes. Keep the area clean to avoid any risk of infection. Do not puncture blisters. If symptoms persist or worsen, or the burnt area is larger in size than the palm of the hand, seek medical advice.

**Aromatherapy** Apply two or three drops of essential oil of lavender to prevent blistering.

**Homeopathy** Take Arnica 30 every 15 minutes for up to three doses for the immediate shock. Take Urtica Urens 30 for stinging and burning pains, and Cantharis 30 for blistering and stronger pains. Homeopathic burn ointment or Urtica Urens ointment can be applied direct to the burn.

**Medical Herbalism** Aloe vera is the best plant to use. The leaves exude a healing gel that can be applied directly to the burn. Marigold and hypericum are also excellent for burns.

## CRAMP

Gently but firmly stretch the affected muscles. If the cramp is caused by cold, warm the affected part of the body gently. Otherwise, drink large amounts of cool water to which salt has been added, about half a teaspoon to one pint.

**Acupuncture** Massage the affected muscle to relieve the spasm and promote the circulation of *Qi* (*chi*) and blood. Burn Moxa over the affected area.

**Homeopathy** Mag Phos 6x tissue salts or Mag Phos 30 can be dissolved in a little warm water and sipped every five minutes. This will particularly relieve leg cramps and growing pains, as well as any cramps ameliorated by hot applications. Colocynthis 30 can be given for colicky cramps that are better for doubling over and holding the affected part.

## CUTS & WOUNDS

Wash the wound thoroughly, removing any foreign bodies, and cover with a clean dressing.

**Homeopathy** Clean with a pad soaked in a solution of hypercal tincture. Apply calendula or hypercal cream to the wound. Give Arnica 30 if there is trauma to the affected area with bruising. Use Calendula 30 to help the wound heal and prevent sepsis.

**Medical Herbalism** Use marigold or comfrey ointment to reduce inflammation and assist healing. Witch Hazel diluted–one tablespoon to one pint of water–can be used to wash the cut and to moisten the dressing.

## DIARRHOEA

It is important to drink plenty of fluids with diarrhoea to prevent dehydration.

**Homeopathy** There are many remedies for diarrhoea. Arsenicum album is the best remedy for diarrhoea from food poisoning with cramping pains, weakness and restlessness. Podophyllum is excellent for watery, gushing stools with gurgling in the guts. Give sulphur for painless diarrhoea and wind smelling of rotten eggs.

**Medical Herbalism** Drink the tea of Meadow-sweet three times daily until symptoms disappear. Combine with Lady's Mantle in equal parts for diarrhoea in children.

**Naturopathy** Grated apple, which can be mixed with live yoghurt, may help. Eat a small quantity of brown rice to bind the stools. Otherwise, eat little until the symptoms have subsided.

## EARACHE

There are many self-help remedies for earache. However, if the earache persists or you have any concerns, seek the help of your health practitioner.

**Aromatherapy** Steam inhalations with essential oils of eucalyptus, peppermint or chamomile added may help to relieve catarrh and soothe internal earache.

**Homeopathy** Belladonna 30 can be given for earache that comes on suddenly and when the ear and cheek are hot, red and inflamed. The earache may be accompanied by a fever. Chamomilla 30 can be given when the pain is severe, causing irritability and restlessness, often worse between 9 p.m. and midnight. Pulsatilla 30 is useful for nagging earache with stopped-up ears, often accompanied by a heavy cold.

**Medical Herbalism** A few drops of warm almond oil or mullein oil can be gently placed in the affected ear. The juice of Pennywort and tincture of Lobelia are also very effective.

**Naturopathy** Apply warmth by using a hot salt pack, made by heating a small muslin bag filled with salt in an oven. Placing a clove of garlic or liquid from garlic pearles helps to relieve the pain. Fasting for 24 hours may also help.

## EYE INJURIES

Gently wash the affected eye with cold water. Eye injuries must be checked by a medical practitioner.

**Homeopathy** Bathe the eye with a solution of Hypercal if there is dirt in the eye, and use Euphrasia tincture in solution if there is pain after a foreign body in the eye has been removed. Give Arnica 30 every hour for three doses after any injury to the eye to prevent bruising. Follow with Ledum 30 in cases of black eye where there is swelling and puffiness. Euphrasia 6 or 30 is suitable if there is pain after the removal of a foreign body from the eye. For injuries to the eyeball with great pain use Symphytum 30 every two hours.

**Medical Herbalism**  In any case of injury to the eye, a compress of Eyebright (Euphrasia) placed over the affected eye for 15 minutes several times a day will bring relief. Marigold and Golden Seal can be used in a similar fashion.

## FAINTING

A person will faint from the temporary disruption of the blood flow to the head. This may be brought on by pain, hunger or emotional shock. The person should be put in the recovery position to keep the airways open if they do not regain consciousness within 15 to 20 seconds. If after a few minutes they have not yet gained consciousness, or loss of consciousness is due to physical trauma, call an ambulance immediately.

**Aromatherapy**  Use essential oil of lavender as a smelling salt.

**Homeopathy**  For fainting due to emotional shock or excitement, use Ignatia 6 or 30 every five minutes up to 10 doses. Give Aconite 30 every five minutes for fainting due to fright or shock, possibly after witnessing an accident or an equally distressing event. Pulsatilla 30 should be used for those who faint in hot, stuffy conditions and who may be anaemic. Coffea 30 can be used for someone who faints from excitement.

## FEVER

A fever is often the immune system's response to infection and other stresses, so it is important not to suppress it. Sponging with tepid, not cold, water will help control the fever as will self-help measures. If fever persists for longer than four days, seek medical advice.

**Homeopathy**  Aconite 30 is the remedy for a sudden high fever brought on by exposure to cold wind or after a fright. The person will be very thirsty, worse at midnight, and restless and frightened. Belladonna 30 can also be given for a high fever with a sudden onset, with red cheeks and burning hot skin but icy cold feet, and dilated pupils. Ferrum Phos is useful at the beginning of mild fevers.

**Medical Herbalism**  A tea consisting of two parts boneset, two parts yarrow and one part Echinacea can be taken every two hours to help the body work through the fever.

**Naturopathy**  Raw garlic can be eaten to help fever. Keep to a cleansing diet based on fruit and fruit juices.

## FOOD POISONING

If you suspect food poisoning, avoid eating and drinking until the symptoms have subsided. Start taking sips of cold water after a couple of hours and continue to take plenty of fluids. Seek medical attention if vomiting persists.

**Acupuncture**  Special points on the wrists and abdomen can be massaged to relieve symptoms.

**Homeopathy**  Vomiting is nature's way of eliminating a swallowed poison. Arsenicum 6 or 30 is the remedy to take for vomiting with cramping pains, thirst for sips of water that are immediately brought up, and weakness and restlessness which may follow a bout of food poisoning. Veratrum Alb 30 is the remedy for severe vomiting and diarrhoea with faintness, chills and complete prostration. Use China 6 or 30 after dehydration.

**Naturopathy**  When travelling in countries where food poisoning is more common, eat more hot, spicy foods because these encourage gastric secretions and hence give protection.

## FRACTURES

If you suspect a fracture after injury, go to Casualty to have it checked.

**Homeopathy**  For immediate physical trauma after injury, give Arnica 30 every 15 minutes for at least three doses and then three times daily for three days. The next remedy to give is Ledum 30 three times daily for three days to reduce any swelling. Once the bones have been set in place, give Symphytum 6 three times daily until the bones have mended. If there is still some residual weakness, give Calc Phos 6x tissue salts three times daily for another two weeks.

**Medical Herbalism**  Use a compress or poultice of comfrey in solution on the fracture to add healing.

## HEADACHE

Minor headaches are best helped by rest, and avoiding loud noise and bright light. Hot or cold compresses may help. If symptoms persist, recur or are the result of an injury, seek medical advice.

**Acupuncture**  Points on the head, neck, hands and feet can be massaged once the precise locations of the points have been learned.

**Homeopathy**  There are many homeopathic remedies for headaches. Nux Vomica is useful for a headache due to a hangover or a sluggish liver. Use Belladonna for sun headaches or migraines with a flushed face that are violent and throbbing, worse for lying down and may be accompanied by fever. Give Bryonia for a headache with sharp, stabbing pains made worse by the slightest eye movement and better for pressure on the forehead.

**Medical Herbalism**  Chamomile, lime blossom and peppermint teas can all help a headache.

**Osteopathy with Naturopathy**  If the headache is caused by tension, press on the back of the head, under the occiput (back of the skull). If caused by food, miss the next meal. If the cause is eyestrain, rest with a cold pad over the eyes. Rubbing lavender oil into the temples can also help.

## HICCUPS

The standard ways to obtain relief include taking sips of water, holding one's breath or having one's attention distracted. If symptoms continue for more than one hour, seek medical advice.

**Acupuncture**  Special points on the hands and feet can be massaged to relieve the hiccups.

**Homeopathy**  Ignatia 30 will most often calm spasm of the diaphragm, which causes hiccups, that may have been precipitated by emotional upset. Nux Vomica 6 or 30 will help hiccups accompanied by belching and retching, especially if they come on one or two hours after eating a large meal.

**Osteopathy with Naturopathy**  Any painful areas around the vertebrae at the same level as the diaphragm can be gently massaged to relieve the symptoms.

## INDIGESTION

If the pain is very severe or persists for some time, seek medical advice.

**Acupuncture**  Special points on the hands and feet can be massaged to relieve pain.

**Homeopathy**  Nux Vomica 6 or 30 is suitable for heartburn that comes on half an hour after overeating, with painful retching that leaves a foul taste in the mouth. Pulsatilla 30 can be given for heartburn that comes on two hours after eating rich, fatty food, with nausea and a feeling of pressure under the breastbone. For a bloated stomach with frequent burping that gives partial relief, use Carbo Veg 30. Use Arg Nit 6 or 30 for windy colic that may accompanied by anxiety and a craving for sweets.

**Medical Herbalism**  Use chamomile, lemon balm or Meadowsweet tea to relieve symptoms.

**Naturopathy**  Miss the next meal. Sip lemon juice. Massage the abdomen gently, stroking rather than probing.

## INSECT BITES AND STINGS

Remove the sting, if it is still present, with tweezers or a sterilized needle. If the sting will not come out, apply a paste of bicarbonate of soda and water to render it alkaline. If the sting is in the mouth or throat, rinse with ice-cold water to prevent swelling and go to hospital. If a sting provokes a severe reaction or anaphylactic shock, call an ambulance immediately.

**Aromatherapy**  Apply a dressing soaked in diluted essential oil of lavender.

**Homeopathy**  Take Arnica 30 for the immediate shock and trauma. Use Apis 30 if the area becomes very swollen and puffy, with heat and redness. If the bite becomes bruised and blue, use Ledum 30. Use Hypericum 30 if the bite is painful, perhaps with shooting pains, and repeat whenever the pain returns. Use Pyrethrum spray on the affected part to help itching.

**Medical Herbalism**  A compress soaked in chamomile can be used on stings, as can the juice from the aloe vera leaf.

## MOTION SICKNESS

Avoid eating large meals and greasy food before a journey.

**Acupuncture**  Special points on the wrist can be massaged to relieve the feeling of nausea. Special wrist bands can be purchased which press these points.

**Homeopathy**  Start taking the indicated remedy up to an hour before travelling as well as during the journey. Cocculus 30 can be used where there is nausea and dizziness with the desire to lie down. Cocculus is particularly effective for seasickness. Petroleum can be used where the nausea is better for eating and worse for fresh air. Use Nux Vomica if you want to vomit but cannot.

**Medical Herbalism**  Chewing small pieces of fresh ginger root can alleviate motion sickness, as can sipping ginger, peppermint or chamomile tea.

## MUSCLE STRAIN

**Aromatherapy**  Diluted essential oils of lavender and rosemary can be rubbed into the strained muscles.

**Chiropractic Therapy**  Apply gentle heat and ice alternately, at least two or three applications of each. Repeat this three or four times daily.

**Homeopathy**  Arnica 30 is the first remedy to consider immediately after the injury to alleviate pain and swelling. Arnica cream can be applied to the strained area. If the affected part becomes very stiff and painful, worse for first movement and better for continued motion, then use Rhus Tox 30 three times daily until the stiffness has subsided. If there is very deep, aching pain, especially in the back, try Ruta Grav 30 three times daily.

**Medical Herbalism**  Gently rub in comfrey ointment to the affected part.

## NOSEBLEEDS

Bend the head forward and pinch the lower part of the nose for up to ten minutes. Do not blow the nose, sniff or do anything that might dislodge the newly formed blood clot. If the nosebleed does not stop after 20 minutes or occurs after a head injury, seek medical attention.

**Homeopathy**  Use Arnica 30 if the nosebleed has resulted from a blow or injury. Phosphorous 6 or 30 is suitable for nosebleeds with heavy colds, from considerable blowing of the nose. Ipecac 30 should be used for heavy nosebleeds with bright red blood, accompanied by nausea.

**Naturopathy** Use a cold compress on the abdomen to draw congestion downwards.

## SORE THROATS

If there is great difficulty swallowing even water or the sore throat persists for a number of days, seek medical advice.

**Homeopathy** Aconite 30 is the remedy for a sore throat that comes on suddenly after exposure to cold wind, with thirst for cold water and aggravation at midnight. The sore throat that requires Belladonna 30 will also have a fast onset, and may well be accompanied by a high fever, flushed cheeks, a bright red or 'strawberry' tongue and a lack of thirst. Mercury 30 is for a severe sore throat where the glands may be swollen, there is a nasty taste in the mouth, excessive salivation and bad breathe, and where the patient cannot tolerate even small temperature changes. Use Hepar Sulph 30 for the sore throat with a splinter-like pain, if you have a desire for warm drinks and are experiencing extreme sensitivity to cold.

**Medical Herbalism** A gargle of red sage or Golden Seal can be very effective in easing pain.

**Naturopathy** Cider vinegar and honey dissolved in equal parts of boiling water is a very soothing drink for sore throats. Gargling with salt water can also help.

## STRAINS

Take any weight off the injured part and apply a cold compress to reduce swelling and pain.

**Chiropractic therapy** Support the injury with a bandage, but if this aggravates the pain and swelling it should be removed at once.

**Homeopathy** Use Arnica 30 immediately after the sprain to reduce swelling and bruising. Ledum 30 will reduce any swelling that follows the sprain. Give Rhus Tox 6 or 30 if the sprained part becomes stiff and difficult to move.

**Medical Herbalism** Use a cooled comfrey solution to make a compress which can be applied to the affected part. Comfrey ointment can also be rubbed in to bring relief.

## SUN-RELATED COMPLAINTS

If the person collapses due to dehydration from the heat or sun, seek medical attention immediately.

**Homeopathy** Sol 6 or 30 (sun rays in dilution) can be taken to help the sufferer acclimatize to the sun when travelling, or for many sun-related complaints. Belladonna 30 is used for sunstroke where there is a throbbing headache which is worse for lying down, when the skin is hot, dry and red, and when the pupils are dilated. Apis 6 or 30 can be given for prickly heat or swollen ankles due to the heat.

**Medical Herbalism** Use essential oil of lavender or a tincture of nettles in solution to soothe sunburn. A solution of diluted vinegar can also help.

# KEY WEBSITES

**www.acupuncture.com/**
Acupuncture subject index for consumers, patients, students and practitioners.

**www.aromaweb.com/**
This web page allows you to view profiles of 90 essential oils, 23 hazardous types of oils to be avoided and 15 carrier oils. You can also enhance your existing knowledge of the subject by reading any of the 22 articles available online. It even gives you hyperlinks to other web pages of interest.

**www.ausflowers.com.au/**
Discover the power of Australian Aboriginal bush flower essences obtained by extracting the most evolved portion of the plant–reputedly the most concentrated in vibrational healing quality.

**www.bachcentre.com/**
This page provides extensive information about Dr Edward Bach, the pioneer behind this remedy system.

**www.cix.co.uk/~mandrake/ayurveda.htm/**
Information on the basic principles of Ayurvedic medicine.

**www.elixirs.com/**
Contains a detailed section on FAQ's (frequently asked questions) about homeopathy and online questionnaires which are then evaluated by a professional practitioner.

**www.gems4friends.com/**
A web page dedicated to informing the public about the healing properties of gemstones and crystals.

**www.geocities.com/HotSprings/4353/iridol.html/**
Selected web link page covering all aspects of the diagnostic tool known as iridology.

**www.healing.about.com/healing/**
Discussion page dedicated to alternative healing therapies and remedies.

**www.herbsforhealth.about.com/cs/chinese herbalism/**
This page provides links to the ancient Oriental practice of Chinese medicine and herbalism.
**www.hir.com/**
Directory of Holistic Internet Resources.

**www.holistic.com/**
Your neighbourhood for healthy living.

**www.homeopathyhome.com/**
A web link page to all homeopathic resources on the Web.

**www.internetlibrary.com/**
One of the most comprehensive online natural remedies libraries. Its menu includes an A–Z directory of health problems, a Medline search, surveys, diet and lifestyle, health headlines, professional associations, self-help organizations, a children's health homeopathic library and online clinics.

**www.majordomo@reliaweb.com/**
This email address enables all users to subscribe to a mailing list for both the general public and practitioners to discuss all aspects of herbalism.

**www.mtwc.com/**
Massage Therapy Web Central (MTWC) – the leading MT professional hub–provides useful information for corporate and individual consumers and gives you handy tips on how to find/hire a qualified massage therapist.

**www.omni.ac.uk**
The UK's gateway to high-quality Internet resources in alternative health and medicine.

**www.organix.net/organix/bach.htm/**
The Bach flower essences are a system of 38 flower essences used to correct emotional imbalances by restoring positive emotion and eliminating negative feelings. Here you will find detailed information about the various essences and their uses.

**www.pandamedicine.com/**
Naturopathic Medicine Network: a comprehensive guide to naturopathic and holistic medicine and alternative health care.

**www.reiki.7gen.com/**
This site is a collection of pages of information on Reiki, the Japanese method of natural healing. Available resources include a historical framework, methods of use and application, practitioner information and recent headlines and updates which have emerged on the subject.

**www.spiritweb.org/spirit/yoga.html/**
Introductions and links to many different schools and traditions of yoga.

**www.theworldofhealth.co.uk/uk**
The World of Health Directory.

# USEFUL ADDRESSES

**Acupuncture Society**
163 Northwood Way
Northwood
Middlesex HA6 1RA
UK
Telephone: + 44 (0) 1923 822 972
Website: http://www.acupuncturesociety.org.uk
E-mail:
info@acupuncturesociety.org.uk

**Alexander Technique International (ATI)**
United States (Main Office):
Jan Baty, ATI Corresponding Secretary
1692 Massachusetts Ave, 3rd floor
Cambridge, MA 02138
USA
Telephone: + 1 (888) 668 8996 (toll free from Canada and the US)
Fax: + 1 (617) 497 26153
Website:
http://www.alexandertech.com
E-mail: usa@ati-net.com

United Kingdom:
Lee Warren, UK Regional
Coordinator
66-C Thurlestone Road
West Norwood
London
SE27 0PD
UK
Telephone: + 44 (0) 7071 880253
E-mail: uk@ati-net.com

**American Alternative Medical Association (AAMA)**
708 Madelaine Drive
Gilmer, TX 75644-3145
USA

Telephone: + 1 (903) 843 6401 or + 1 (903) 764 2237
Website: http://www.joinaama.com/

**American Association of Drugless Practitioners (AADP)**
708 Madelaine Drive
Gilmer, TX 756644-3140
USA
Telephone: + 1 (903) 843 6401
Fax: + 1 (888) 764-AADP
Website: http://www.aadp.net

**American Association of Oriental Medicine (AAOM)**
433 Front Street
Catasauqua PA 18032
USA
Telephone: + 1 (610) 226 1433
Website: http://www.aaom.org
E-mail: AAOM1@aol.com

**American Botanical Council (ABC)**
PO Box 144345
Austin, TX 78714-4345
USA
Website: http://www.herbalgram.org
E-mail: abc@herbalgram.org

**American Chiropractic Association (ACA)**
1701 Clarendon Blvd.
Arlington, VA 22209
USA
Telephone: + 1 (800) 986 4636
Fax: + 1 (703) 243 2593
Website: http://www.amerchiro.org

**American Holistic Health Association (AHHA)**

PO Box 17400
Anaheim, CA 92817-7400
USA
Telephone/Fax: + 1 (714) 779 6152
Website: http://www.ahha.org/
E-mail: ahha@healthy.net

**American Holistic Medical Association (AHMA)**
6728 McLean Village Drive
McLean, VA 22101-8729
USA
Telephone/Fax: + 1 (703) 556 8729
Website: http://www.holisticmedicine.org/
E-mail: info@holisticmedicine.org

**American Massage Therapy Association (AMTA)**
820 Davis Street, Suite 100
Evanston, IL 60201-4444
USA
Telephone: + 1 (847) 864 0123
Fax: + 1 (847) 864 1178
Website:
http://www.amtamassage.org/
E-mail:
jschlesinger@inet.amtamassage.org

**American Medical Massage Association (AMMA)**
PO Box 272
Gainesville, VA 20156-0272
USA
Telephone: +1 (540) 351 0807
Fax: + 1 (540) 351 0041
Website: http://www.americanmedicalmassage.com/
E-mail: rdeperio@americanmedicalmassage.com

## American Naturopathic Medical Association (ANMA)

PO Box 96273
Las Vegas, Nevada 89193
USA
Telephone: + 1 (702) 897 7053
Fax: + 1 (702) 897 7140
Website: http: www.anma.com /

## American Oriental Bodywork Therapy Association (AOBTA)

Website: http://www.healthy.net

## American Polarity Therapy Association (APTA)

PO Box 19858
Boulder, CO 80308
USA
Telephone: + 1 (303) 545 2080
Fax: + 1 (303) 545 2161
Website: http://www.polarity
therapy.org/
E-mail: hq@polaritytherapy.org

## American Reiki Masters Association (ARMA)

PO Box 130
Lake City, FL 32056
USA
Telephone: + 1 (904) 755-9638

## American Society for the Alexander Technique (ASAT)

PO Box 60008
Florence, MA 01062
USA
Telephone: + 1 (800) 473 0620
Website:
http://www.alexandertech.com/

## American Society of Alternative Therapists (ASAT)

PO Box 703
Rockport MA 01966
USA
Telephone: + 1 (978) 281 4400
Website: http://www.asat.org
E-mail: asat@asat.org

## American Yoga Association (AYA)

PO Box 19986
Sarasota, FL 34276
USA
Telephone: + 1 (941) 927 4977
Fax: +1 (921) 9844
Website: http://www.americanyogaas-
sociation.org/
E-mail: info@ americanyogaassocia-
tion.org

## Ancient Traditional Chinese Medical Association (ATCMA)

3149 N Cowney Pkwy
Merritt Island, FL 32953
USA
Telephone: + 1 (321) 454 9259
Fax: + 1 (321) 454 9974
Website: http://www.hantang.com

## Aromatherapy & Allied Practitioners' Association (AAPA)*

8 George Street
Croydon
Surrey
UK
Telephone/Fax: + 44 (0) 208-680
7761
Website: http://www.AAPA.org.uk
E-mail: aromatherapy@aol.com

## Aromatherapy Organizations Council (AOC)

The AOC Secretary
PO Box 19834
London
SE25 6WF
UK
Telephone: + 44 (0) 208 251 7912
Fax: + 44 (0) 208 251 7942
Website: http://www.aromatherapy-
uk.org

The AOC is the governing body for the aromatherapy profession in the UK. It is comprised of aromatherapy associations, not individual aromatherapists.

The following associations marked with an asterisk are all members of the AOC. The first to be established was the International Federation of Aromatherapists (IFA) (set up in 1985 with over 1200 members) and the largest is International Society of Professional Aromatherapists (ISPA).

## Association of Holistic Therapies International (AHTI)*

8 Llys Soar
Scott Street
Tynewydd
Rhondda
Mid Glam
CF42 5NA
UK
Telephone: + 44 (0) 1443 332 4924

## Association of Medical Aromatherapists (AMA)*

Abergare
Rhu Point

Helensborough
G84 8NF
UK
Telephone/Fax: + 44 (0) 141 332 4924
Website:
http://www.dunromin.demon.co.uk/aromatherapy/

**Association of Natural Medicine (ANM)**
19a Collingwood Road
Witham
Essex
CM8 2DY
UK
Telephone: + 44 (0) 1376 502762

**Association of Physical & Natural Therapists (APNT)***
27 Old Gloucester Road
London
WC1N 3XX
UK
Telephone: + 44 (0) 966 181 588

**Association of Reflexologists**
27 Old Gloucester Street
London
WC1N 3XX
UK
Website: http://www.62.232.45.43/
E-mail: aon@reflexology.org

**Beaumont College of Natural Remedies**
MWB Business Exchange
Hinton Road
Bournemouth BH1 2EF
UK
Telephone: + 44 (0) 1202 708887
Fax: + 44 (0) 1202 708720
Website: http://www.beaumontcollege.co.uk
E-mail: info@beaumontcollege.co.uk

**British Acupuncture Council (BacC)**
63 Jeddo Road
London
W12 9HQ
UK
Telephone: + 44 (0) 208 735 0400
Fax: + 44 (0) 208 735 0404
Website:
http://www.acupuncture.org.uk
E-mail: info@acupuncture.org.uk

**British Essential Oils Association**
15 Exeter Mansions
Exeter Road
London
NW2 3UG
UK
Telephone: + 44 (0) 208 450 3713

**British Medical Acupuncture Society (BMAS)**
Newton House
Newton Lane
Whitley
Warrington
Cheshire
WA4 4JA
UK
Telephone: + 44 (0) 1925 730 727
Fax: + 44 (0) 1925 730 492
Website: http://medical-acupuncture.co.uk
E-mail: bmasadmin@aol.com

**British Osteopathic Association (BOA)**
Langham House East
Luton
Bedfordshire
LU1 2NA
UK
Telephone: + 44 (0) 1582 488455

Fax: + 44 (0) 1582 481533
Website:
http://www.osteopathy.org/main/home.html
E-mail: enquiries@osteopathy.org

The largest professional association for osteopaths in the UK.

**Centre for the Study of Complementary Medicine**
14 Harley Street
Upper Harley Street
London
NW1 4PR
UK
Telephone: + 44 (0) 207 935 7848
Fax: + 44 (0) 207 224 4519
Website:
http://www.complemed.co.uk/
E-mail: enquiries@complemed.co.uk

**Dr Edward Bach Centre**
Mount Vernon
Bakers Lane
Sotwell, Oxon
OX10 0P2
UK
Telephone: + 44 (0) 1491 834 678
Fax: + 44 (0) 1491 825 022
Website: http://www.bachcentre.com

**English Société de l'Institute Pierre Franchomme (ESIPF)***
Belmont House
Newport
Essex
CB11 3RF
UK
Telephone: + 44 (0) 1799 540 622
Fax: + 44 (0) 1799 541 294

**Foundation for International Spiritual Unfoldment (FISU)**
Foundation House
58 Marlborough Road
London
E4 9AL
UK
Telephone: + 44 (0) 208 523 3133
Fax: + 44 (0) 208 523 2028
Website: http://www.fisu.org/
E-mail: fisu@fisu.org

**Guild of Complementary Practitioners (GCP)***
Liddell House
Liddell Close
Finchampstead
Berks RG40 4NS
UK
Telephone: + 44 (0) 1189 735 757
Fax: + 44 (0) 1799 541 294
Website: http://www.gcpnet.com
E-mail: info@gcpnet.com

**Holistic Aromatherapy Foundation (HAF)***
65 Bradenham Avenue
Welling
Kent
DA16 2JQ
UK
Telephone: + 44 (0) 208 303 8019

**Institute of Biodynamic Psychology & Psychotherapy**
126 Rainville Court
Rainville Road
London
W6 9HJ
UK
Telephone: + 44 (0) 207 381 9075
Fax: + 44 (0) 207 381 6110
Website: http://www.biodynamic.org
E-mail: ibpp@biodynamic.org

**Institute for Complimentary Medicine (ICM)**
ICM
PO Box 194
London
SE16 7QZ
UK
Telephone: + 44 (0) 207 237 5165
Fax: + 44 (0) 207 237 5175
Website:
http://www.icmedicine.co.uk
E-mail: icm@icmedicine.co

**International Association of Infant Massage (IAIM)**
1891 Goodyear Avenue, Suite N. 622
Ventura, CA 93003
USA
Telephone: + 1 (800) 248 5432
Fax: + 1 (800) 644 7699
Website: http://www.iaim-us.com
E-mail: iaim4us@aol.com

**International Association of Reiki Professionals (IARP)**
PO Box 481
Winchester, MA 01890
USA
Telephone: + 1 (781) 729 3530
Fax: + 1 (781) 721 7306
Website: http://www.iarp.org/
E-mail: info@larp.org

**International Federation of Aromatherapists (IFA)***
182 Chiswick High Road
Chiswick
London
W4 1PP
UK
Telephone: + 44 (0) 208 742 2605
Fax: + 44 (0) 208 742 2606
Website: http://www.int-fed-aromatherapy.co.uk

**International Federation of Essential Oils and Aroma Trades (IFEAT)**
6 Catherine Street
London
WC2B 5JJ
UK
Telephone: + 44 (0) 207 836 2460
Fax: + 44 (0) 207 836 0580
Website: http://www.ifeat.org.uk

**International Massage Association (IMA)**
PO Drawer 421
Warrenton, VA 20188-0421
USA
Telephone: + 1 (540) 351 0800
Fax: + 1 (540) 351 0816
Website: http://www.imagroup.com
E-mail: info@imagroup.com

**International Society of Professional Aromatherapists (ISPA)***
ISPA House
82 Ashby Road
Hinckley
Leics
LE10 1SN
UK
Telephone: + 44 (0) 1455 637 987
Fax: + 44 (0) 1455 890 956
Website:
http://www.ispa.demon.co.uk
E-mail:
LisaBrown@ISPA.demon/co.uk

**Loving Life**
Telephone/Fax: + 1 (775) 358 1432
Website: http://www.lovinglife.org/
E-mail: feelgood@lovinglife.org

**National Acupuncture Detoxification Association (NADA)**
NADA UK
PO Box 208
Oldham
OL2 8FL
UK
Telephone: + 44 (0) 161 232 7564
Website: http://www.nadauk.com/
Email: nadauk@btinternet.com

**National Association for Holistic Aromatherapy (NAHA)**
4509 Interlake Ave.
N. 233
Seattle, Washington 98103-6773
USA
Tel: + 1 (206) 547 2164      Fax: + 1 (206) 547 2680
Website: http://www.naha.org
E-mail: info@naha.org

**National Centre for Complementary and Alternative Medicine (NCCAM)**
NCCAM Clearinghouse
PO Box 8218
Silver Spring
Maryland 2097-8218
USA
Telephone (outside US): + 1 (301) 231 7537, ext. 5
Toll free number: 1-888-644-6226
Website: http://www.nccam.nih.gov

**National Institute of Medical Herbalists (NIMH)**
56 Longbrook Street
Exeter
Devon
EX4 6AH
UK
Tel: + 44 (0) 1392 426022   Fax: + 44 (0) 1392 498963
Website: http://www.btinternet.com/~nimh/
E-mail: nimh@ukexeter.freeserve.co.uk

**Register of Qualified Aromatherapists (RQA)**
PO Box 3431
Danbury
Chelmsford
Essex
CM3 4UA
UK
Telephone: + 44 (0) 1245 227 957
Website: http://www.rqa-uk.org
E-mail: admin@rqa-uk.org

**Renbardou Institute**
Acorn House
Cherry Orchard Road
Croydon
Surrey
CR0 6BA
UK
Telephone: + 44 (0) 208 6499 291

**Shiatsu Society**
Eastlands Court
St Peters Rd
Rugby CV21 3QP
Telephone: + 44 (0) 1788 555051
Fax: + 44 (0) 1788 555052
Website: http://www.shiatsu.org
E-mail: admin@shiatsu.org

**Society of Teachers of the Alexander Technique (STAT)**
129 Camden Mews
London
NW1 9AH
UK
Telephone: + 44 (0) 207 284 3338
Fax: + 44 (0) 207 482 5435
Website: http://www.stat.org.uk/

**Study Society (Meditation)**
Colet House
151 Talgarth Road
London
W14 9DA
UK
Telephone: + 44 (0) 208 748 9338
Fax: + 44 (0) 208 563 0551
Website: http://www.studysociety.org
E-mail: info@studysociety.org

**Touch For Health Association**
PO Box 392
New Carlisle, OH 45344-0392
USA
Telephone: + 1 (800) 466 8342
Fax: + 1 (937) 845-3909
Website: http://www.63.238.164.1001

**Traditional Acupuncture Society (TAS)**
1 The Ridgeway
Stratford-upon-Avon
Warwickshire CV37 9JL
UK
Telephone: + 44 (0) 1789 298798

# BIBLIOGRAPHY

## Acupunture and Acupressure

De Morant, George Soulie & Grinnel, Laurence, *Chinese Acupuncture* (Paradigm Publishers, 1994)

Devi, Dr S. & Nambudripad et al, *Living Pain Free With Acupressure* (Delta Publishing Co., 1997)

Forem, Jack & Shimer, Steve, *Healing with Pressure Point Therapy: Simple, Effective Techniques for Massaging Away More Than 100 Common Ailments* (Prentice Hall Press, 1999)

Frangles, Nora, *Simple Guide to Using Acupuncture* (Global Books Ltd., 2000)

Hicks, Angela, *Principles of Acupuncture* (HarperCollins, 1997)

Pratt, George J. & Lambrou, Peter T., *Instant Emotional Healing: Acupressure for the Emotions* (Broadway Books, 2000)

Seem, Mark, *A New American Acupuncture: Acupuncture Osteopathy: The Myofascial Release of the Body's Mind* (Blue Poppy Press, 1993)

Stux, G. & Pomeranz, B., *Basics of Acupuncture* (Springer-Verlag Berlin & Heidelberg GmbH & Co. KG, 1997)

## Aromatherapy

Catty, Suzanne, *Hydrosols: The Next Aromatherapy* (Inner Traditions International Ltd., 2001)

Johnson, Maria, Donna & Coles, *Making Aromatherapy Creams and Lotions: 101 Natural Remedies to Revitalize and Nourish Your Skin* (Storey Books, 2000)

Lavery, Sheila & Ness, Caro (Eds.), *Aromatherapy: A Step-by-Step Guide* (Element, 1997)

Lawless, Julia, *The Illustrated Encyclopedia of Essential Oils: The Complete Guide to the Use of Oils in Aromatherapy and Herbalism* (Element Paperbacks, 1995)

Maria, Donna & Coles Johnson, *Making Aromatherapy Creams and Lotions: 101 Natural Remedies to Revitalize and Nourish Your Skin* (Storey Books, 2000)

Valnet, Dr Jean & Tisserand, Robert (Eds.), *The Practice of Aromatherapy: A Classic Compendium of Plant Medicines and Their Healing Properties* (Inner Traditions International Ltd., 1990)

Worwood, Valerie Ann, *The Complete Book of Essential Oils and Aromatherapy* (New World Library, 1991)

## Ayurveda

Johari, Harish, *Ayurvedic Massage: Traditional Indian Techniques for Balancing Body and Mind* (Inner Traditions International Ltd., 1996)

Tirtha, Swami Sada Shiva, *The Ayurveda Encyclopedia: Natural Secrets to Healing, Prevention & Longevity* (Ayurveda Holistic Center Press, 1998)

Tiwari, Bri Maya & Benedict, Dirk, *Ayurveda Secrets of Healing* (Lotus Press Paperback, 1995)

Warrier, Gopi & Deepika, Gunawant, *The Complete Illustrated Guide to Ayurveda: The Ancient Indian Healing Tradition* (Element Paperback, 1997)

## Bach Flower Remedies

Ball, Stefan, *Teach Yourself Bach Flower Remedies* (2000)

Chancellor, Philip M., *The Illustrated Handbook of Bach Flower Remedies* (C.W. Daniel Company Ltd., 1971)

Holden, Susan, *Bach Flowers* (Astrology Publishing House, 2000)

## Chinese Medicine and Herbalism

Brinker, Francis et al, *Herb Contraindications and Drug Interactions* (2nd edition) (Electric Medical Publications, 1998)

Flaws, Bob, *The Secret of Chinese Pulse Diagnosis* (Blue Poppy Press, 1997)

Hael, R., *Samuel Hahnemann: His Life and Works* (Homeopathic Publishing Company, 1922, 2 volumes)

Lee, Helen, *Tao of Beauty: Chinese Herbal Secrets to Feeling Good and Looking Great* (Bantam Books Paperback, 1999)

Master Hong Lui, *The Healing Art of Qi Gong* (Time Warner International, 1999)

Miller, Lucinda M. (Ed.) & Murray, Wallace J. (Ed.), *Herbal Medicinals: A Clinician's Guide* (Haworth, 1995)

## Herbalism
Beyerl, Paul, *The Master Book of Herbalism* (Paperback, 1984)

McCaleb, Robert S. et al, *The Encyclopedia of Popular Herbs: From the Herb Research Foundation, Your Complete Guide to the Handy Medical Plants* (Prima Publishing, 2000)

Ody, P., *The Herb Society's Complete Medicinal Herbal* (Dorling Kindersley, 1992)

## Holistic Medicine and Health
Courteney, Hazel, *500 of the Most Important Health Tips You'll Ever Need: An A–Z of Alternative Health Hints to Help Over 200 Conditions* (Cico Books, 2001)

Luker Robert S. & Nelson, Todd H., *Arthritis Survival: The Holistic Medical Treatment Program for Osteoarthritis* (J.P. Tarcher Paperback, 2001)

## Homeopathy and Complementary Medicine
Bach, Edward, *Heal Thyself* (C.W. Daniel Company, 1978)

Bach, Edward, *The Twelve Healers and Other Remedies* (C.W. Daniel Company, 1973)

Cummings, S. & Ullman, D., *Everybody's Guide to Homoepathic Medicines: Taking Care of Yourself and Your Family with Safe and Effective Remedies* (Tarcher, 1997)

Tandon, R.K., Bajaj, V.R., *Homeopathic Guide to Family Health* (Gazelle Books Seneca, 1997)

Vannier, L., *Typology in Homeopathy* (Beaconsfield Publishers, 1992)

## Massage and Reflexology
Cosway-Hayes, Joan, *Reflexology For Everybody* (Footloose Press, 1999)

Gillanders, Ann, *The Joy of Reflexology: Healing Techniques For the Hands and Feet to Reduce Stress and Reclaim Health* (Little, Brown and Co., 1996)

Schneider McClure, Vimala, *Infant Massage: A Handbook for Loving Parents* (Bantam Doubleday Dell Publishers, 2000)

Wills, Pauline, *The Reflexology Manual: An Easy-To-Use Illustrated Guide to the Healing Zones of the Hands and Feet* (Healing Arts Press, 1995)

## Naturopathy
Bowling, Allen C., *Alternative Medicine and Multiple Sclerosis* (Demos Medical Publishing, 2001)

Bratman, Stephen M.D. & Kroll, David (Ed.), *The Natural Pharmacist: Natural Health Bible from the Most Trusted Alternative Health Site in the World: Your A–Z Guide to Over 300 Conditions, Herbs, Vitamins and Supplements* (Prima Publishing Paperback, 2000)

Murray, Michael, T. & Pizzorno, Joseph E., *The Encyclopedia of Natural Medicine* (2nd Ed.) (Prima Publishing Paperback, 1997)

Shealy, Norman C. MD PhD (Ed.), *The Illustrated Encyclopedia of Healing Remedies* (Element Books, 1991)

## Reiki
Lubeck, Walter, *The Complete Reiki Handbook* (Lotus Light, 1995)

Vennells, David, *Reiki for Beginners* (Llewellyn Publications, 2000)

## Yoga and Meditation
Singh Kalsa, Dharma et al, *Meditation As Medicine: Activate the Power of Your Natural Healing* (Pocket Books, 2001)

# BIOGRAPHIES

## AUTHOR

Karen Sullivan is a best-selling author and highly regarded journalist specializing in natural health and childcare. She has written over 20 books on health and health issues, including *Natural Healthcare for Children, Healthy Eating, Vitamins and Minerals, The Complete Illustrated Guide to Natural Home Remedies, Organic Living in 10 Simple Lessons* and *Kids Under Pressure.* She writes regularly for national newspapers and magazines, and lectures widely in the UK.

## GENERAL EDITOR

Tricia Allen has been a practising homeopath for the last 11 years. She studied at the College of Homeopathy in London, and since then, as well as running a busy practice in South East London, teaches new students in the field and lectures at the Centre for Homeopathic Education in London. Tricia is the registrar of the Alliance of Registered Homeopaths (ARH).

# PICTURE CREDITS

# INDEX